REVELATION UNCOVERED

BY

ART MOKAROW

Revelation Uncovered

Evanow Publishers
P. O. Box 1197
Montgomery, TX 77356

Copyright Pending

Written by Art Mokarow

REVELATION UNCOVERED

CONTENTS

REVELATION UNCOVERED

PREFACE

There are more interpretations about the mystical, symbolic <u>Book of Revelation</u> than any other book in <u>The Bible</u>. Are you able to decipher its meaning? <u>Revelation Uncovered</u> or "The Apocalypse" means "the uncovering" in the Greek. What is <u>The Book of Revelation</u> uncovering? You will see the unveiling of world history, from **"biblical times"** to present-day conditions and circumstances. In addition, your future reward in God's Kingdom is foretold, along with everyone's eventual **salvation** and eternal life. It will explain everyone's personal reward! A special thanks to Clyde Brown who he co-authored Chapter 4, 'Who Is The Beast.' His expertise is History, and has added the **historical** events as they relate to the time frame of <u>The Book of Revelation</u>. Also, thanks to David McMullen for his outlines on <u>Revelation Uncovered</u> and **the temple** at the end of the book. Before the reprinting of this book, we were humbled by a reader's comment: "I just wanted to write you and say thank you. I just received Revelation Uncovered and started reading it and I must say it has been awesome having someone help me to understand The Book of Revelation. I think what you are doing is incredible and it is also nice to see someone spreading The Word of God and not doing so to make money. I never understood how Jesus told His Disciples to give it freely and how people thought it is acceptable to get rich off it. Keep up the great work."

No monies can ever be accepted, but feel free to offer any comments or criticisms. Ask for your free CD disk containing all 6 books which you can read on your computer. Also, feel free to ask biblical questions by mail or e-mail.

Art Mokarow

Mailing Address: Box 1197, Montgomery, TX 77356
Email: art@mokarow.com
Website: www.godspuzzlesolved.com
(download all books free of charge)

<u>God's Puzzle Solved</u>   <u>The White Throne Judgment</u>   Children's Books:
<u>God's Work</u>   <u>Discovering God</u>
<u>Revelation Uncovered</u>   <u>God's Original Bible</u>   <u>God's Two Trees</u>
<u>Christ In You</u>   <u>God's Story</u>   <u>God's Magical Ten Words</u>
<u>The Great Apostasy</u>   <u>Faith With Works</u>

INTRODUCTION

SYMBOLISM EXPLAINED   Would you be amazed to find a book in The Bible, which covers world history from the birth of Christ and The Roman Empire until God's Kingdom comes? **The Book of Revelation does just that!**

A problem for **biblical readers** and **scholars** is to comprehend the mysteries, which are filled with symbols. Once you have the key, God's mysteries and symbolism will show you true world history and its events. Not only is The Book of Revelation prophetic but it will also allow you to understand much of world history (Revelation 19:10).

BEFORE THE BIBLE   In The Garden of Eden, God through His **messengers** spoke directly to Adam and Eve. But, once Adam and Eve sinned and were cut off from The Tree of Life (God's Holy Spirit), humanity was left to itself. Only special people such as Shem, Noah, Abraham and The Prophets had contact with God. These special, chosen people became God's Prophets or **witnesses** of **the truth**. It seemed God had left humanity isolated from His Gospel of The Good News. Yet, God states in Hebrews 4:3 that God's Work was finished or completed right from the beginning. How could this be?

Hebrew 4:4 reveals on that first seventh day God's Work was completed and The Gospel was known. How? There was no Holy Bible or The Scriptures as an informed or **written source** for **humanity**. God no longer would deal with the world from that point forward except with His **chosen witnesses**. How did God preach The Gospel to an ignorant world?

NOAH'S FLOOD   At the time of the flood, the entire world had become evil except for Noah – His Witness. Noah as the only witness could not preach The Gospel to every human in the known world.   Yet, Noah forewarned the world would be destroyed by a world flood and they needed to repent. Repent of what? They wouldn't even know what sin was. Would God destroy anyone because they were ignorant? Would a loving forgiving God destroy those who didn't know better? Of course not.   Today, we have The Holy Bible, but in Noah's time, they had nothing in writing to tell them God's **truth**. Christ said, **"Man shall not live by bread alone, but by every word that proceedeth out of the mouth of God"** (Matthew 4:4). The world in Noah's day did not have The Word of God or did they?

TOWER OF BABEL   Ironically, just before the flood, God said if He had not stopped the human race every thought conceived or imagined by them would end up in evilness (Genesis 6:5).   God flooded the earth leaving only Noah and his family. After the waters receded, Noah and his family with his sons and their wives departed the ark and repopulated the earth. World society was all of one language. Communication was simple because everyone understood each other. Suddenly, their leaders such as Nimrod, a hunter of renown against God and Nimrod, himself was worshipped as a god, began to be concerned the people would begin to form separate societies and ethnic groups. Why?

Noah had three sons – Shem, Ham and Japheth. From these three sons, all the races and ethnic groups developed and repopulated the earth. Their wives were of the basic three races and Noah was Caucasian. The races began to intermix during the time of The Tower of Babel. Genesis 10 records these races and where they began. Genesis 10:6-10 relates the chronology of Ham, Noah's Son. Ham had Cush and Mizraim. History records Mizraim as Egypt. Then Genesis 10:8 states Cush begat Nimrod. Nimrod as a progenitor of the Egyptians, with his wife, Semiramis, became the Egyptian gods (Osirus and Isis). How did this occur?

BIRTH OF BABYLON   As mentioned, Nimrod and his followers wanted to keep humanity as ONE EMPIRE, which would have included all races and ethnic groups. How could they do it? Now for a big surprise anthropologically. History's critical EVENT, which changed the world from that time to The Return of The Messiah or Christ was about to happen. Surprisingly, this monumental occurrence laid the foundation for how historians would eventually see world history. From this point forward, researchers and historians **view their world paradigms from false knowledge**. The Tower of Babel affected all future philosophers and historians except for the FEW who searched for **the truth**. Before The Tower of Babel, The Gospel of God's Good News was recorded, not in a book or scroll but in the heavens. True ASTRONOMY and not ASTROLOGY was prevalent in Noah's day. Noah knew the stars and the constellations gave the true story of The Gospel of God and His Son, Jesus. King David loved God's Law, The Torah, because The Law was a shadow or prophecy of things to come (Hebrews 10:1). David pondered God's Law day and night as a shadow or prophecy of the future. David knew history, past, present and future and recorded it in the last third of THE SCRIPTURE or TANAKH known as THE BOOK OF PSALMS. Psalm 19:1-5 reveals **the truth** of this period of historical change, which occurred at the time of THE TOWER OF BABEL. Verses 1 to 5 DECLARE the HEAVENS manifests The GLORY of God. God's Glory or **the shekinah** declares all of GOD'S GOODNESS as was revealed to Moses (Exodus 33:18-19). God's Glory is the totality of The Gospel. All of God's **goodness**, His riches, creativity, power, etc., is inherent in God's Glory, **the shekinah**. The Messiah, Himself, was in God's Glory. Read this record or witness by David in Psalm 19. Verse 2 states the heavens utter or speak this truth of God's Glory – day after day and night after night. Verse 3 validates there is NO SPEECH or Word of God that shows this knowledge better than the STARS IN HEAVEN. The Prophet said God teaches KNOWLEDGE BY LINE UPON LINE (Isaiah 28:10). This is exactly what David said in Psalms 19:4. This LINE goes out THROUGHOUT THE EARTH and THEIR WORDS to the END of the WORLD (Verse 4). In them, God has set THE TABERNACLE or TEMPLE for the SUN. Then, astounding as it may seem, Psalms 19:5 declares this SUN in the heaven is a BRIDEGROOM (Christ). In Revelation 12:1, the woman is clothed with the sun, Jesus, as The Light Bringer (John 1:6-9) who received this light (the sun) from His Father. Revelation 2:2 states the woman, Mary, gave birth to Jesus, Her Son. Christ is likened to the SUN IN HEAVEN. Virgo in **the heavens** is the virgin giving birth. Draco is Satan.

In Revelation 22:16, Jesus states He is **the bright and morning star**. Revelation 1:20 symbolizes stars as angels. Angels are spirit beings as Jesus is The Firstborn Son, the FIRST bright and morning star. The Book of Revelation defines the heavenly host, the constellations, as revealing The Gospel written in the heavens. When Noah, Abraham and The

Prophets looked to the heavens and understood THE WHOLE PLAN OF GOD. What more proof does one need? The very GOSPEL OF CHRIST was manifested in the CONSTELLATIONS of the heavens before The Holy Bible was written. Wow! Adam and Eve knew. Their children knew – Shem, Noah, Abraham and King David knew. The world knew and Satan wanted to deceive them just as he did before the flood. Only Noah remained **faithful** to The Gospel.

REPROBATE MIND   The Apostle Paul also knew The Gospel had been revealed as prophecy or a TESTIMONY (witness) in the heavens. The invisible things of God (mystery) are UNDERSTOOD by things CLEARLY SEEN (Romans 1:20). Every night the constellations of the stars disclose The Words of God as prophesied by King David (Psalm 19). Now for Satan's **deception**.

The Tower of Babel was the beginning of The Babylonian Mystery system of religion (Baal). Nimrod CHANGED The TRUTH of The GOSPEL, which was declared in the heavens from astronomy to ASTROLOGY. Satan did the same to The Christian Church at the time of Constantine. Romans 1:22-24, Paul continues and states God's Glory (**goodness**) was changed to worshipping the CREATION instead of The CREATOR, GOD! There it is clear as a Biblical **bell**.

Genesis 11:4 states what was being said in Nimrod's Day: **"Go to, let us build us a city** [Babel] **and a tower, whose top may reach into heaven** [the stars]**; and let us make us a name** [Babylon]**, lest we be scattered abroad upon the face of the whole earth."** Notice Nimrod's Kingdom began in the City of Babel (Genesis 10:10). This was the genesis of The

Babylonian Mystery System stated in The Book of Revelation – Babylon The Great (Revelation 18 and 19).

What was this TOWER and why was God so opposed to it? This tower was to be built as high as they could to be able to see the STARS in the heavens to mathematically start The Babylon System of Astrology. True astronomy with the true meaning or declaration of God's Gospel message would be changed forever. Satan's great deception was at work again. He instilled half-truths or lies of what the heavenly stars were actually declaring in Psalms 19. The world bought this lie. The Egyptian Pyramid at Giza, The Pyramids in South America and all over the known world are **witnesses** that astrology became the religion of the priesthood. **The truth** was twisted and eventually completely lost.

SYMBOLISM   Now you can understand the true symbolic mysteries revealed by His Son, Jesus, in The Book of Revelation. The Book of Revelation manifests the true meaning of the original Gospel of God. The heavenly host is clearly defined as The True Gospel in The Book of Revelation.

There is one more mystery in Revelation, which is defined in this last Book of The Bible – **the temple** on earth and **the true temple** in heaven. The Book of Revelation is replete with **the temple**. Each statement as well as every event in **the temple** on earth, as well as **the heavenly temple** is filled with prophecy or THE TESTIMONY OF JESUS.

The Law or Torah is a shadow of things to come (Hebrews 10:1). One third of The Law deals with **the temple** of God. **The temple's divine**

services are prophecy in action. Every event in <u>The Book of Revelation</u> is significant as to its prophetical history of events, which will shortly come to pass (Revelation 1:1). The Levitical Priesthood, also, carried out their daily divine services, which prophesied **the end-time**.

The first chapter in this book is 'The Schoolmaster,' which explains The Prophet's meaning of God's **temple**.

This introduction was written, so you can understand the importance of the symbolism and the mystery about **the temple**. At the same time, you will gain an understanding of the real meaning of the prophecy of <u>The Book of Revelation</u>. You will read in the following chapters, the historical and prophetical events covered in <u>The Book of Revelation</u> bringing greater understanding from Christ's birth and the genesis of The Roman Empire to the establishment of God's Kingdom on the new earth.

The word "Revelation" in The Greek is "Apokalypsis" or "the uncovering." As you read this book while checking and proving everything in <u>The Book of Revelation</u>, you, yourself, will uncover the **hidden** truths of God's Gospel.

Chapter 1

SCHOOLMASTER

Did you know "the tabernacle" built by Moses and the temple in Solomon's day are a prophecy of the END OF TIME? Paul said The Law or <u>Torah</u> is a shadow of things to come (Hebrews 10:1). The "temple," including everything in it, foretells the future. One third of The Law is about "the temple." The Law is your "schoolmaster" or "teacher" (Galatians 3:24). You will get excited learning about the wonderful purpose of this "schoolmaster," along with God's "temple" and its prophetical meanings.

When Adam and Eve sinned by eating the fruit of The Tree of Good and Evil, God removed them from **the garden**. They were expelled from God's **rest** or **paradise**. When they lost access to The Tree of Life – **salvation** was lost.

Adam and Eve's sin or offense did not transgress God's Law since at that time The Law was not legally enforced. They, however, broke <u>The Ten Commandments</u> in **"spirit"** by dishonoring God, The Father. They, in **"spirit"** transgressed The Fifth Commandment. Since The Law was not enforced legally until Mt. Sinai, no sin was imputed (Romans 5:13). That is why Paul called Adam and Eve's sin **"an offense."** They offended (injured) God, The Father. They lacked **"faith."**

PARADISE LOST   Adam and Eve's **offense** brought death to them and their posterity. Cain and Able and all humanity lost access to God, and all the riches God would have bestowed upon everyone had Adam and Eve chosen The Tree of Life instead. God's **rest**, or **paradise**, was truly lost.

Many do not realize Adam and Eve had complete liberty and freedom in The Garden of Eden. They could do whatever they chose to do. God's **rest** in **paradise** had no laws, restrictions or even any conditions. They truly had total liberty to do whatsoever they wanted.

Even when God told Adam and Eve not to eat of The Tree of Knowledge of Good and Evil, there was **no legal law against it**. Adam and Eve had **complete freedom of choice** to do anything they wanted. Adam and Eve were **totally free** to do anything just as God The Father could. God told them not to eat The Tree of Good and Evil because they and their children would die or lose **salvation**. God never instituted a legal law for them not to eat The Tree of Knowledge. God totally left the choice up to Adam and Eve. They had absolute liberty without adhering to laws or any legal requirements.

God was giving humanity (through Adam and Eve) the right of free choice to live any way they chose. He merely warned them what would happen if they made the wrong choice. They made the wrong decision and all humanity had to suffer because of that wrong choice. No one could say God did not give humanity a free choice. Under Christ, you still have free choice or liberty just as Adam and Eve had. Once Jesus ended the curse of The Law, you, as a Christian, would have no condemnation. Christians are dead to The Law (Romans 7:1-7). You have total liberty through

Christ (Galatians 5:1).

RESTORATION   Jesus said He came to **restore** what was lost (Matthew 18:11).   When Adam and Eve were removed from **the garden**, besides losing **salvation**, they lost God's **rest** or **paradise**.   They, also, lost the liberty to be totally free (Romans 8:21).   Christ came to **restore all** that was lost, which includes liberty and total freedom.

THE PROCESS   Once Adam and Eve lost **paradise**, they were told "**a seed**" would come from their progeny who would defeat Satan, and **restore the garden** and God's **rest**.   Until then, the earth and everyone on it have been and are under Satan's rulership.   Until Christ defeats all of God's enemies, which includes death, Satan is in control of the world.   Everyone lives in Satan's world or system on this earth, which he rules and does his best to deceive.   What was God's **plan** to **restore paradise** lost?

THE FIVE COVENANTS   God instituted **five covenants** so humanity could receive **salvation**:   (1) Adam and Eve were given a **life** or **death** choice.   They could have eaten from The Tree of Life, but they chose death by eating The Tree of Good and Evil.   (2) Melchisedec, as The High Priest of God, made a **covenant** with Abraham through **the promised seed** that God's **rest** would be **restored**.   (3) This agreement was made because of a sin.   Israel, as a nation, sinned by building a golden calf to worship.   This is **"the genesis"** of The Old Covenant or administration of death (II Corinthians 3:1-7).   This **"covenant"** was an agreement based upon The Law (a legal contract),   which in turn is based upon **statutes** and **judgments** with **blessings** of human existence and

curses, or **penalties** in God's Court of Law – **The Temple** (Deuteronomy 28-30). This **covenant** was designed to bring Israel to **repentance** or to The Messiah, The Christ, or back to Melchisedec (Galatians 3 and 4). This **covenant** was known as **"the schoolmaster"** to bring them to Christ (Galations 3 and 4). (This is the **focus of this chapter**). (4) The **new covenant** came and **restored** The Melchisedec Priesthood, based upon **faith** and not human works to fulfill The Abrahamic Covenant of Salvation or The Restoration of Paradise (Hebrews 7and 8). (5) This **covenant** will occur in God's **kingdom** when God makes all things new and continues paradise for all of Adam and Eve's children, which has yet to occur (Revelation 21 and 22).

INSTITUTION OF THE SCHOOLMASTER   The Third Covenant (The Old Covenant) made and ratified with Israel was an **intermediate agreement** with God because Israel had sinned. This system based upon The Letter of The Law or <u>Torah</u> bound The Nation of Israel under Moses as **a way** to come to Christ, The Messiah (Galatians 3 and 4). God made this Law a legal requirement in a **court of law**. It was made for a carnal society to know **"right"** from **"wrong."** It was only a shadow of **true righteousness**.

Since Israel sinned and was carnal, God devised a **covenant** but only for **carnal people** with a bondage of **"works" as shadows**. In fact, the entire Letter of The Law was only a shadow – not the real thing! The Law and everything in it was a **"schoolmaster"** as a method to teach them about Christ. It was only through Christ, **the promised seed,** who would restore liberty to humanity.

Israel totally misunderstood what God wanted this **covenant**, based upon the **total** keeping of The Letter of The Law, to do. They believed in doing literally everything in The Law. They thought The Law would be their **"righteousness"** (Deuteronomy 6:25). Instead, God wanted The Law to reveal to them they couldn't be **"righteous"** (Romans 5:20). The Law was **righteous**, but Israel couldn't keep it because of the weakness of their flesh. The Law was to be a **"schoolmaster"** (Galatians 3) to bring them to Christ and **"repentance."** It was truly to be a **"schoolmaster."** The Law was a teacher to show them how sinful they really were. Israel was always carnal and unrepentant, and had to be reminded over and over again.

THE SHADOW The Law with the sacrifices was **a shadow** of things to come (Hebrews 10:1). The Sabbath, Holy Days, meal offerings, new moons were shadows of how Jesus would restore Israel and bring the whole world to God's **rest** or **paradise** (Colossians 2:16-17). In John 5:46, Jesus told The Pharisees if they had understood what Moses wrote, they would have known Moses was writing about Christ, The Messiah. Moses wrote The Law, which was a **shadow** of all that Jesus would do to **restore salvation** in **the garden** (Revelation 21 and 22).

SHADOW OF THE RESTORATION What was **the shadow** of The Law? What did The Law do to reveal The Messiah? Most of The Law is **history**. Books Genesis to Deuteronomy give the history from the creation of the universe to the time Israel became a nation and was about to enter God's **promised land** with Joshua as their leader. Even this history had **shadows** or revealed Christ.

Scripturally, Adam was a **type** of Jesus (Romans 5). Abraham was a type of God, The Father, with his willingness to sacrifice His Son, Isaac. The sacrifices, with The Lamb as Christ, and all the other offerings as the peace offering, literally pictures God's **rest**, or The Garden of Eden – "**restored**" (Revelation 21 and 22). Yes, **the temple**, itself, was a shadow of Christ bringing humanity to The Real Mercy Seat in The Holy of Holies (Hebrews 9:9). The entire Law was a true shadow of things to come hopefully to bring Israel to **"repentance"** and a change of heart. But, they failed and they never did repent. A vail was over their eyes blinding them to understand God's real **purpose** of The Law. The Law was only a **"schoolmaster"** to try to teach them by doing **homework** so they could pass their test, and the test they were to pass was to **"repent"** (I Timothy 1:7-10). **The temple**, which covers one third of The Law, was the largest part of **the shadow** of The Law. Without **the temple** you cannot keep The Law (James 2:10).

THE TEMPLE In The Torah or The Law, much of it covers **the temple** and its furnishings. Since the **entire** Law was a **"schoolmaster," the temple** was to be a **"schoolmaster"** as well. It was to be the exact figure of **the true temple** in heaven (Hebrews 9:9). The Law told Israel how to be **righteous** and a witness of God to the world. If Israel obeyed, they would be accepted by God even though they were still carnal. This Law was given to Israel because they were **unrighteous** (I Timothy 1:7-10). Truly, keeping The Letter of The Law could never change their human nature. They were still carnal. The Law was only a **schoolmaster** to teach them how carnal they were (Romans 5:20), so they could **change** and come to Christ. The Torah or The Law pictured Jesus, The Christ, and so did **the temple**. The Law was only **a shadow**. Christ was **the rock** (God's **glory**) or **"the shekinah"** (I Corinthians 10:4).

When Israel sinned, they came to **the temple** and made sacrifices for all their sins. **The temple**, being a place to worship God, was also God's **courthouse** to **try** the sinner, whether **guilty** or **not**. It was to continually remind them they were sinners (Romans 5:20) and to try to bring them to Christ.

TWO TEMPLES   Now, for a surprise: One **temple** was a **physical temple** and the other a **spiritual temple**.   Only "**Spirit**" is real. Remember, the **temple** in **Israel** was only a **shadow** (figure), not real, but merely a type of the temple in heaven (Hebrews 9:9). Just as The Law was only **a shadow** and could not make anyone **righteous** neither was the **physical temple** able to make one worthy to enter The Holy of Holies – only Christ could. **All of The Law**, **including the temple**, could only bring one to Jesus or truly **restore** God's **rest** in **paradise**. This **temple** and The Law were really only **shadows** or a type as a **duality**. Read Hebrews 9, and you can prove this point. You will see **the real temple**, in **heaven**, defines the real meaning of the **earthly temple**, which was only a **shadow** of the real. Revelation uncovers the true meaning of the earthly **temple**.

TWO HOUSES   Hebrews 3:1-6 speaks about **two houses,** or **temples**. In John 14:1-2, Christ told His Disciples not to trouble their heart for **"in my Father's house are many mansions"** (or fabulous palaces of abode). Then Jesus continued, **"I go to PREPARE A PLACE FOR YOU!"** How wonderful. Christians are to live in palaces and mansions. Of these

two houses – one is God's **real house** and the other is merely **a shadow**.

Moses was faithful in **all** his house (Verse 2). Why? Moses was faithful in his house (Israel's **temple**), for a **testimony** or **witness** of those things, which were to be spoken (Hebrews 3:35). The Law and the physical **temple** only looked like what will be **real** in the future through Christ. Notice, Jesus warned about this **temple**, which was only **a shadow**.

During The Passover (John 2:13), Jesus went to **the temple**, and found the people selling animals for sacrifices in **the temple**. They created a business of God's **physical house** on earth. He was furious and drove the moneychangers and animals out. Christ said "not to make a **business** out of My Father's "**house**." Then, He made an astonishing statement. **"Destroy this temple, and in three days, I will raise it up"** (John 2:19-21). He was referring to His **body** or a **spiritual temple**. The **physical temple** and The Letter of The Law were only **shadows** and not able to make the worshippers **spiritual**. The **physical temple** continually reminded them they were still carnal. Jesus spoke of both a physical temple and a **spiritual temple**. This was the physical temple of Moses.

THE REAL TEMPLE   Hebrews 3:6 speaks of Christ being over **His Own House. Whose house are we**! Christians are to hold fast with confidence to **the end**. God's **spiritual** house or temple in heaven, are **Christians** growing **spiritually** with God's Law written in your hearts and minds or a **real change of your nature** to be Holy, as God. This is God's Spiritual Temple. That is why no physical Law is necessary when you become **"spirit"**. God's Holy Law is now in your heart. How was the **physical temple, a schoolmaster** under Moses?

THE PHYSICAL TEMPLE   To learn how this **temple** is to be built, read Exodus 25:26, 27 and 28. Paul said **the temple** being built on earth must be an **exact duplicate** or a precise figure of the one in **heaven** (Hebrews 9:9). Always keep in mind, this **temple** on earth was only a **schoolmaster** or a **teacher** to bring them to Christ. The one in **heaven** is real where Jesus shares His Father's **throne** and intercedes for Christian's sins as Melchisedec, The High Priest. Jesus said **the temple** in **heaven** is a "**spiritual one**" (John 2:19-21). What does the **physical temple** as a "**schoolmaster**" foreshadow?

The Chapters in The Bible were created by men and are not in the original scrolls. Many times a subject is mistakenly cut off when a new chapter was begun before the subject was completed. With that in mind, Hebrews 10:1 is a summary, which really belongs with the subject in Hebrews 9.

Hebrews 10:1 states The Law given to Moses with the **sacrifices** were **a shadow** of things to come. The Torah, or The First Five Books of The Bible were written to be **a shadow** or **type** of what would happen in the future. As Paul said, **"The Law was our schoolmaster to bring us unto Christ"** (Galatians 3:24). This Law was to be a **schoolmaster** or teacher to make you aware you needed Jesus (Romans 5:20). The Law could never make you perfect or **righteous**. And yet, Christians' goal is to become perfect (Matthew 5:48). Hebrews 9 - a major part of The Law, reveals **the temple** was a **figure** or type of Christ as well (Hebrews 9). You will see that **without the temple** as part of The Law, you never really understand the shadow or prophecy, which The Law was to reveal. That is why one cannot keep or observe The Sabbath and Holy Days without **the temple**. The **shadow** or prophecy of things to come would not be complete. One could not come to Christ without **the temple**. Keeping just one part of The Law profits nothing. That is why keeping a part of The Law is a sin. It is like a **schoolmaster** teaching only part of the subject.

The Law, without **the temple**, gives you the history of the world, along with what **righteousness** is and what **sin** is. The Law also reveals God's **plan** of **salvation** and the need for Jesus, The Christ.   But, without understanding the prophecy or the **figure**, which **the temple** portrays with specific details about God's **plan**, which cannot be understood without it. **The temple** brings you to God or The Holy of Holies. In fact, this earthly **temple** explains   the   entire   meaning   of   The Book of Revelation. The **temple** on earth, first and foremost, pictured **God's real temple in heaven**. Moses was admonished to copy **the temple** of God, and build it exactly as it was in **heaven** (Hebrews 9:9). It was to be a **figure** or **type** of the heavenly. Since **the temple** was also **a shadow** of The Law, just what did it foreshadow?   How was **the temple** a **schoolmaster** to bring you to Christ? Revelation opens up.   It reveals how to come to Jesus and God, The Father.

FINDING FAULT What was the weakness based upon **The Law** or **The Old Covenant**? What was wrong with The Old Covenant based upon all the works or **Divine Ordinances** of The Law? Simply, Hebrews 10:1, **The Law with those sacrifices** could **never make them perfect**. Christianity, however, **demands perfection** (Matthew 5:48). This Old Covenant based upon The Law could not make them true worshippers. It changed no one. It was only **a shadow** or **prophecy** about Christ. What did this **temple** on earth foreshadow? In <u>The New Covenant</u>, God would **write His Laws** in your hearts and minds (Hebrews 8:10). How is God going to do that? Does prophecy tell you? What this prophecy foreshadows will, indeed, reveal how God will make you perfect? **The earthly temple discloses the process**. It is a figure of **the true** or **real temple** in **heaven**, which descends as a Bride when God's **kingdom** comes to The New Earth (Revelation 21:10 and Revelation 19:7). <u>The Book of Revelation</u> prophesies what the real **temple** in **heaven** discloses about **the earthly temple**, which was only **a shadow**. <u>The Book of Revelation</u> is **Christ's "will"** or "testimony" to enter The Holy of Holies (Revelation 19).

TEMPLE FIGURES   Read the description of **the temple** Moses was to build. Hebrews 9 depicts **the temple** and what is in **the temple**. You are about to discover that **the temple** foreshadows The Lake of Fire, "The Two Witnesses," The True Church, **the place of safety** during The Great Tribulation, and ultimately, who will be the **Bride** of Christ. All this and more is **foreshadowed** in **the temple** with its divine services or ordinances. <u>The Book of Revelation</u> reveals it all! It is the "**testimony**" or "**will**" of Christ, Your Savior (Hebrews 9:15-22).

TEMPLE OVERVIEW   To understand **the temple**, which Moses was ordered to build on earth, you need to picture it in your mind first. After that, you need to go through **each part** of **the temple** to understand its prophetic **shadows**. **The temple** itself was relatively small in comparison to the **entire temple area**. **The temple**, built by Solomon, was on one of the mountains in the southeastern corner of Jerusalem. Across from its Eastern Gate was a bridge going over to Mt. Olivet or The Mount of

Olives where Christ died.

The temple itself was located in the rear part of **the temple area** facing **The Eastern Gate**. Jesus will return upon The Mount of Olives facing this gate. **The temple** has two compartments, one in its back half (part), called The Holy of Holies where The Mercy Seat was, and the front half (part), which was divided by a vail and had **the seven golden candlesticks** on the table with **the shewbread**.

Another vail in the front of this chamber, called **The Holy Place**, with its entrance that led to some steps going down to what is known as **the court area**. Going down these steps there were two pillars one on each side. The pillar on the right was called Jachin and the one on the left was called Boaz. These pillars **did not support any part of the temple**, but each merely stood on the left and the right. In front of the steps is an altar. This was the sacrificial altar for the animal sacrifices. Between **the altar** and **the temple** was the basin to purify oneself. This symbolizes baptism.

The court area was divided by its front court, which was for The Nation of Israel or The Twelve Tribes. The second court was for all circumcised Gentiles or strangers. In both courts, the men were on one side and the women on the other. Surrounding this court area and **the temple** was a high wall with four gates. It had an east gate, west gate, north gate and south gate. This was the **entire temple** area.

HEBREWS NINE   Paul describes **the temple**, The Holy of Holies and The Holy Place with its major pieces (Hebrews 9). You will discover each section in its appropriate place – with the court area as a **shadow**, or a **teacher** or **schoolmaster** to **reveal future prophecy** concerning

Christ and His **church**. Jesus, Himself, gives you the answer to their meanings. In fact, the **entire end time** is uncovered or revealed in <u>The Book of Revelation</u>. Jesus is The Revelator!

The **first covenant**, which included **the temple** on earth, had **ordinances** of **divine** service (Hebrews 9:1). In Greek, the word "ordinances," conveys the meaning of "**works**, which had **legal rights**." Everything done in **the temple** by The Priests with **each temple piece** carrying a legal meaning by God as a divine or Godly service even though it was only a worldly (type of) sanctuary. Paul, first, describes The Holy Place where the **candlestick** was kept.

Paul states this Holy Place had a candlestick, a table and the shewbread called **the sanctuary** or holy place (Hebrews 9:22). A vail divided The Holy Place from The Holy of Holies (Verse 3). The Holy of Holies contained the **Golden censer,** the **Ark** of the **Covenant**, the **Golden Pot** with manna, Aaron's **rod that budded,** and **the tables of the covenant**, or The Ten Commandments in stone (Verse 4).

Only The High Priest could go into The Holy of Holies, once a year, because The Holy Spirit was signifying the way into The Holiest "of all" was not possible (Hebrews 9:7-11). This **first tabernacle** was merely **a shadow** of the real **temple** in **heaven**. No one legally had access to God, The Father, because they were still carnal. They, therefore, could not be forgiven for their sins and receive mercy. Paul said all these divine services in this **temple** were only a **figure** or a **type** of the real **temple** in **heaven**. All the sacrifices, gifts, etc. could not make those **worshipping in the temple perfect**. These services couldn't change one's conscience or heart to have **God's Laws written in their hearts and minds**. One could be keeping the entire Letter of The Law, which was only **a shadow**, but attempting to keep them could not make them Holy or **perfect** as God (Matthew 5:48). This **temple** and the entire Letter of The Law had a different purpose. It was designed to convert **carnal people** into **repentant** Christians (I Timothy 1:7-10).

Paul states only Jesus, The Christ, was A High Priest in a greater and more **perfect temple** than the earthly (Hebrews 9:11). You are ready now to prove how this **earthly temple** was a **schoolmaster** to bring you to Christ!

PURPOSE OF BOOK OF REVELATION   John, The Apostle, was on The Isle of Patmos and in a vision a loud voice told him to write a letter (The Book of Revelation) **to The Seven Churches in Asia**. The Seven Churches were: **Ephesus, Smyrna, Pergamos, Thyatira, Sardis, Philadelphia** and **Laodicea**.   This Book of Revelation was written exclusively to these **seven churches**. Why? Because this "**revelation**" was coming directly from Jesus, The Christ (Revelation 1:1). Revelation 1:19 relates The Purpose of The Book of Revelation and why it was written. The Book of Revelation was written to tell **the seven churches such things which shall be in the future**. This is prophecy and Jesus, Himself, is The Revelator. These **seven churches** as Christ's **"witness,"** have the "**testimony**" of **Jesus** (Revelation 19:10).   What is His "**testimony**?"   Christ's "**testimony**" is The Spirit of Prophecy.   This prophecy is **Christ's "will."** The Book of Revelation is written specifically to **the seven churches** because they are to be **the witnesses** of this prophecy until God's **kingdom** comes to this earth.   These Seven Churches continue to exist as Christ's **church – the seven candlesticks –**

until the entire prophecy of Revelation is completed. Christ, Himself, reveals what is going to happen to His **seven churches** until His return.

What could this prophecy reveal? Jesus will come with the clouds and **every eye shall see him** (Revelation 1:7). This **book** covers the events of the actual **return** of The True Messiah and the establishment of God's **kingdom**. All events pertaining to Christ's **return** and God's **kingdom** are foretold by this prophecy. Let Christ reveal **the truth** to all His **witnesses – the seven churches** of Revelation 2 and 3.

THE TRUE CHURCH OF GOD   Every Christian denomination or group claims to be The True Church of God. Catholics claim one must become a Catholic or go to hell. The Orthodox and Protestant Churches make the same claim – only they regard themselves as The True Churches. All others – Evangelicals, Independents and even **sects** say the same. All **churches** believe they are The True Church and one must believe **their doctrine or their faith** to be a member in their **church**. The Jews claim Christ has not come yet and only they are God's **chosen people**. All this is complete confusion! Who is right? Where is The True Church of God? Who are the **elect** or **called-out ones**?

JESUS, THE REVELATOR   Study the **shadows** to see if you can distinguish **The True Church**. Paul starts describing what was in **the temple**. The Holy Place or sanctuary contains the **candlestick**, the **table** and the **shewbread** (Hebrews 9:2). What do these items foreshadow? The word "sanctuary" in Greek is "hagios:" "a **sacred thing**" or "**a Holy thing**." The candlestick, table and shewbread are all sacred or Holy and undefiled. What is this **candlestick** in **prophecy**?

Jesus states in His right hand, He held **"seven golden candlesticks"** (Revelation 1:20). These **Seven Golden Candlesticks** are **the candlesticks** in The Holy Place in **the temple**. The Jews call these **seven candlesticks – the menorah**. What are they? To The Jews, this candlestick is highly prized and included in most of their religious services. These candlesticks provide light – **a witness**.

Christ reveals these **"seven candlesticks are the seven churches"** (Verse 20). They are to be **witnesses** of Christ (Acts 1). Revelation 1:12-13 states John saw Jesus, Himself, in the middle of these **seven candlesticks**. Christ states The Menorah in The Holy Place represents **"the seven churches"** in Asia. These **seven churches** are The **True** Churches of God; God's **church** does not exist as **one candlestick or one church but seven candlesticks** or **seven churches**. These **seven churches** in Asia represent The True Churches of God. They are The Menorah or candlestick in The Holy Place. Jesus only regards these **seven** as His, since He is in their midst. Jesus is not in the middle of any **other** seven candlesticks – only these seven. That is why Revelation is written to them about Christ's **return** since these **seven** are being told their future in **prophecy**. Jesus is revealing how His **churches** are to be **true witnesses** to be able to **"inherit"** from His **"will."**

A BIG ERROR Some Christian groups believe these **seven churches** are The Seven Eras of God's Church from Christ's death until His **return**. What an error! There is **no biblical proof** to think they are **"eras."** One can never understand The Book of Revelation and its prophecy under such delusion. Read Revelation 2 and 3 where each of these **seven churches exists** from the time John wrote about them until The Return of Christ.

Each and every one of these **seven churches** exist until The Return of Jesus in the clouds. They are not **church eras** but include the **whole Church of God** throughout history until The Return of Christ. These **seven churches** represent The True Church of God! The physical "**temple**" The Holy Place will validate where you find **the candlestick** with **the seven lamps** – The Menorah! Christ is in their midst.

DOCTRINE **All Christian churches**, as well as those in The Jewish "**faith**," **claim** they are God's True Chosen Ones or The Church of God. Acts 7:38 calls Israel, those of Jewish **faith**, The Church in The Wilderness. How can this be? Whose is **the true church**? All those of The Jewish and Christian **faiths** are separate one from the other based upon **doctrine** or **creed**. It merely means a specific church's teachings differentiating one group from another group. Is this true? Is The True Church of God different because of doctrine? What does Christ, The Head of The Church, have to say about this?

THE SEVEN So far, you have proven **biblically** that **God's true church** consists of **the seven churches stated** in **Revelation 2 and 3**. Did they all hold to the same teaching, doctrine or creed? Amazingly, not at all! Each of The Seven True Churches of God were either **slightly** or **grossly** different in belief, one from another. Doctrine was not what constituted them as a True Church of God. Something else does.

THE ECCLESIA In Greek, the English word "church" is "**ecclesia**." It means the "called-out ones." Called-out for what? In its Greek root, "ecclesia" carries the meaning of a "**general public assembly**." What is **the purpose** of the assembly since it merely refers to the **general public**?

The Greek word for "church" is **not** an **exclusive** club. It is all-inclusive. Its **purpose** is not to be private but a **public assembly**. But, for what **purpose**? The Apostle Paul said this **general** public assembly can have the **learned** as well as **unlearned** congregating in it (I Corinthians 14:12). They just are naturally all at different levels of **faith** or **belief** (Romans 14). The "**church**" is not a matter of **doctrine** or different faiths, but an invitation to a calling for **a purpose**.

In Matthew 24:1-5 Jesus answered the question regarding the destruction of Herod's "**temple**" and His **return**. Christ prophesies the future: Christ said, **"Take heed that no man deceive you"** (Verse 4). Why? Many shall come in **Christ's name** or The Church of God. What will they say? They will say **Jesus is The Christ**. Those are exactly the words Peter said to Jesus in Matthew 16. Christ said only God could reveal it to a person. One can be called and know Jesus is The Christ, **The Anointed Messiah** and still deceive others. It is not a matter of doctrine, but a **calling** because Jesus is The Christ. You are invited to **the church** when you know Jesus, is The Christ – The Anointed High Priest, Melchisedec, who died for your sins. You are invited to **The Wedding Feast**. To know Jesus, The Christ, is all that is required to be in The Church of God! One merely needs to **repent** and be **baptized** for one's sins. It is not a matter of doctrine or creed. It is your entrance ticket – from that point you must **grow spiritually**.

There is a warning that many in **the church** will be deceived by the preaching they hear (Verse 5). Prove from **Christ's own "Words"** in Revelation 2 and 3 that each of The Churches of God had a **diverse** set of doctrines or beliefs. Remember, Christ walked in the midst of all these "**seven churches**" as True Churches of God.

THE SEVEN   **Ephesus** was the first of **the seven churches**, but this **church** has something wrong with it (Revelation 2:1-7). Jesus states He has a two-edged sword and only speaks The Word of God (Revelation 1:16 and Matthew 4:4).   What was wrong with this Christian **church**? They lost their first love (Verse 4). What was this **love**?

The Apostle Paul calls a meeting of all The Elders of The Ephesian Church, and states they are to be the overseers (episcopae) of the flock (Acts 20:17). The Elder's responsibility is to feed them **the truth** of God and Christ (Acts 20:28).

Paul said after He leaves, other men will arise speaking **perverse false things** about God and His Son (Acts 20:29). Not only will false teachers come into **the church**, but within the group of **bishops**, there will be false preachers. As prophesized, The Ephesian Church lost their first love. They needed The Book of Revelation.

John said the early Ephesian Church "**tried**" those Apostles to see if they were **Jews** or the original Jewish Apostles, but they were not (Revelation 20:2).   Paul said the same in II Corinthians 11:13.   These were **false apostles** who were making a **business** out of **the church** (II Corinthian 11:4-11). They were preaching a **false Jesus**, not "**the true**" Christ. That is the **first love they lost**. These **apostles** were of **Satan**, but **the church was a true Christian church** even though they followed a **false** Christ!

Now, Christ's **startling statement** concerning His **true church**, which followed a **false Christ** (Revelation 2:5) clearly prophesies this Ephesian

Church **is not an era,** but **exists all the way to The Return of Jesus**. **Your Savior** makes an amazing announcement by His **angel** who stated when The Christ **returns**, this Ephesian Church is still in **existence**, and He, Jesus, will then remove them as a **candlestick**. Not only is this **church** not following every Word of God (Matthew 4:4), but **rejects** the two-edged sword coming out of Jesus' mouth. The Ephesian Church, which is **Christian** or **the true church** doesn't even believe in The True Jesus at His **return**! Their **doctrinal belief** completely rejects "**the true Christ**," and Jesus tells you they are His True Church of God! Wow! How about the next church, **Smyrna**? This **church** goes through tribulation, but only for ten days (Revelation 2:10). Why? Revelation 2:9, explains they, too, accept **false Jews, false apostles**, and are of Satan's church. That's why. But notice, Revelation 2:11, Jesus promises this **church will not** go into **The Lake of Fire**. Smyrna, as The Ephesian Church, exists all the way to God's **kingdom**. Amazing! No era, but an ongoing True Church of God till God's **kingdom** comes.

The **third church, Pergamos**, is warned by **the angel**, that Jesus is telling them to stick to what Christ preaches as the sharp two-edged sword coming out of His mouth (Matthew 4:4). What **false doctrine** is being taught in this Christian Church of God? First, they make a **business** out of The Church of God. They follow the doctrine of Balaam (Revelation 2:14). Read Numbers 22 through 31. You will see God's Prophets make a **business** or profit from God's **truth**. What do they teach? They teach **fornication** or idolatry for money. They, also, teach **pagan myths** about The Nicolaitenes, which Christ hates; including Easter rabbits having eggs, Christmas, The Son's birth during the solstice of winter. Paganism was in this **true** Church of God. They are teaching **wrong doctrines** and yet they are **still Christians** as a **candlestick**. Pergamos will still be existing at **the return** of Christ (Revelation 2:16). This is no church era.

The **fourth church, Thyatira** is warned that Jesus is a flaming fire (Revelation 2:18). Why? They teach the doctrine of Jezebel who claims to be a prophetess (Revelation 2:20). Jezebel teaches and supports Baal, **the god of fertility** or **sex** (Read II Kings 9-21). Jezebel followed the pagan prophets. Wow! This church Christ's candlestick preaches **pagan, idolatrous** religion. This **Christian** Church of God **will go** into **The Great Tribulation** to **repent** (Revelation 2:22). This **church still exists** at the Return of Christ as one of The True Churches of God (Revelation 2:25).

The **fifth church** is The **Sardis** Church and is called a **dead** church, but nevertheless, it is Christ's **candlestick** and a **Christian church** (Revelation 3:3). This **church** makes one feel good because they think they have the only **truth** about God. They are The Only True Church of God. Jesus states when He **returns**, this Sardis Church exists, and He will come upon this church as a **thief in the night** (five unwise virgins) (Matthew 24:43). Again, Sardis is not a church era, but is a **church** that exists at **Christ's return**.

The **Philadelphia** Church, of all the seven, keeps **the truth** of Christ as Jesus reveals it to them, and because they are **faithful**, they do not have to go through **the tribulation** (Revelation 3:10). This **church** continues to grow and continues to seek **new truth**. Also, since they don't follow Satan's teaching (Revelation 3:9), they will go to a place of safety during **the tribulation** (Revelation 12). This **church** also exists at **the return** of

Christ (Revelation 3:11).

The seventh church is **Laodicea** outlined in Revelation 3:14-21. This **church** is neither **cold** nor **hot**, only lukewarm. Why? If they were atheists (not believing in God), they would not be held responsible because they would be only ignorant. If they were **true witnesses** of Christ (not merely attending church, giving money and keeping days), but would instead expound Christ's nature by **doing good works** as Jesus told them, then they would be **hot**!

What does Jesus say of this **true** Christian Church of God? Christ said He counsels them to buy **gold** or go into **The Lake of Fire** – hell, to truly repent (Revelation 3:18). There you have it. The Laodicean **candlestick** – God's **church**, will exist when Jesus **returns** for His Bride (Revelation 3:20). What **a group of churches**! The only common **faith** or **belief** or **doctrine** is they all believe Jesus is The Savior who paid for everyone's sins. This is truly a **general public assembly** or **called-out ones**. Read their **real history** in **the parable of the SOWER and the SEED** (Matthews 13:24-30). This is Christ's true parable of **The True Churches of God with their history**. Then, Revelation 2 and 3 gives you God's True Christian Churches from **the fall of the temple** in 70 A.D. until God's **kingdom** comes. Doctrine is not what makes **True Christians** – **"Christian."** All The Churches of God do not have the same **faith**. That is why Paul said, **"What is not of faith is sin"** (Romans 14:23). The Parable of The Ten Talents reveals all are at different levels of **spiritual growth** or **doctrinal understanding** (Matthew 25). Nevertheless, **all** are **Christians**, regardless of **the seven types of churches** you may attend or are affiliated with. But, Jesus issues a **warning** to **all** those who are **not**

true witnesses of Christ in The Parable of The **Ten Virgins**. Only half are **wise** and continue to **grow** in God's Holy Spirit or continued **truth** until **the return** of Christ (Matthew 25:1-13). Be sure you will be invited to The Wedding Feast. Continue to grow and be considered the **called-out ones** who are faithful (Matthews 25:13)! You may be **invited** to The Wedding as The True Church of God but "**MANY are CALLED** [ecclesia], **but few are chosen**" (Matthews 22:14). That is why Revelation 18:4 is a warning to God's Seven Churches, "**COME OUT OF HER MY PEOPLE!**"

SUMMARY OF THE SEVEN   At the very **birth** of Christ, Satan **started** to infiltrate The Church of God. Through Herod, at Jesus' birth, Satan attempted to kill Christ (Revelation 12). From that point on, Satan infiltrated The Churches of God. He even tried to sift The Apostle Peter as wheat. By the time The Thessalonian Church was established, Satan began his deception of **the falling away**. Once **the temple** ended in 70 A.D., "**the church**" was scattered. Some went to Pella. In time, by the end of the first century, Christ accepted **the seven churches** in Asia as His "**candlesticks.**" All of them, in some way, were deceived by Satan except **The Philidelphians**. They only had a **little strength** or **truth**. But all are The True Churches of God until the very **return** of Christ. The Catholics, Orthodox, Protestants, Evangelicals, Independents and those of The Jewish Faith are God's **called-out ones** (Revelation 12).

In the parable of the sower and the seed, Jesus said, "**Let the TARES and the WHEAT grow together until the end.**" By 325 A.D., at The Council of Nicea, The Roman Empire, under Constantine, took over The Christian Church with 250 bishops present. In Daniel, The Roman Empire is "The Fourth Beast," which Christ at His **return** destroys. God and Christ allowed His "**church**" to be taken over by Satan. The **tares** and **wheat** are **now together**. They are all in Babylon. The rest of <u>Revelation</u> explains how **God separates** the two, so **Christ's Bride** and **Guests** can be invited to The Wedding Feast. **"Many are CALLED but few CHOSEN"** (Matthew 22:14). All of **the seven churches** are Christian and are **the shadow** or "**the schoolmaster**" in "**the temple**" as "**the menorah**" in The Holy Place.

<u>**THE TABLE AND THE SHEWBREAD**</u>   Hebrews 9:2 reveals the table where "**the shewbread**" was placed, as well as, "t**he seven candlesticks**." In Luke 22:15-16, Jesus desired to eat that Passover with His Disciples. Then   He   said He   would   eat this Passover meal with them in "**the kingdom.**" **The shewbread** with **the church** is The Wedding Feast, which completes The Marriage Ceremony between Christ and His Bride. Remember, only a few are chosen as His Bride, with only a few Guests. The rest of **the temple** and **courtyard** for both The Israelites and The Gentiles are a **shadow of events** revealed in <u>The Book of Revelation</u>.

<u>**KING – PRIESTS**</u>   From this point on, Revelation 5 to Revelation 22 deals with prophecy where Jesus reveals what he and God, The Father must do to **correct "the seven churches" so they can come out of Babylon** (Revelation 18:4).

In Revelation 5:9 the heavenly host sings a new song, which declares, The Lamb – Christ, is worthy to open **the seals** of <u>The Book of Revelation</u>. What does <u>The Book</u> reveal?   It is His "**testimony**" or "**will**."   It prophesies the future of "**the seven churches**" – Jesus' death so He could **redeem** you to God by His **blood**. Why did Christ **redeem** you? Jesus has **redeemed** Christians to be **Kings** and **Priests,** and you will reign on **the earth**. This is The Millennium (Revelation 5:10).

There it is: The Seven Christian Churches who have been infiltrated by Satan's false teachings are to become Priests and Kings in God's **"kingdom."** However, this only happens if all Christians and Israelites come out of **the false teachings** of Babylon. Chapter 6, 'Babylon and The Two Grails' explains in depth the specific details. After Jesus cleanses His **"churches,"** just before His **"millennial reign,"** Satan is cast into prison for one thousand years, and many voices proclaim, **"They** [saved of the seven churches] **lived and reigned with Christ a thousand years"** (Revelation 20:4). The second death will not have **any power** over them.

These **Kings** or **Priests** are those of **the seven churches** who reign with Christ for one thousand years. These are **the chosen** or **the saints** who become The **Bride** of **Christ** (Revelation 19:7-8).

Now, you are ready to trace **the schoolmaster** in the earthly **temple** to discover how Jesus cleanses His Bride and Wedding Guests to come to The Wedding. Remember, many from **"the seven churches"** are **called** but only a few chosen (Matthew 22:14). The rest of <u>Revelation</u> depicts how those who are chosen to attend must have a proper wedding garment to be a part of The Groom's Wedding. The early **temple** will give you the answer.

CHURCH IN THE WILDERNESS   Revelation 12 summarizes **church history** until Christ comes and establishes God's **"kingdom."** Read it **all** carefully. Revelation 12:6 shows the woman – God's **"church"** – during the time of world trouble known as **The Great Tribulation,**

taking "**the church**" into a **place of safety** where God supplies all her needs. This Great Tribulation lasts for three and a half years or 1,260 days. Satan and his **demon** angels had a war in heaven with God and His **angels**. Satan and his demon angels were defeated and cast to the earth. Because Satan knows his time is short, he determines to make war with the remnant of God's "**church**" who keep God's "**commandments**" and "**the testimony**" or prophecy from "**the true**" Christ (Revelation 12:17). **The Church** is in **The Wilderness**.

THE QUESTIONS   The first twelve chapters in <u>Revelation</u> present many questions about the history of "**the true church**" (**seven candlesticks**). Prophetically to understand <u>The Book of Revelation</u>, you need to know the answers to these questions:

       1   What is the wilderness?

       2   What is the place of safety?

       3   What part of "**the church**" goes into safety?

       4   What part of "**the church**" is persecuted and martyred by Satan?

Once you find **the biblical answer** to these questions, you will know who will be able to attend The Wedding Feast, and who will not be allowed to attend – "**many are called but few chosen.**"

Those in <u>The Book of Life</u> are those attending The Marriage Feast of The Lamb. <u>The Book of Life</u> is a **Marriage Registry**. **The temple**, as part of The Law, is **a shadow**, and **the temple** with The Holy Days are also **a shadow**, which will lead everyone eventually to Christ in **the last days**. The Last Days begin with The Birth of Jesus and will be explained in Chapter 4, 'Who Is The Beast?'

THE TWO PILLARS   From The Holy Place in **the temple (seven candlesticks)**, going East as one goes through the veil, are **two pillars**. Each of these two pillars has a name. The pillar on the right is called Jachin, and on the left is called Boaz (I Kings 7:21-22). Who or what are these two pillars? These two pillars do not support **the temple** at all. They are two columns standing in front of The Holy Place and The Holy of Holies. What do they **represent** as **shadows**? Revelation 3:12 prophesies if The Philadelphia Church **overcomes to the end** they will be a **pillar** in **the temple** in New Jerusalem. Remember, the two pillars in Solomon's **temple** are Christians who overcome **till the end**. Just who does The Book of Revelation say they are?

THE TWO WITNESSES So much has been written and preached about the **two witnesses** being **two humans**. Some say one is a young man and the other an elder. When you allow The Bible to interpret, amazingly, you will find out they are **not** two people at all. Some, among Christians, are bold enough to   believe   they, themselves, will   be one of **the two witnesses**. Revelation 11 describes these **two witnesses**, so let The Bible unravel **the mystery** for you.

John was told to measure God's **temple** (Revelation 11:1-2). Then, John was told not to measure **the court** of The Gentiles because for three and a half years The Gentiles will control God's **temple**. This is the time period when the anti-Christ will be in **the temple** claiming to be God. This is the time of The Great Tribulation.

The importance of **this temple** is that **the court** of Israel is to be measured because Christ knows **the exact number of Israelites who will occupy The Court of Israel**. Remember, in John 14:1, Jesus said, **He was going to God, The Father to prepare a place for you** [Christians] **in God's house, "the temple."** Revelation uncovers the process or order that Christians will or will not be in The Father's "**house.**" The **two witnesses** tell who will be in that **temple**. On the same subject, John reveals in Revelation 11:3 that his **two witnesses** will prophecy (The Book of Revelation) for three and a half years or during The Great Tribulation. Who are these **two witnesses**? Revelation 11:4 states these **two witnesses** are **two olive trees** and **two candlesticks** who are standing before God on the earth. Now you have the definition!

1   They are **two olive trees**.

2   They are **two candlesticks**

3   They **stand before God's throne**

Does The Bible define these three points, which reveals who these **two witnesses** are? Yes, it does! An **angel** awoke Zechariah and showed him a candlestick, of gold with a bowl on top which had seven lamps (Zechariah 4:1-4). This is an Old Testament prophecy – **"the menorah"** in The Holy Place representing **"the seven churches"** in Revelation 2 and 3.

"There are two olive trees" by this **seven-lamp candlestick** (Verse 3). Then, Zechariah asked what are these **olive trees** and **candlesticks** (Verse 4)? Who or what are these **"two olive trees"** by **"the menorah"** or **"the candlestick?"** (Zechariah 4:11-14) These **"two olive"** trees empty themselves into **"the candlestick"** (Verse 12). Then **the angel** states clearly these two olive trees are God's **two anointed ones** who stand before God. Now, you have solved **a part** of the mystery. **"These olive trees"** represent God's Holy Spirit providing the fuel for **the candlestick – The Seven Churches** to have a light and be witnesses during the **three and a half years** of "tribulation." Can you prove who these two olive trees are? Yes, you can. Remember, Jesus was **not** going to have **the court** of The Gentiles measured (Revelation 11:1-2). Who is The Revelator of these **two olive trees?** Who are **the two witnesses**? The Apostle to The Gentiles – **The Apostle Paul** clearly tells you who the **two olive trees** are.

In Romans 11:1 Paul said God will not throw Israel – His people away. For a short time The Nation of Israel is **blinded** by The Law because they do not understand The Law was only **a shadow** or a stepping stone to bring them to Christ. The Law's **purpose** was not to make them **righteous**. The Law is just **a shadow** pointing to Christ who only can make you **righteous** (Hebrews 10:1 and Colossian 1:27). The Letter is not a point of sin but a **shadow** or **type** of what is **real** or **the truth**.

Ultimately, **all Israel** will be **saved** (Romans 11:26). The blindness of Israel will last until The Gentile **rule** on the earth **ends**. Only a **remnant** of Israel (during The Gentile **rule**) will be **saved** (Romans 11:25). Why? So **The Gentile** "world" can be **saved** (Romans 11:15). Now, who are "The Two Olive Trees?"

Romans 11:16-24 simply reveals **The Two Olive Trees** are The **Israelites** and The **Gentiles**. This is God's **purpose** to be **ALL AND IN ALL** (I Corinthians 15). This all fits perfectly with the story of <u>Revelation</u>. God, through His people **Israel** and the converted **Gentiles** (The Seven Candlesticks) are **the two witnesses.** Jesus already revealed "**candlesticks**" represent "**churches**" **not** two people (Revelation 1:20). The two candlesticks are **not two humans** but "**two churches**" – The Church in The Wilderness (Israel) and The Church of God (Gentiles) who **witness** during The Great Tribulation and finally, are martyred and resurrected (at **the return** of Christ) (Revelation 11:7-12). Where are they killed? In The Great City of Babylon – **the whore**, where Christ was crucified (Revelation 11:8). Can you know how many will be killed? Yes.

Revelation 7:1-17 prophesies that of Israel only **144,000** from The Tribes of Israel do **the witnessing** and the **innumerable multitude** from The Gentiles are **the witnesses.** Revelation 7:14 states these one hundred and forty-four thousand **(144,000) Israelites** and **an innumerable Gentile multitude come out of The Great Tribulation.** Plain as day! The **two witnesses** are the **144,000 of Israel** and **the innumerable multitude from The Gentiles.** They are "**The Two Olive Trees.**" The Apostle Paul proved it (Romans 11). The **natural olive tree** represents Israel, God's Church in The Wilderness, and the **wild olive tree** represents The Gentiles **converted** to the **natural** tree as Christians.

PHILADELPHIA   The reward of The Church of Philadelphia, if they overcome, is to be of these **two pillars** (Revelation 3:12). They will be invited to The Wedding in New Jerusalem.

THE SHADOWS   Remember, Jachin and Boaz are **the two pillars** before God's **throne** and **the candlestick** with **the seven lamps.** Jachin in Hebrew is in "the male gender." Boaz is in "the female gender." Why?

Boaz is of **the church** (The Gentile Church), through Ruth, The Moabites. Ruth was Gentile, and she was grafted into the **natural** olive tree – Boaz of Israel. Boaz is female because it is "**the church**" or woman in Revelation 12. Israel is Jachin or **the remnant** of Israel who is **saved** to be the 144,000 of Israel. Israel is male because **the inheritance** must pass through the male line. You now have the true story of **the two witnesses** and "**the schoolmaster**" leading you to Christ in **the temple**.

THE ALTAR   When one descends the steps from **the temple**, you find the **sacrificial altar**. Why is the altar located right in front of **the temple**? Remember, between **the temple** and **altar** was the basin to cleanse or baptize. First, you must be **repentant** or your human nature must die. Hebrews 9:2 Paul said for you to be able to be accepted of God, **all things** are by Law **purged** by **blood**; and without shedding of blood there is no remission. Christ gave that sacrifice for sinners but what about the rest of the unconverted world? Remember, The Law, which includes **the temple**, is only **a shadow**.

In The Law, God requires animal sacrifice by The Priest for his sins and the sins of the people (Hebrews 9:9-10). These animal sacrifices did not make The Priest or the people "**perfect**." That is why they offered clean animals **only** as a sacrifice. Why only clean animals? Clean animals can be trained and are far more docile than the unclean animals, but they still were animals. For example, lions and tigers are wild. Lambs are able to be led. That is the difference. This is why God gave a Law about clean and unclean animals?

Peter, who was given **the keys** to "**the kingdom**," reveals the difference.

After Peter had the vision concerning clean and unclean animals, Cornelius, The Gentile (who was without God), was converted. God revealed the meaning of **the shadow** in The Law and why God instituted clean and unclean animals. Peter now said there was no difference between clean and unclean animals (Acts 10:28). God revealed **the clean animals were Israel**, and **the unclean animals were The Gentiles**, who were without God. Now, both were clean, but **only** if they **repented** and **accepted** Christ. Both were still not perfect and still had carnal natures, but now both, The Israelites and The Gentiles, were **teachable**. Psalms 95:1-11 covers the answers so you understand **the place of safety, the wilderness**, as well as, those who go through **The Great Tribulation** – including **The Lake of Fire**!

What is **the place of safety**? The **rock** is your **salvation**. In Hebrew, the word "rock," signifies "a place of safety" or "fortress of protection." Some Christians, fallaciously, believe Petra (a rock city) in South Jordan is **the place of safety**. This is false. Read Psalms 94:22. It clearly interprets **the place of safety**. **"But The Lord is my refuge** [place of safety] **and my God is THE ROCK** [not Petra] – **God is my refuge."** This is **the place of safety for some** Christians during The Great Tribulation. Christ will protect you (I Corinthians 10:4).

Now, what is **the wilderness** where Christ protects you? David states **harden** not your heart as Israel did and wouldn't **enter God's rest**, but had to spend **forty years** in **the wilderness** being **tested of God** (Psalms 95:8). That is why Stephen called Israel **The Church in The Wilderness** (Acts 7:38). Of a truth, Israel is **the pillar** (Jachin) in **the temple**, and must be tried and tested in **the wilderness** just like **the pillar** of Boaz –

"the seven churches" of Revelations 2 and 3. Both must have their trial of **faith** in The Wilderness to come out of Babylon (Revelation 18:4).

The woman – **"the church"** flees from Satan into **the wilderness** just as Israel had done (Revelation 12:14). It is in **the wilderness** and not God's **rest** where **"the church"** is safe. This part of **"the church"** is kept safe during The Great Tribulation by Christ, **"our rock"** or **place of safety.** How? As Satan pursues **the spiritually growing** Christians (five wise virgins), Christ **causes** natural disasters to occur around them to keep them safe (Revelation 12:15-16). These are The Seven Trumpets. God protects His **worthy Christians** by natural disasters and wars as a shield to keep them safe (Revelation 11). No one will be after Christians if the enemy is running for their lives. The wilderness is the world under Satan's control with all its wars, famines, diseases and its struggle for the fittest to survive. It is the time of worldwide trouble. John 16:20-21 speaks of **"the church"** just before Christ **returns**. Christ prayed to The Father even though **spiritually** growing Christians are **in the world** (wilderness), they are not of it (John 17:11-15). They have come out of Babylon – The Wilderness.

Now, what happens to those in The Seven Churches of God who will not be coming out of Babylon. Hebrews 4:10-11 states those **resting** (safe) in Christ will cease **from their works**. But notice what happens to the Christians who do not come out of Babylon. Those who do not **in faith** believe **in Christ** as their **place of safety**, they will not enter into **God's rest** or **safety**, but will receive **His wrath**! (Psalms 95:11)

Back to **the sacrificial altar** and its meaning. Since God protects the

faithful Christians in safety, Satan is angry (Revelation 12:17). Satan goes to make war with the remnant of God's **church** who keep His Ten Commandments and the prophecy of Christ. What happens to them? These Christians do keep "**the commandments**" and will be **saved** but what do they lack?

The **unfaithful part** of "**the seven churches**" go into **The Great Tribulation** to gain total **faith** in Christ which they lacked, and only then will live by every Word (logos) of God (Revelation 7:14-15). Israel also lacked **faith** (Matthew 4:4). These are the 144,000 and the innumerable multitude who are Gentiles who **witness "the true"** Christ during The Tribulation. These are **the two candlesticks** or **two witnesses** of God who are martyred (Revelation 11:7-11). Then at Christ's "**return**" at

The **Seventh Trump**, they are in The **First Resurrection** – The Spring Barley Harvest. Pick up the story in Revelation 14:1, where you see the 144,000 with Jesus on Mt. Zion. A voice cries out to the dead, "wait, you, too, will also be resurrected" (Revelation 14:13-20). There are two more "**harvests**" – The **Wheat Harvest** and **The Grape Harvest** (Verses 14 to 20). For more insight read Chapter 7, 'The Mystery Harvest.'

Those in The Grape Harvest, Revelation 14:18 states this **angel** comes out of the **altar**, not just **the temple**, why? Because this **angel** takes **fire from the_altar** and starts the **seven last plagues** which is finalized with **The Lake of Fire** or hell. There you have it. **The altar** is **a shadow** of God's **wrath**, since God is a **consuming fire** (Hebrews 12:29). All those who haven't come out of **Babylon** or false teaching (The Seven Churches and Israel) will be brought to complete repentance by **God's wrath** and **The**

Lake of Fire. Not everyone will be invited to The Wedding Feast in New Jerusalem. Many are **called** (The Churches) but **few are chosen**. THE **TEMPLE** IS TRULY THE MAJOR **SHADOW** OR **SCHOOLMASTER**, WHICH WILL EVENTUALLY BRING YOU TO CHRIST AND THE WEDDING FEAST.

CHAPTER 2

WHO IS GOD'S CHURCH?

Why are there so many Christian denominations? Every Christian group claims they, only, are "the true church." Those of The Jewish faith have the same problem. There are the Reformed, Orthodox, Kabalists, along with others. What and where is The True Church of God?

You will discover God has a specific purpose for His people and the answer is God's "two witnesses" in The Book of Revelation. Discover the truth of God's church and it's diversified groups.

After God broke the engagement in <u>The Old Testament</u> with Israel, Christ came in <u>The New Testament</u>. Christ became The Groom and contractually was married to **the church** by an engagement. But before the consummation of **the marriage**, The Bride, His Virgin, had to make herself ready. Read Ephesians 5:24-32. God is preparing for The Wedding Feast, but who will be The Bride? Those in The Jewish Faith firmly believe they will be The Messiah's Bride. On the other hand, Christians, as **"the church,"** believe they will be The Bride. Who is right?

<u>THE MARRIAGE FEAST</u> Jesus gives a parable about a certain King – (God) who prepared to marry off His Son, Jesus (Matthew 22:1-14).

Israel and The Church of God, including The Guests, all made some excuse not to attend. What is important for you to know is not all of Israel nor all **the church** are **chosen**. Jesus said, **"For MANY ARE CALLED, but few are CHOSEN!"** (Matthew 22:14) Wow! Neither the whole of Israel or the whole **church** are The Bride. The Bible states only the **few** are **chosen** to be at The Wedding.

WHO ARE THE CHOSEN?   Jesus, then relates the parable of the **ten virgins** (Matthew 25:1-10).   Five of them are wise, the other half are unwise. Remember, all of them are **virgins** – and are acceptable to be brides.   Notice the problem.   Only half of them are prepared to be **a proper bride**. Matthew 25:10 states the five wise virgins **were ready**, and when Christ, The Groom, returned, they were the only ones ready for The Wedding Feast. Some of Israel and some in **"the church"** are not picked.   Even The Guests who are invited are not prepared for The Wedding. Five are **chosen** to be The Bride and the other five who are not chosen are only bridesmaids. "Always a bridesmaid (virgins) but **never** a **bride**." They will be part of The Wedding, but not included as The Bride.

Read The Book of Esther. It took her nearly two years to get ready to be The King's Bride. Esther was a type of Israel and **"the church."** What is the distinguishing requirement to be Christ's Bride? Since only half of The Ten Virgins, are to be The Bride, you need to know.

THE ANSWER   The Book of Revelation reveals   exactly   who Christ's Bride will be. Revelation 19:7-9 prophesies who will be Christ's Bride and those who will be allowed to come to The Wedding as Guests. New Jerusalem, coming down out of Heaven from God, is **prepared** as a

Bride adorned for her husband (Revelation 21:2)! Pretty clear. Jerusalem, coming from **heaven**, will be the location ready for The Wedding Feast. Who can come? **No one** who **defiles** can come (Revelation 21:27). One must be **perfect** (Matthew 5:48), and only those written in The Lamb's Book of Life. The Book of Life is The Marriage Registry. If you are not written in The Book of Life (**Christ "living in you"**) (Colossians 1:27), you cannot even come to The Wedding Feast. Now, who is The Bride?

Revelation 19:7-8 reveals The Bride. **"⁸And to her was granted that she [bride] should be ARRAYED in FINE LINEN."** The Bride has to wear a particular dress. What is that dress? Going on, **"For the FINE LINEN is the RIGHTEOUSNESS of SAINTS."** The Bride will only be those who continue to grow **spiritually** to become **a saint, a righteous one** or as the word in Hebrew reveals, a "hassidim." One must **spiritually** grow where they neither **offend God** or **His creation**. They must be one who becomes a Christian, whether Israelite or Gentile, and **continue to grow spiritually** to become Holy or perfect (Matthew 5:48). These are the five wise virgins. If you are an Israelite or of The Church of God doesn't mean you will be chosen as **"a saint"** or a **"righteous one."** One can end up being **"a guest"** or a **bridesmaid but not a bride**. When you read Chapter 9, 'What is Sin,' you will know the difference. Paul told Timothy, **"But in GOD'S GREAT HOUSE (Israel or Gentile) there are not only vessels of gold and silver, but also of wood and of earth; and some to honour, and some to dishonour"** (II Timothy 2:20). Those, ultimately to dishonor, go into The Lake of Fire or hell. First, you know who Israel is, but who, of The Gentiles, is Christ's Bride? To answer that question, one must understand who is The Church of God?

CHURCH CALLING   The Greek word for "**church**" in <u>The New Testament</u> is "**ecclesia**" or "**the called-out ones**." You know that God, The Father, is having A Wedding for His Son. Ephesians 5 proves His Bride is being prepared by Christ, The Husband, through **the gift of Jesus – The Father's Holy Spirit**. Notice what event **the church** is called to attend.

The Bride is made ready just before The Return of Christ (Revelation 19:7-9). The Bride is now **prepared** for **The Wedding Feast**, but The Guests, right at this moment in time (Christ's second coming), are only **invited to attend The Wedding** (Verse 9). The Barley Spring Harvest shadows The First Resurrection, which is about to take place. What does Revelation 19:9 reveal? **"Blessed are they which are CALLED unto the marriage supper of the lamb."** Then, the rest of the chapter relates **the return** of Christ on **The White Horse**.

Notice, who is **invited** to The Marriage Feast – "**the called**," The Churches of God. Clear as a bell! <u>The Book of Life</u> is a <u>Marriage Registry</u>.

THE REAL CHURCH ERAS   Go to the parable of "**the sower and the seed**" in Matthew 13:18-30. Each person is called to "**the church**," but as you have proved, only a few will be **chosen** to come to **The Wedding Feast**. Whether one is to be The Bride (**saint** or **righteous ones**) or The Guests (**the faithful**) – only a **few are chosen**. Jesus said some who are called into "**the church**" and accept **the truth** in their heart quit when Satan deceives them.

The second group receives **the truth** and is so excited, but when they are tested as in the **tribulation** or **persecuted**, they give up or are offended. The third group receives **the truth**, but is more interested in the earthly affairs of this life and is too busy to keep **growing spiritually**.

Of those who are called in the fourth group are The Christians who are the ones **chosen**. All the **other Christians in "the church"** who have been called are not listed in <u>The Marriage Registry</u> – <u>The Book of Life</u>. They cannot come to The Wedding Feast. They are called and invited, but wear the wrong garment to attend. Why?

<u>TARES AND WHEAT</u> This is a great mystery according to The Apostle Paul in Ephesians 5:32. What is it about **"the church"** and Christ's Bride? The Words of Christ about The Parable of The Sower and The Seed explains it to you.

Jesus adds **a new understanding** to The Parable of The Sower and The Seed (Matthew 13:24-30). Christ said someone sprinkled tares in between the seeds of the **seedlings** – **the growing wheat**. He asked who did this? It was an **enemy** of **the sower**. It was suggested they pull out the tares so the wheat can grow without hindrance or deceit. Christ continued and states, **"Let BOTH** [seed and tares] **grow TOGETHER UNTIL the HARVEST."** Why? So, that no **wheat** is pulled out or lost with the tares. Then at the harvest, the tares are removed and burned. The wheat, then, is harvested and put into the barn. Do you understand what Jesus is telling you? The tares are of Satan and **his false teaching**, which are **mixed** with the **wheat** while **the church** is trying to **grow spiritually**.

THE SEVEN CANDLESTICKS   Chapter 1 on 'The Schoolmaster' proves "**the seven candlesticks**" in Revelation 1:20 are "**the menorah**," or "**the seven candlesticks**" in The Holy Place in **the temple** (Hebrew 9:2). As Christ states **these seven candlesticks** are "**the seven churches**" in Revelation 2 and 3. In Revelation 1:12-13 Jesus is the one in the **midst** of these seven candlesticks, which are a **shadow** or **type** of these churches. Since these are seven churches, which define "**the menorah**" in **the temple**, these **seven churches** are "**the seven churches**" of God. Whatever Jesus defines as these "**seven churches**," they are **the true** and **only** Churches of God. They are **candlesticks** because they are to be Christ's **witness** to the world. You will see <u>Revelation</u> is the prophecy of the future witnessing of what Christians are doing in their daily lives. Jesus relates to John that <u>The Book of Revelation</u> is to be written to "**the seven churches**" (Revelation 1:11). Why?

<u>The Book of Revelation</u> is "**the testimony**" or "**will**" of Jesus Christ (Revelation 19:10). With His death this **testimony** went into force and this "**will**" of Jesus is **the spirit of prophesy**. <u>The Book of Revelation</u> is bequeathed to "**the seven churches**" as their **inheritance** from Christ. This **inheritance** is a **prophecy** of what "**the seven churches**" **must do** to receive **their inheritance**!   These "**seven churches**" are The True Churches of God. What does Jesus demand of His "**seven churches**."

REVELATION 2 AND 3   In error, some claim these **seven churches** are seven eras. This according to **<u>Revelation,</u>** cannot be. Why? Simply, because you will see each of "**the seven churches**" existing when Christ

returns. It is, therefore, **impossible** for "**the seven churches**" to each be separate periods from the genesis of "**the church**" on Pentecost to "**the return**" of Christ.

These "**seven churches**" represented by "**the seven candlesticks**" in **the temple remain** until **Christ's second coming** to receive their **reward** or **inheritance**. These "**seven churches**," therefore, are a **type** from the genesis of "**the church**" until **the return** of Jesus in the clouds. That is the very reason The Book of Revelation is written to them. The Book of Revelation is their prophecy or future until God's "**kingdom**" comes. Open this testimony of Jesus and see the future of God's **true church**:

EPHESUS: Jesus warns them they have **left their first love** (Revelation 2:4). Christ warns them that if they do not repent, He will **remove their candlestick when He comes**! (Verse 5) The Ephesian Church of God will still be in existence upon Christ's **return**.

SMYRNA: If this "**church**" remains faithful, their reward is – they will not be hurt or thrown into The Lake of Fire (Revelation 2:11). They exist at **the return** of Jesus.

PERGAMOS: Jesus warns them He will **come** quickly and will fight against them at His Second Coming (Revelation 2:16). Pergamos exists until the end.

THYATIRA: Christ tells those in Thyatira to hold fast until He **returns** (Revelation 2:25). This Church still exists at Christ's **second coming**.

SARDIS: Jesus tells them to hold fast to what **truth** they know until He

returns (Revelation 3:3). Those of The Sardis Church will continue to exist until He **returns**.

PHILADELPHIA: Christ tells The Philadelphians to hold fast because He will quickly **return** (Revelation 3:11).

LAODICEA: Jesus warns them He stands at the door at His **return** (Revelation 3:20). Laodiceans exist when Christ **returns**.

These **seven churches** are not **eras** but seven types of **Christian "churches."** All exist from their beginnings when Christ first came until Christ's second coming. These **"seven churches,"** as **"the menorah"** in The Holy Place, are to be **witnesses** of Jesus right until God's **"kingdom"** comes. That is why they receive this Book of Revelation so they can understand prophecy and witness about the **real** God and **true** Savior, Jesus, The Christ. These **"seven churches"** are The True Churches of God **throughout** human history until God's **"kingdom."** This is your Savior, Jesus Christ, telling you who are the real Churches of God. What do these churches believe? What **faith** or **doctrine** do they hold?

CHURCH OF GOD DOCTRINE   The Seven Churches of God in Revelation are **The True Churches of God**. All of them had different beliefs and doctrines.   Whether Catholic, Orthodox, Protestants, Evangelicals, Independents, etc. – **all are Christians**. They are all the **called-out ones**. They are all invited to **The Wedding Feast**. Jesus said those originally **called to The Wedding Feast were not worthy** (Matthew 22:8-13). What did Christ say to do? He told His servants (ministry) to invite **everyone, both good and bad**. Paul said in His

Father's House are vessels of honor and dishonor – good and bad. That is The Church of God. That is why Jesus said when He **returns** many are **called** but **few chosen**. Being in The Church of God does not mean **you will be invited** to The Wedding Feast. Read Revelation 2 and 3 so you can prove all these **churches** had a variety of doctrinal teachings. Some had more **truth** than others, but all had to **hold fast** and/or **overcome**.

Teachings ranged from a **false Christ** and a **false God** to belief in pagan days and Baalism through Jezebel. What confusion and what a doctrinal **mess** of a mixture. The major outstanding **sin** or **missing the mark** for most of them is **to believe they are the only "true church."** In fact, that was the **major sin** of **The Laodiceans**. They thought they **all** had **the truth** they needed. That is why they weren't growing in **spiritual talents** from one to two or five to ten. They are the **five unwise virgins**, but they **are still virgins** or **God's "church."** What was their penalty? Christ said, **"I counsel of you to buy gold"** – where? In Fire or The Lake of Fire (Revelation 3:18). **All "seven churches"** of God had to **hold fast** or **overcome**. That is why Jesus said, **"Come out of her** [Babylon] **my people!"** (Revelation 18:4) All are in Babylon and Christians are to come out of all the false teachings. How? Paul said if you do not **prove**, **biblically**, what is being preached from God's **"Word,"** you **will have to learn the truth in The Lake of Fire** (I Corinthians 3:9-15). Paul said, **"Let the prophets** [or preachers] **speak two or three, and let the other judge"** (each **one** by The Word of God) (I Corinthians 14:29). How is Christ helping you to come to **the truth**?

THE TWO WITNESSES Many believe **the two witnesses** are two men. Some think one will be old and the other young. Others say it is Moses and Elijah. Over the centuries, many have wondered who these **two witnesses** are.

The truth is they are not two people at all. In fact, **the two witnesses** are a major part of the entire <u>Book of Revelation</u>. It is how God prepares His Bride and Guests for The Wedding Feast. Let <u>The Bible</u> reveal who **the two witnesses** are.

<u>TWO CANDLESTICKS</u>   Revelation 11:3-4 states **the two candlesticks** are **two witnesses** for a period of forty-two months or three and a half years. Later, you will see this covers the period known as The Great Tribulation. These **two candlesticks** are, also, **the two olive trees** before God (Verse 4). Does <u>The Bible</u> tell you who these two olive trees are? Yes, it does.

One of the olive trees is The Nation of Israel (Jeremiah 11:15-17). Also, it states Israel followed Baal just like **"the churches"** in **Revelation**. The Prophet Zechariah even gives you more biblical proof as to who **the two witnesses** are. In Zechariah 4:3-4, **the angel** asks who are the two olive trees? The angel tells Zechariah that the candlestick with seven lamps is fed olive oil from these two olive trees. The angel continues and says these two olive trees empty into the seven lamps just as Revelation 1:20 mentions **the seven candlesticks** (Verses 11 to 14). Jesus reveals **the candlesticks** are "the seven churches." Zechariah 4:14 states the two olive trees that feed **the candlestick** or "**menorah**" in The Holy Place are God's **two anointed ones**. Before the call of The Gentiles, **the anointed ones** were Judah and Israel. Acts 7:38 states that Israel is The Church in

The Wilderness. Who is the other olive tree? The Apostle to The Gentiles tells you: Romans 11:16-25, The Apostle Paul states **one of the olive trees is Israel,** The Natural Olive Tree and the second is The Wild Olive Tree – The Gentiles, who are grafted into the natural (Israel) and both are, **the two witnesses** of God. Israel (The Natural Olive Tree) and The Gentiles (The Wild Grafted-in Olive Tree) are **the two witnesses**. Israel is The Church in The Wilderness, and the other Wild Olive Tree is The Church of God. There, you have **the biblical proof. The two candlesticks** or **two witnesses** in Revelation 11 are **not two people**, but **God's "two churches,"** Israel and The Gentile Church of God. They are God's **two witnesses** during The Great Tribulation. Read what <u>Revelation</u> has to say about these **"two churches"** which are **God's two witnesses**.

144,000 AND INNUMERABLE MULTITUDE   Revelation 7 speaks of 144,000 and an innumerable multitude from all nations or The Gentiles. These individuals are all **sealed** by God as His **servants**. God **seals** them because they are being protected by God from The Seven Trumpets. Who are these 144,000 and innumerable multitude of Gentiles?

Revelation 7:4-8 states the 144,000 are from The Twelve Tribes of Israel. Then Revelation 7:9-10 tells you these are from all The Gentile Nations, and they, with the 144,000 Israelites, are clothed in white robes to attend **the wedding feast**. How did these Israelites and Gentiles become **the righteous ones with white robes**? Revelation 7:14 reveals these **two** witnesses of Christ received **the proper** Wedding Garment because they came through **the great tribulation**. The 144,000 and the innumerable multitude of Gentiles are the **two witnesses**. They **aren't two men**, but

two churches, The Church in The Wilderness (Acts 7:38) and The Church of God in Revelation 2 and 3. Revelation 11:3 states these two churches, 144,000 of Israel and The Gentiles witness for three and a half years as they go through The Great Tribulation. How does God bring them through The Great Tribulation?

REVELATION 12   Jesus reveals the history of **the true church** from The Birth of Christ (Revelation 12:1-2) until The Great Tribulation (Revelation 12:5-17). Part of **"the church"** is protected by God in **the wilderness** during The Great Tribulation. They are in a place of safety (Revelation 12:14). Then, in Revelation 12:17, Satan is angry because part of **"the church"** is protected, and he goes after **the two witnesses** who keep God's **"commandments,"** and murders them (Revelation 11:7). The difference between those **Christians** going to a **place of safety** and those **martyred** are those of "the seven churches" who **weren't faithful**, as well as, The **144,000 Israelites**. This is **scripturally** clear. Revelation 2:18-22 states those of Thyatira who do not **repent** have to go into The Great Tribulation. Now you have it. **The two witnesses** are The 144,000 Israelites with The Gentiles who are not **faithful** and must **witness the true** Christ in **the tribulation** and then are martyred. Then, they are resurrected after three days at **The Seventh Trump** or **the return** of Christ (Revelation 11:11 and Revelation 14:1-5).

THE WILDERNESS   What part of **"the church"** is in safety in **the wilderness**? Simply, just as in Acts 7:38, Israel – **"the church"** in **"the wilderness"** is in **"the world"** and not in God's **rest**. **The wilderness** is the world without God's **rest**, and by the great eagle with its two wings, they will be protected (Revelation 12:14). Christ prayed that Christians are to be **in the world but not of the world** (John 17:14-18).

The place of safety is not some physical place in the world. The place of safety is in **"the wilderness"** or **"the world."** These Christians are witnessing God's **truth**, and they are protected, but how? They do not go into The Great Tribulation because they are a light or witness to the world (five wise virgins).

THE WINGS OF AN EAGLE   Does The Bible tell you who the eagle with the wings is? It certainly does and Revelation tells where to look. Revelation 14:1-5 states at **the return** of Christ, these 144,000 sing a song. No one else was allowed to learn to sing this song. What is this song?

Revelation 15:3 reveals in **the resurrection**, The 144,000 and The Gentiles sing two songs. Only The 144,000 can learn to sing the one song. What is it? Verse 3 states it is **'The Song of Moses.'** Amazingly, **'The Song of Moses'** is recorded in Deuteronomy 32. Read it.

Deuteronomy 32:4 states **the rock** is Israel's **Lord**. I Corinthians 10:4 Paul tells you **the rock** is Christ. Then, it is this **rock, Christ,** who is **the eagle,** and that He bears them on His **wings** (Deuteronomy 32:11-12). The Bible interprets itself. **The eagle** is Christ who protects **the church** by carrying them on His **wings** just as He did with Israel in **The Wilderness.** Psalms 95 – read it all. **"The churches" place of safety,** is not Petra or some other physical place. The Israelites in The Wilderness had no faith. Only the **faithful** of **"the seven churches" rest** in Christ,

God's **rest**, and therefore, are protected by Jesus, **the rock**, while this prophecy is witnessed to the world (or wilderness). Now, you know who **"the true church"** is and those protected in safety and those who must go through The Great Tribulation. The Seven Trumpets protect those in safety, which lasts for three and a half years or the time of The Great Tribulation (Revelation 11:4-6).

To learn the rest of the story on how **the marriage feast** takes place, read Chapter 3, 'The Marriage Registry.'

CHAPTER 3

THE MARRIAGE REGISTRY

The Book of Life – you and everyone else would like your name to appear in this book; but the name not in **The Book of Life** will burn in The Lake of Fire. A primary question you should ask is what is **The Book of Life**? Read the surprising answer revealed by Jesus, Himself, in **The Book of Revelation**.

Every marriage has a registry or written invitational list of who is invited to the wedding. God, also, has a **Marriage Registry** for His Son, Jesus (Revelation 19:7-9). A great multitude of voices said, **"Let us be glad and rejoice, and give honour to him: for the marriage of the lamb is come, and his wife hath made herself ready."** How does she make herself ready? The Bride has become **righteous**, by **repenting** and becoming a **saint** in one of **"the seven churches"** or 144,000 Israelites (Verse 8). She has her Bride's **wedding gown**. The **wedding gown** is her **righteousness** by coming out of Babylon as Christ said in Revelation 18:4. She is of the five wise virgins who kept **growing spiritually** in God's Holy Spirit. The Bride does not think she **alone** has **the truth** of God. She knew she was to continue coming out of Babylon or false teaching until the very coming of Christ. Elijah also thought only he had **the truth**. God had to tell Elijah, in The Old Testament, in addition to him, there were seven thousand others He reserved as His. The Churches of God feel they are the only churches, with **the truth**. But the facts are it is not just one group of people who alone have **the truth**. That is why God tells **all of His people to come out of Babylon** (Revelation 18:4). Everyone is in **Babylon** (false god and teaching). You must continue to have **spiritual growth**!

In John 14:1-2, Jesus tells you He is going to God to prepare a place for you. <u>Revelation</u> is that story. In Christ's **"will"** <u>The Book of Revelation,</u> states what God's people, Israel and The Christians must do to **inherit** God's **"kingdom."** It all depends upon **spiritual growth** and not a church's creed of faith. Entering The Kingdom of God is based upon the degree of **spiritual growth** you are able to achieve while living in this Babylonian **system**, (as long as you repent after sinning). This is the **point** of <u>The Book of Revelation.</u>

Revelation covers the time period, in prophecy, from Christ's **birth** until God descends and starts **the new heaven** and **new earth** on this very earth. The Seven Seals covers the entire prophecy. These **seven seals** start from the birth of **the church** on Pentecost until God's **"kingdom"** comes. Revelation 6 reveals the events up to The Seven Trumpets. <u>The Book</u> covers **the last days**. The Seven Trumpets covers the three and a half years of The Great Tribulation when Jesus returns at The Seventh Trumpet and commences The Kingdom of God. Revelation 6:1-11 describes **the first five seals**. These seals represent the time period of Constantine, when Rome took control of The Christian Church of God. It includes the martyrdom, which took place during the dark ages all the way until 1947.

The well-known Four Horses of The Apocalypse takes place beginning with Constantine – The Emperor of Rome. The First Horse was **white,** carried out by Constantine with his horse when he took over **The Roman government**. The Second Horse was **red,** and came from the earth. The Third Horse was **black** during the time of famine and the black plagues. The Fourth Horse was **pale** and is during a time of **war** and **hunger**.

The Fifth Seal was extremely significant to God's **people**. Israel and growing Christians – both go through persecution and martyrdom. Read Foxes Book of Martyrs which brings the persecution of The Jews and Christ up to the end of World War II.

Jesus told His prophecy of these events in Matthew 24:1-8. Christ was asked two questions: First, when would **the temple of Herod** be destroyed? This event occurred in 70 A.D. by Titus. Not one stone was left upon another. The second question was when will be **the return** of Jesus and **the end-time** events. The first question was answered with the fall of **the temple** in 70 A.D., and then Jesus continued world history from 70 A.D. until the completion of the prophecy of The Four Horses in Revelation 6.

First, Christ said Christianity would be taken over by false teaching, paganism **mixed** with Christian teaching. Then, there would be a series of wars between kingdoms (large and small wars). Next, there will be pestilence and famine and earthquakes in the world. This, Christ said, is the beginning of sorrow and completes the prophecy up to The Fourth Seal. The Fifth Seal was grievous for Israel and the growing Christians who were coming out of Babylon.

The Lamb opens The Fifth Seal (Revelation 6:9-11). There were people under the altar in **the temple**. The altar is the shadow or symbol of martyrdom and fire or sacrifice. What happens? These are **spiritually growing Christians** and **Israelites** coming out of Babylon. They are persecuted and killed by "**the church**." This includes the time of Genghis Kahn up to World War II including The Holocaust.

When this dispensation is concluded, the martyrs are told to rest until their brothers will be martyred in The Great Tribulation (Revelation 6:11 and Matthew 24:9-13). Then in Matthew 24:14-20 Jesus answers the second question about **the end-times** and His **return**. Finally, Matthew 24:28 shows The First Resurrection, which states where the carcass is, The Battle of Armageddon, where the eagles will be gathered. Who are **the eagles**? They are The Christians and The Israelites who are with Christ on Mt. Zion, not far from The Valley of Jehoshaphat. How can you know who the eagles are? 'The Song of Moses' in Deuteronomy 32 reveals that Christ is **the rock**, who is **the eagle** who carries the baby eagles on His **wings** to safety while in **the wilderness** (world). Now, those witnessing The Gospel during The Great Tribulation in **the wilderness** (in safety), and those **two witnesses** going into **the tribulation**, after having been martyred are now **mature** (spiritually grown) **eagles** and are in the first, Barley Harvest, as The Bride of Christ, by Mt. Zion, not far from the slaughter at Armageddon.

OUR PRESENT TIME   Where is the world at present in the prophecy of The Seven Seals? **Five Seals of Prophecy** are now history. The **Sixth Seal has not been opened** as yet since its prophecy has not occurred. Those living now are in **those times**. **Christians are near the**

time of The Sixth Seal. Those martyred during the dark ages through World War II are asked to rest or sleep in death until their brothers also die for Christ (Revelation 6:10-11).

Then Revelation 6:12 states that when The Sixth Seal is opened and a great earthquake begins to rumble, and **the sun becomes black** and **the moon becomes as blood**. This must still come to pass. Then The Sixth Seal will reveal heavenly disturbances such as when MOUNTAINS, ISLANDS and COASTLANDS are moved and literally changed. **This earthquake** will be the most horrific ever seen by mankind. Perhaps, the recent tsunami is a type of what is to come to pass all over the world. Now you know where you are in prophecy. You are at the beginning of The Sixth Seal since The Fifth Seal has been completed (Matthew 24:9-13). This Sixth Seal is also the prophecy in The Book of Joel. Read it.

THE 7TH SEAL Revelation 7. Read all of it, as this is the future of those who go through **The Great Tribulation** – The Seventh Seal (Revelation 7:14). Then, as The Seventh Seal is opened, there will be silence in **heaven**. Another angel stood by the altar in **the temple**, and he had **incense**, which are the **prayers of "the saints**." These are those martyred in The Great Tribulation, and **the faithful witnesses** in safety during this time. It is very important to understand this time period of three and a half years, which is the **duration** of **The Seven Trumpets** (as you will see).

Since this is Christ's **"will"** and **"testament,"** you need to know those coming out of Babylon are God's people (Revelation 18:4). What is required of those Christians and Israelites to be in The First Resurrection of The Barley Harvest? These comprise **The Bride of Christ**. Who are they?

THE SEVEN CHURCHES   In Revelation 11:1-2, you see only **the court** of Israel is measured, but The Gentile **court** is not measured. Why?

Revelation 7 denotes only 144,000 Israelites coming out of The Great Tribulation.   That is why only **the court** of Israel is measured.   The Gentiles have an innumerable multitude or are not measured, and therefore, The Gentile "**court**" is not known.   To answer this question, you only need to know **how many Gentiles** go through The Great Tribulation.   That is why The Book of Revelation is written **only** to **the seven churches**.   The number for The Israelites is already known but not the number of The Seven Churches of God.   Most of them are **not growing spiritually** as they should.   Christ informs them what these "**seven churches**" must do, although the number is not revealed.

1   Jesus tells The Ephesian Church if they do not return to their first love, **the true** God and Christ, He will **remove** their **candlestick**. They will not be The Bride or even The Guests at The Wedding. They must be **tested** in **The Great Tribulation**, and come out of Babylon or Christ will **remove** their **candlestick** when He **returns** (Revelation 2:1-5).

2   Smyrna will only need to go through The Tribulation for a short time.   They have **false apostle teachings** as they are not of the original **Jewish** Apostles but of Satan.   Because of this, they will be tried and tested briefly.   Those from Smyrna who come out of Babylon will not have to go into The Lake of Fire to repent.   No second death (Revelation 2:8-11).

3   Pergamos has a problem because this **"Christian church"** accepts pagan teaching and doctrine of The Nicolaitanes as well as making a **business** out of God's **"church"** like Balaam and Balak (Revelation 2:1-17).   Notice, if they **repent** of this Babylonish system, they will be a stone or part of the wall in Jerusalem. However, they will not be The Bride.

4   Thyatira followed Jezebel, which held the pagan doctrine of Baal. However, as they are **"tried,"** their last works are better than when this Church of God started.   There are those in this Christian-pagan Church who do not accept Jezebel's teachings.   Those who come out of Babylon will be in The First Resurrection and rule with Christ with a rod of iron (Revelation 2:18-28).   Also, **the spiritually growing Christians will be Christ's Bride.   Jesus** is the **bright and morning star** as **God's firstborn**.   He is the first light of the stars in the morning.

5   Sardis as God's **church** is a **social club**.   Going to church, giving money and fasting and praying is good enough for them.   **Growing spiritually** from one talent to two, five and ten takes too much work and energy.   Physical works can never change human nature. They believe being in **the church**, and following its days or doctrines is sufficient.   When Christ comes, as a thief in the night, they will **not be ready**.   They are the **unwise** virgins.   A **few** of them grow **spiritually**, and will be in The First Resurrection. Those who remain only **satisfied** with **the milk** of **the truth** must go into **The Lake of Fire** (Revelation 3:1-6).

6   The Philadelphia Church of God has the **key** of **David**, A RIGHT HEART AND HAVE CHRIST IN THEM. Because of this, they have a **little strength** or Christ in them. They are **growing spiritually**. They have not denied the **real Jesus**, and therefore, will not be tried, but will be able to go into a **place of safety (the rock)** and will not go through The Great Tribulation. Jesus said to The Philadelphians, **"I come quickly: hold that fast which thou hast, that no man take thy crown"** (Revelation 3:11). This word "crown" in Greek is not "royalty," but "having Christ's banner around their head." Christ lives in them. Their reward will be a **pillar**, Jachin and Boaz, and will enter The Marriage Feast as Christ's Bride. They will share Christ's **throne** as He shares His Father's **throne** (Revelation 3:7-13).

7   The last of the seven is The Laodicean Church. They have real problems. Pagan teaching is not their sin. It is worse. They are **lukewarm**. They are barely a **witness** of **the true** Christ. They have made Christianity a religion. It has rituals of dos and don'ts. They believe they have to do human works, such as The Letter of The Law. Real change is for you to be as Christ is. Instead, they are self-satisfied with **the limited truth** they have. They are those with **one talent**. They, truly, are **lukewarm**. Jesus will **spit** them out of His mouth when He comes. Why? They do not **grow spiritually** with God's **"word" or "logos."**

If they were **cold**, as atheists or agnostics, they wouldn't know better. They would only need a few stripes to wake up. But, since they are satisfied with **their truth** as **the ONLY truth**, Jesus gives them this advice in Revelation 3:18: Christ said, **"I counsel thee to buy of me gold."** How? By going into The Lake of Fire. Read Luke 12 about this **"church."** They will burn until they wake up, and **repent** and **grow in spiritual truth** (I Corinthians 3).

There you have it – <u>Revelation</u> prophesies Christ's "will." Who will **inherit "the kingdom"** as a Bride, or a Witness, Ushers, Bridesmaids or Guests? These are those who will be written in The Marriage Registry. What is The Marriage Registry?

<u>REVELATION 21</u>   **"Be glad and rejoice."** Why? The Marriage of The Lamb – The Feast, is ready, and The Bride has made herself ready (Revelation 19:7-9). Verse 9 tells you, **"Blessed** [happy] **are they which are called** [Israel and Gentiles] **unto the marriage supper of the Lamb."** Who is **called** to this **marriage supper**?

New Jerusalem is The Bride adorned (righteousness) for her husband (Revelation 21:2). Who gets to attend besides The Bride? **The gates** to New Jerusalem will always be opened. Who can enter? (Revelation 21:25-27) Verse 27 states, **"there shall in no wise enter into it** [New Jerusalem] **anything that defiles."** The **Marriage Registry** allows only **those written** in <u>The Lamb's Book of Life</u>. This is Christ's Marriage Registry – <u>The Book of Life</u>!

Then Revelation 22:14 reveals the garment you must wear to enter through **the gates**. You are blessed if you **keep** the **sayings of this** prophecy – **Christ's "will"** in <u>The Book of Revelation</u>. Revelation 22:14 says only those will be blessed who eat of **The Tree of Life** if they keep God's **"commandments."** Those **left out** or **without the city** are those thrown into The Lake of Fire. <u>The Book of Life</u> is <u>The Lamb's Marriage Registry</u>. Now, you must learn what Christ requires of you, so you can enter the city to eat of The Tree of Life!

CHAPTER 4

WHO IS THE BEAST?

The beast is known in the Christian world as a hideous creature with seven heads and ten horns. Every imaginable horrendous image has been drawn to depict this beast. Who or what is this monster? Surprisingly, the true biblical answer reveals prophetically a time when the "times of The Gentiles" will be fulfilled and Christ returns. You will be amazed to discover this beast began during The Day of Nebuchadnezzar and The Babylonian Empire. This beast ends with The Return of Christ as revealed in <u>The Book of Revelation</u>.

Many have attempted to explain exactly who and what the beast is in <u>The Book of Revelation</u>. Some say it is Rome, or The European Common Market. On and on it goes, compounding one assumption after another. The common mistake made by most is to isolate **the time period** referring only to **the end-time**. Part of the problem exists because of an error in understanding **the last days**. You may be surprised to find **the last days** started thousands of years ago.

<u>A BEAST</u> Biblically, <u>The Bible</u> refers to someone or some thing that is **beast-like** and very evil. A beast is carnivorous or is driven by the desire to survive at any cost. Even wild animals, such as lions or tigers, once fully fed, are generally not interested in devouring more animals. In fact, after animals have eaten, they can be quite gentle. A carnivorous beast,

once driven by hunger, stops at nothing to be able to eat. **Survival of the fittest comes first,** and humans, themselves, often act the same way. The Bible refers to such behavior as carnal or beast-like (I Corinthians 3:1).

REVELATION'S BEAST   The Apostle John had a vision (Revelation 13:1). He could have been standing on the sand or some rocks on a beach looking out to the sea. What was he looking at? He saw, rising out of the **sea** a hideous **beast**, which had **seven heads** and **ten horns**, with the name of "**blasphemy**" upon the heads. **Blasphemy** denotes deception and falsehood in claiming to be something it is not. This beast **"was like unto a leopard, and his feet were as the feet of a bear, and his mouth as the mouth of a lion: and the dragon** [or Satan] **gave him his power"** (or authority to this beast) (Revelation 12:2). The **entire world** worships this beast (Verses 3 and 4). This worship by the world, which has given power to the beast lasts for three and a half years (Revelations 13:5). This beast has been given a number, **666** (Revelation 13:18). If you have wisdom, you will discern this beast and its number. (Chapter 5, 'Mark of The Beast,' goes into further details). Revelation 17:9-18 states he who has wisdom can know the seven heads are **seven mountains** or **governments**. The **ten horns** are **ten kings** or **world rulers** in the future, which shall make war against Christ when He comes. The beast coming from the waters or the sea represents **peoples**, **nations** and **languages** – a worldwide system. Who is this future beast, which emerges from the world and is ruled by Satan?

THE LAST DAYS   When do **the last days** literally start? What are **the last days**? You will find the answer in The Books of Daniel and

Revelation. Daniel, a **righteous** Prophet of God, is asked to interpret a dream that Nebuchadnezzar, King of The Babylonian Empire had. It was a horrific dream, which loomed as a **huge image**. This standing image had a head of **gold**, his breast and arms of **silver**, the belly and thighs of **brass**, his legs of **iron**, his feet were part iron and part clay (Daniel 2:31-33).

In Daniel 2:28, Daniel tells The King that only God in **heaven**, reveals secrets and God is letting Nebuchadnezzar know what is going to happen in the latter or **last days**. Daniel said that God was going to let him see the future – beginning with Nebuchadnezzar's day until Christ's **return** (Daniel 2:29). When do these latter or **last days** start? Remember, this image of Nebuchadnezzar's dream represents **the future** from King Nebuchadnezzar's time until Jesus establishes The Kingdom of God on earth. It is when Christ destroys all the human kingdoms of the world. After which, only God's **"kingdom"** will continue forever.

The Apostle Paul knew **the last days** and **the end-time** do not necessarily refer to **the same period**. Paul said in these **last days**, God speaks to you through His Son, Jesus (Hebrews 1:2). Paul is letting you know **the last days** began when Christ **first** came. The English word "end" is "eschatos" in Greek and means **"the farthest point**."   The English word "eschatology," means "the study of the last days." Paul said "the last days" **started** when Christ was born. Peter confirmed **the last time** or **the last days** started when Jesus was born (I Peter 1:20). John also said, it was the **last time** or **last days**. In Peter and John, the words in English, "end days," are translated "times;" and in the Greek, it is "eschator," which is also interpreted "days" or "**last days**." So, Paul, Peter and John all knew they were in **the last days** starting with Jesus at His **birth**. Why do **the last days** begin at the time of Christ's **birth** and not at **the end-time**, when God's "**kingdom**" becomes "**the kingdom**" of this world?

END-TIMES   At the end of <u>The Book of Daniel</u>, God tells Nebuchadnezzar he will die or go to his rest and stand in his lot (resurrection) at **the end of the days** or **the end-time**. The Hebrew word for "**end**" is "qets." In Hebrew, it carries the meaning of "extremity," "utmost," or "border." Truly "**the end-time**" or "**end of days**." You find a big difference between **the last days** and **the end of days**. Both do not refer to the same period of time in history or prophecy. Why the difference?

GRAPH
2,000-Year Time Frame

Roman Empire
Birth of Christ------------------LAST DAYS----------------Kingdom of God
THE TIME OF THE END
THE LATTER TIMES
THE LAST TIME
THE END

Seven Trumpets
Christ Returns--------------------END-TIME----------------Kingdom of God
END OF DAYS
END-DAYS
END OF THE TIME
END OF TIME

THE IMAGE AND THE BEAST   In Daniel 2, the image with its **four parts** constitutes a time period from Nebuchadnezzar's day until Christ **returns** and establishes The Kingdom of God, which will last forever. From Daniel's time, this image exists until human history ends. **There is no missing period of time.** This horrible image in Nebuchadnezzar's dream relates to all of humanity's future till the very **end-time** (when Christ **returns**). Why is this so significant? Later, you will **biblically** prove this image of Nebuchadnezzar ties directly to the beast prophesied in Revelation 13. Without understanding these Four World Empires in Nebuchadnezzar's dream, you can never know who the beast is in Revelation 13.

THE FOUR WORLD EMPIRES   Daniel 7 covers **the four beasts**, which came out of the sea. Each beast is different one from the other. The first, was like a **lion**; second, like a **bear**; the third like a **leopard**, and the fourth beast was stronger and worse than the preceding three.

This Fourth Beast absorbs all of the former beasts. Who are these beasts? These great beasts are four kings, which shall come from the earth (Daniel 7:17). God's **saints** will take over these four kings or kingdoms and reign over them forever (Verse 18), **just as the dream** in Nebuchadnezzar's image when Christ takes over God's "**kingdom.**" These four beasts and the image are **one** and the same. **They cover the world's future.** Daniel 8 covers another vision which tells you what happens after The Kingdom of Babylon, The Kingdom of Media and Persia takes over. Then, The King of Grecia or Alexander The Great defeats The Medio-Persian Empire (Daniel 8:22). Now, you have three of the four beasts revealed. The **first**

kingdom is The Babylonian Kingdom, which is **the head of gold**. **The second kingdom** is The Medio-Persian Kingdom, represented by **the chest and arms of silver**. **The third kingdom** of **brass** is Alexander's Kingdom. The Fourth Beast made of **iron and clay** was The Roman Empire, which absorbed all the other governments. This **fourth kingdom** or The Roman Government occurs in **the latter times** or **the last times** (Daniel 8:23). In Hebrew, the word "latter" denotes "hinder" or "last times." There you have it. **"The last days"** are **the days of The Fourth Kingdom of Rome** during the 2,000-year time-period.

When did **the fourth kingdom** begin? It began during the days of Jesus Christ when He was walking this earth. The Roman Empire existed during the time of Jesus, Peter, John and Paul. This was **the beginning** of **the last days** – the day of The Fourth Kingdom of Rome. You are living in **the last days** just before **the end days**, when Christ **returns**.

Jesus said The Gentiles would control Jerusalem until **the time** of The Gentiles is fulfilled (Luke 21:24). What is **the time** of The Gentiles? Christ said this **Gentile "rule"** ends immediately when they see Jesus returning in the clouds (Luke 21:27). Now, you have it. **The last days** started with The Roman Empire at the birth of Christ, and lasts until **Jesus' return** to establish God's "**kingdom**." This Roman system is to exist until **the end-time** or **end of days** just before Christ **returns** and establishes The Kingdom of God. The Gentile **rule** ends in Jerusalem, which is at **the end-days**, and began at the end-time frame of **the last days**. The **time of The Gentiles** ends when Christ **returns** in the clouds. The Gospel will have been preached to the world (Revelation 14:6).

AT THE TIME OF THE END TILL THE END-TIMES   The Fourth Beast Empire begins with the expression "**at the time of the end,**" the 2,000-year time-frame.   The major mistake most commentators make is to take **at the time of the end** and regard it the same as **the end of the time** when Christ **returns**.   **The end** should be applied to the transition from **the third kingdom,** which was Greece, to **the fourth kingdom**, which **was and still is** The Roman Empire system, which begins to incorporate the whole world.   The legs on the composite beast of Daniel 2 never ceases to exist until **"the stone cut out of the mountain without hands,"** smashes those ten toes. It is then, **the kingdoms of this world cease to exist** and Jesus brings The Kingdom of God to this earth (end-days). The Roman Empire, which is dominating the old world, continues to spread its abomination until it covers the whole world.   Within the two legs of the composite beast which begins **the time of the end** (the 2,000 year period) and end with the **end of the time** (Christ's **return**) of human rule.   When the commentaries on The Book of Daniel make at **the time of the end**, or **last days** (the 2,000 year period) **the same** as **the end of the time** (Christ's **return**), they confuse the long history of The Roman Empire system.   This in turn interrupts the understanding of The Book of Revelation, which follows the same pattern as The Book of Daniel.

Where the historical **fulfilled prophecy** ends and the events of the **end-time** begin is left in utter confusion.   Once the **last days begin** with the emergence of "**the fourth empire**" more than two thousand years occupy the space between **the time of the end**, until the **end of the time** or **end-days** when Christ **returns**.   The Fourth Empire begins with the rise of Julius Caesar. After the murder of Julius Caesar his name became a title for the Emperors who ruled in his name. Julius Caesar received a deadly wound in 44 BC, after ruling from 49 BC. This name or title "Caesar" comes from the Hebrew word "sar," or "Prince of Princes" – "the top ruler of the world."

FROM DANIEL TO THE BOOK OF REVELATION   A 120-year period of **fulfilled prophecy** occurs from 49 BC when Julius Caesar takes control of The Roman Empire until 70 AD, when the second temple in Jerusalem lay in smoldering ruins. When correctly discerned through historical evidence, the predictions in Daniel 7, of the ten + one kings, end with The Roman King, **Vespasian** as "**the seventh head**," which ends the nation of The Jews in 70 AD. What does **not** end is **the fourth empire** that extends from its beginning in 49 BC with Julius Caesar. While Julius Caesar begins **the biblical "fourth empire"** of Daniel, it continues the long historical periods in history until the prophesied events that are to occur when The Son of Man comes "in the clouds." Unless you understand the difference between **the last days – the time of the end**, the 2,000-year period, which begins with Julius Caesar, you will fail to read the signs in the events at **the end of the times** (end-days), you will be blinded to the coming of The Son of Man "in the clouds." **Christ will not come in secret**.

From the end of The Jewish Nation in 70 AD both <u>The Book of Daniel</u> and <u>The Book of Revelation</u> reveals **the end of the time** (Christ's **return**) of man's rule, and the establishment of The Kingdom of God upon the earth. At that time, Gentile **rule** ends, and <u>The Gospel</u> is preached to the world (II Thessalonians 2). Although most of the prophetic historical events of Daniel 7, the two legs of the composite beast of Daniel 2 have already extended more then two thousand years. (Western Empire of Rome and The Eastern Empire of Rome under Constantine).

The Book of Daniel has been likened to looking at several mountain peaks in a row. The events represent the significant events, each as a mountain summit. What is not always disclosed in the narratives of Daniel is the distance between the mountain peaks. What can be said for The Book of Daniel applies as well to The Book of Revelation. From prophesies that have either had partial fulfillment of completed history, to the future events must be discerned through **the scriptural** texts and the future events themselves. At **the time of the end**, beginning **the end** of **"the third beast kingdom"** and the emergence of **"the fourth beast"** is a 33 year period from 3-2 BCE, the **birth, life, death**, and **resurrection** of Jesus Christ.

From the rise of Julius Caesar (49 BCE) to the birth of Jesus was 47 years, and from the birth of Jesus to His death and resurrection – 33 years. From His death to the desolations of Jerusalem and **the second temple** was just 6 months shy of 40 years. The total number of years for the emergence of the head Julius Caesar to the desolation was 120 years. Jesus said as in the days of Noah a **120-year period** was allotted for **repentance**, and then destruction came (Matthew 24:36-39). The fact that Jesus connected these **scriptures** to the coming of The Son of Man **"in the clouds,"** you must understand that even if you had a 120-year period as in the days of Noah, there is a long gap of time between the 70 CE desolations and **the end-times,** with The Return of Christ. It is as though the mountain itself **peaks** again. From the 120-year period of time that ended in 70 CE, to the coming of The Son of Man in the clouds has already been nearly 2,000 years. This means you must find the historical events that fulfilled this prophecy before you can separate these events from those in **the end-times**, just before The Son of Man comes in the cloud. Believe it or not **bible scholars** have ended prophecy that found fulfillment in historical events, TWO CENTURIES TOO SOON! In Daniel 11:35, scholars have closed **fulfilled prophecy** with the exploits of Antiochus Epiphanes and his overthrow by The Hasmonaean Family. These historical facts tell a different story, as the rush to fulfill the prophetic Word of God. The mountain peak of the significance of 70 CE, the time gap before The Son of Man appears in the cloud to that last mountain peak **the end-times**, are revealed by the significant events. **The end-times** (Christ's **return**) meaning the closing of the times of The Gentiles, are in Daniel 2. One Gentile Kingdom after another swallowing up the preceding – until the first three kingdoms became part of The Fourth Kingdom of Rome. From the beginning of <u>The Book of Daniel</u> to the ending in Chapter 12, The Fourth Empire never ceases to exist until **"the stone cut out of the mountains"** smashes the toes and causes all of The Roman Empire to collapse upon itself (Daniel 2:45).

<u>THE RISE AND FALL OF EMPIRES</u> The Babylonian Empire began the times of The Gentiles when The Jewish **people** were carried out of the land of Judea in three deportations. The first occurred in 605 BC, when Daniel was carried to Babylon. The second invasion was 597 and lastly 586 BC when The Babylonians destroyed The City of Jerusalem and **the temple. "As kingdoms come" and "kingdoms go,"** the powerful

Persians along with The Medes who had merged under The Great King Cyrus, defeated The Babylonians, to establish themselves as the world power.

What lies ahead and perhaps nearer than many might suppose, is the formation of the ten toes into a **global configuration**. What began in one part of the old world – The Roman Empire system – has insidiously, and almost unnoticed spread and crept in and **encompassed the whole world**.

Jerusalem shall be trodden down by The Gentiles, until **"the times of the Gentiles are fulfilled"** (End of their rule) (Luke 21:24). Even though there is The State of Israel in the modern world, The Gentiles continue to tread down Jerusalem. When will **"the times of The Gentiles"** end and cease to tread down Jerusalem? When the stone cut out of the mountain in Daniel 2, which is The Son of Man coming in the clouds when **the end of time,** brings Jesus and The Kingdom of God to this earth. What are the events that usher in the fulfillment of the two legs and ten toes of Daniel 2? What are the events in The Book of Revelation, which have direct relevance to Daniel 2? These explanations will be explained later.

The main purpose in the continuing story is to correlate history with fulfilled prophecy. The Medes and Persians under Cyrus, The Great overcame and swallowed up The Babylonian Empire. Cyrus had married a daughter from The Mede **royal linage**, and The Medes were incorporated into The Persian Empire. This is how it became The Medo-Persians as **the second beast empire** in The Book of Daniel.

THE MEDO-PERSIAN EMPIRE   Daniel 11:1-2 does not cover the entire Persian reign. <u>The Book of Daniel</u> is about his people and the nations. Only the important highlights are covered: **"And now will I shew thee the truth. Behold, there shall stand up yet three kings in Persia; and the fourth shall be far richer than they all: and by his strength through his riches he shall stir up all against the realm of Grecia."**

The translators broke up the story between Chapter 10 and Chapter 11 by making a chapter break in the middle of a subject when the narrative should not have ended until the thought was completed. The historical time period is that of Darius, The Mede.   What becomes important from the historical perspective is when Xerxes, The King who became the **husband of Esther**.   It was Xerxes who was richer than all the others, from the accumulation of wealth from the pillage of many nations. Xerxes made an effort to take The Kingdom of Greece, and though his advance on Greece failed, it was never forgotten. Although other kings followed Xerxes, The Persian Empire was in rapid decline. This leads directly into The Fourth Empire of Alexander, The Great – the mighty king who advances to swallow up the nations before him. So great were the exploits of Alexander, The Great, the head of the future Roman Empire sought to follow his example. At the young age of 33 Alexander was dead, and the kingdom he established was split among **four of his generals**. Only two of the four become important in relation to the people of Daniel, The Jews. The General of Alexander – Seleucus I Nicator occupied the territory **north** of Jerusalem in Syria. Out of Egypt, was Ptolemy I Soter as The King of The **South**. In Daniel 11: 5-35, are the wars between The Seleucids Kings of The North and The Ptolemy Kings from The South.

The worst of them all was Antiochus IV Epiphanes in Daniel 11:21- 31, when he was defeated by the sons of Mattathias – later called The Maccabees. The downfall of the kingdom established by Alexander, The Great, became the rise of "**the fourth kingdom,**" which never ceases to exist in The Book of Daniel until the stone cut out of the mountain crushes the toes, and causes the entire historical beast to fall to the ground. This will be explained later since **the stone kingdom** is yet for a time in the future.

THE RISE OF ROME   You can pick up the historical fulfillment and the rise of The Roman Empire in Daniel 7. Commentaries on The Book of Daniel are not as helpful as you would like them to be.   The most misunderstood concept of all commentaries on prophecy is where they determined – at **the time of the end** being **the end of the time** of The Gentiles. The failure to understand – "the time of the end" (last days) is not the same as **the end-times** (end-days).   There is a wide time-span between **the time of the end** – and **the end-times**. The two legs and ten toes on the metallic beast image set up by Nebuchadnezzar, should not be confused with the ten + 1 kings of the historical **fourth empire** (Hosea 1).

The ten + 1 "Kings of Daniel 7" have become history and their reign is from 49 BCE to 74 CE, **the time of the end** the 2,000-year period of **The Nation of Judah** (Hosea 1). From this historical fulfillment time jumps ahead to when The Roman Empire is transformed. But for now, you should concentrate on the historical Roman Empire where Judah was given a 120-year period as in the days of Noah.   The Bible speaks of "Kings" but no "Emperors." Daniel 7 speaks of kings – "ten kings" were to arise. Then in the midst of these kings comes up **a little horn** "king." He is different from the first kings.

In Daniel 7, Daniel is having a dream, where visions pass through his mind. Daniel writes down the substance of those visions. What troubled Daniel most was the terrifying **"fourth beast."** Daniel wanted to know the true meaning of **"the fourth beast"** with its iron teeth and bronze claws – which was different from all the others and most terrifying, crushing and devouring its victims, and trampled whatever was left.

(Daniel 7:19). The Jews were given into the hands of the little horn (the 11th king) under whose authority Jerusalem and **the great second temple** were destroyed. Josephus, The Jewish **historian**, furnishes all the details in **The War of The Jews**. During the first year of the war the victory went to the zealots. This was in the year of 66 CE. But from the spring of 67 to the fall of 70 CE, it was all downhill for Judah. Vespasian, The General (from The South in Egypt) was chosen to put down The Jewish rebellion.

To prevent attack from the backside, Vespasian began his siege in Galilee defeating one city after another. The Roman Kings (or Caesars) came after him, but fell before him in the space of one year. In Daniel 7, the record is that three kings were plucked up by the roots, from before this 11th "little horn" king. The **"little horn king"** was put over the entire Roman Empire when those three kings were plucked up from before him. In Revelation this king is said to be **the eighth king** but still **the seventh head**. How can this be? If **Vespasian** is historically **the seventh head** after the three plucked up from before him, how can he also be **the eighth**

king?

The beginning of **the time of the end** (last-days) was the emergence of **Julius Caesar, "first king"** of The Roman Empire in Daniel 7. **Augustus** was the second king, and the third king was **Tiberius**. Fourth was **Guis**, to be followed by the fifth – **Claudius**. The **sixth was Nero** at the time of John recorded in The Book of Revelation. The three kings which were plucked up by the roots were: (1) Galbo (2) Otho and (3) Vilellius; all came and fell before Vespasian. The three plucked up by the **roots** means **although they were**, but **they are no more**, and **Vespasian** becomes the **seventh king of the historical beast.**

What perhaps is more than a coincidence is when Vespasian began to besiege Judah in the spring of 67 CE, (exactly two periods of three and one half years), making the war of The Jews **a seven-year war**. From the spring of 67 CE to the fall of 70 (three and one-half years), The City of Jerusalem and **the second temple** lay in smoldering ruins. A remaining three and one-half years were needed to end the war of Jews in taking of the last strong hold of **Masada**. Is there a connection to the last seventieth week of **the seventy-week prophecy** in Daniel 9?

A certain amount of prophecy has been fulfilled beginning at **the time of the end** (2,000-year period). **The Roman Empire swallowed up The Gentile Church** and made it subject to The Emperor or **Constantine**, The Great (as a false prophet). The change in The Roman Empire, which began to be ruled from Constantinople, eventually split into The Orthodox of The East and Catholicism in Rome. These two Christian groups were forced to accept all **pagan teachings** (which were changed to Christian

names) from Emperor Constantine at The Council of Nicea in 325 A.D.
When the two legs appeared, one in The East the other in The West, the
two legs on the image in Daniel 2, began to emerge. These are The
Western and Eastern **"two legs"** in Daniel's Image of The Roman Empire.
Although the beast changed its form, it is prophesied to exist until the ten
toes are crushed which causes the image to fall. Then, The Kingdom of
God replaces it forever and ever. To understand the chronology of the
beast and its part in ending The Nation of Judah, the desolation of the
second temple, and the destruction of Jerusalem in 70 CE, you must study
The Gospel of Luke.

LUKE'S GOSPEL AND THE OLIVET PROPHECIES   Luke, the
traveling partner of The Apostle Paul, observes the need to compose a
correct chronology of the things that have been fulfilled. Luke has
carefully analyzed those things which occurred – the miracles performed,
and the words spoken by Jesus during his historical ministry. Jesus and
His Disciples are teaching in **the temple** (Luke 21). In departing from **the
temple**, The Disciples were remarking how **the temple** was adorned with
beautiful stones. At which time, Jesus follows with a shocking statement.
**"As for these things which ye behold, the days will come, in the which
there shall not be left one stone upon another, that shall not be thrown
down"** (Verse 6).

Pay careful attention to what Luke records. Since two questions were
asked by The Disciples, each question relates to **two different events**.
The first question is when will these things be, and the second question,
what will be the sign when these things shall come to pass? **The**

destruction and desolation of "the temple" will be so great that not one stone will be left upon another. The Disciples were wondering when the destruction to **the temple** would occur. Josephus, The Jewish historian, has carefully recorded the historical desolations of 70 CE, in his War of The Jews.

The general and crown prince, firstborn son of Vespasian, was assigned to bring Jerusalem into obedience under Rome. The siege began by Vespasian in upper Galilee when he took one city after another. With the death of Nero, three more kings stood up claiming the crown. The Legions in The East went over to Vespasian, and the three kings fell before him, all in a one-year period. Vespasian returned to Rome to stabilize the government while Titus with The Eastern Legions came from Egypt to besiege the Jerusalem stronghold. From the spring of 67 when Vespasian began to besiege Judah to the fall of 70 CE (a three and one-half year period), sacrifices had ceased as **the temple** lay in smoldering ruins.

Luke describes this fulfillment after The Disciples asked Jesus these questions. In order to retrieve the gold that had melted from the burning temple (70 CE), the very foundational stones were toppled. Amazingly, what Jesus had predicted nearly 40 years before, came to pass in the fall of 70 CE. As Jesus predicted, not one stone was left upon another. In Luke 21:24, the preceding verses are those events, which occurred from 67 to 70 CE. Remember to always discern the difference between at **the time of the end** (2,000-year period), from those predicted for **end-times**, at Christ's **return,** otherwise you cannot separate the two predicted events.

Luke in Chapter 21:24, points back to the desolations of **the temple** and The City of Jerusalem.

The term at **the time of the end** (2,000-year period) is split between the historical and the future, which must be termed as **the end-times (when The Son of Man returns in the clouds)** (Verse 24). If you mix the two separate events, the one ending in 70 CE, relating to the geographical locations of Galilee and Judah, you will miss **the global tribulation**. Luke 21:24 gives the correct chronology of what came to pass, and what in **the end-times** is yet to be fulfilled. This verse, also, separates at **the time of the end** of The Jewish Nation, from those events just prior to **the return** of The Son of Man.

"And they shall fall by the edge of the sword, and shall be led away captive into all nations: and Jerusalem will be trodden down of The Gentiles, until the times of The Gentiles be fulfilled" (Luke 21). Not only has The Nation of Judah come to its end, **the temple** was destroyed; Jerusalem is laid waste. From this point, The Gentiles will tread down Jerusalem until Christ **returns**. How long shall The Gentiles tread down Jerusalem? Luke tells you **until the times of The Gentiles be fulfilled**. This is THE END of **"the fourth beast"** when Christ **returns**. When will that be? When the stone cut out of the mountain without hands crushes the nations – The whole Roman **"system."** When the times of The Gentiles begin to come to their end, Luke 21:24-25 leaves the historical fulfillment at **the time of the end**, (the 2,000-year period) meaning **the end of The Nation of Judah**.

THE TIMES OF THE GENTILES TO THE END-TIMES   Read

carefully the transition from at **the time of the end** (the 2,000-year period) of The Nation of Judah, to the global Great Tribulation to come upon the nations. **"And there shall be signs in the sun, and in the moon, and in the stars; and upon the earth distress of nations, with perplexity; the sea and the waves roaring;"** (Luke 21:25). This is during The Sixth Seal (Revelation 6:12). **"Men's hearts failing them for fear, and looking after those things, which are coming upon the earth: for the powers of heaven shall be shaken"** (Luke 21:26). Luke sets straight the chronology from those things that have come to pass, to those things, **yet**, for **a future time**. Luke takes you from the geographical tribulation upon Judah, to the global tribulation upon the nations. Luke gives the answers to the two questions asked by The Disciples of Jesus. **The second temple** is no more – even to such desolations that one stone has not been left upon another. (From **the time of the end** (the 2,000-year period), beginning with **"the fourth empire"** in Daniel, when **the fourth empire** has covertly taken its system and extended it to global proportions, to **the end-times** (Christ returning.) Luke records the signs of this global tribulation. What are those signs that precede The Son of Man coming in the clouds? To understand those things relating to **the end-times**, turn to The Book of Revelation since it continues from The Book of Daniel.

THE SAME BEAST Revelation 13:1 reveals this beast, rising out of the sea, having **seven heads** and **ten horns** and each horn has **ten crowns**. Verse 2 states this beast was like a **leopard**, feet of a **bear**, mouth of a **lion** and the **dragon** or **Satan** controls these governments. Who is this beast? Remember, Satan is **"the god"** of **this world**. Revelation 17:8-16 prophesies this beast coming out of the **sea** (Mediterranean) constitutes many nations and languages of **the whole world**. The seven heads are seven kings, five are fallen, and **one is** (when John wrote <u>The Book of Revelation</u>), and the other **is yet** to come. When the **seventh comes**, he continues a **short time**. The beast finally has an **eighth head** and is of **"the seventh."**

The **seven heads** are **all Roman Emperors** who think they are "gods." Remember, Daniel tells you God sets up the **basest** of **men** (and they think they are God), and as Nebuchadnezzar learned, only God in **heaven** actually gives men or women their rulership. These kings **are not God**! When they think they are God, then He removes them like Belshazzar in Daniel 5. That is why only Nebuchadnezzar, tried by God, is the head of **gold**. All the others are inferior and each deteriorates to silver, brass and finally, to iron or The Roman Empire. The **emperors** in this Roman Empire, who think they are God, are removed. These are the **seven heads** of the beast – the last Gentile beast.

Some churches believe these heads are represented by future rulers such as Charlemagne, Napoleon and Hitler. This is preposterous. The **seventh head** lasts only a **short time after** the **sixth,** and they all refer directly to The Roman Government of John's time. The **sixth head exists** while John is writing <u>The Book of Revelation</u>. The **seventh head** comes **shortly** after the **sixth head**. All **seven heads** must be Roman Emperors and not some future European leaders. Stick to **<u>The Scriptures</u>** and not what mankind dreams up in their minds.

Who does this beast look like? Is it exactly like another beast? Yes, it is. In Daniel 7:1-18, **four great beasts** come out of the sea (world) just as the beast in <u>Revelation</u>. Also, these **four beasts** look like a **lion, bear** and a **leopard**. Again, just like the beast in <u>Revelation</u>. Verse 8 states a little horn comes along and devours the previous three which leaves only **"the fourth beast"** or The Roman Empire.

One of **the angels** is asked the interpretation of the four beasts (Daniel 7:16-26). The interpretation reveals this fourth beast (Rome), devours the entire world. This fourth beast speaks **great words** against God and claims to be God and represents God's government on earth. Constantine claimed he was the 13th Apostle after The Twelve Apostles and declared Rome was God's **"kingdom."** This government persecutes **true** Christians for three and a half years or The Great Tribulation. These are God's **two witnesses** (Revelation 7 and 11) going into The Great Tribulation, Israel (Church in Wilderness) and Gentiles (Church of God) (Revelation 14).

This **fourth beast** uproots three of the kings of the ten which leaves seven (Daniel 7:24). These four beasts with only the fourth remaining, is the **same** beast which also comes out of the seas (world). What is left? Seven horns (governments) and seven kings just like the beast in Revelation 13. The Revelation 13 beast is the same beast in Daniel 7 and continues as the seven heads of The Roman Empire and not any future European or world rulers. <u>The Bible</u> and history combined have now proved who the beast is – The Fourth World Ruling Empire – The Roman Empire. What happens to it?

THE IMAGE   This **fourth beast** of Daniel is the last ruling Gentile Kingdom, although still ruling **during The Great Tribulation** for forty-two months or three and a half years (Revelation 13:5-8). How does this happen? The Roman Empire ceased to exist hundreds of years ago. The two little horns answer the question. These little horns get the whole world, to worship The Roman Empire's **image** or **system**.

THE TWO HORNS   When horns are mentioned in The Bible, they symbolize a government, although not necessarily a nation. In this case, it is a religious government. Revelation 11:9-12 declares anyone who has **ears** and is willing to **listen** to **the truth** will know who this **religious government** is.

Then, another beast comes out of the earth and not out of the sea like the other beast (Verse 11). This government is human, out of the earth (like Adam) and claims to be God's **"kingdom"** on earth. It also has **two horns** or two religious governments, but both are human and not God's **"true kingdom"** of **rule**. These are of **the seven churches** of Christ and are Christian – **the called-out ones**. Also, it states both of these religious systems speak as **Christians** or as a **lamb**, but Satan deceives them, and they are really led by Satan.   Remember, Christ warns The Seven Churches He knows where Satan's seat is. These **two Christian churches** are being deceived by Satan, (Revelation 2 and 3). These **two horns** are Christ's **two churches**. That is why Jesus wants them to come out of this Satanic system, which is mixed with pagan and Christian teaching. Martin Luther is just an example of one trying to come out of it. This confused Babylon/Christian teachings. Jesus states, **"COME OUT OF HER my people"** (Revelation 18:4). Then Revelation 14:12 prophesies that these two Christian **churches** promote the ideas and teaching of the former,

fourth beast, The Roman Empire, by Constantine, as Rome's Emperor, at The Council of Nicea in 325 A.D. Constantine as Rome's Emperor **took over** the **control** of the **two Christian churches** which were The Catholic and Eastern Orthodox. They had **no choice**. Christianity, from this point on, belonged to Rome, including its Eastern and Western domain. From those two segments, all Christian **churches** have been spawned to this very day. A mixture of **truth** and **paganism**. Babylon prevails in today's world in all **denominations and splits**. All the while, **true** Christians are trying to **grow spiritually** to continue in God's **truth** from His Holy Word, The Bible. That is why Christianity and Judaism are **divided** into so **many groups**! Revelation 18:4 warns **growing Christians** to come out of the false teachings of **the fourth beast**, The Roman Empire, which Christ will defeat at His **return**.

These two lamb horns (Christian) are able to do great **false miracles** just like the **magicians** in Pharaoh's day with Moses (Revelation 13:13-18). God's **"two witnesses," The 144,000 Israelites** and **the innumerable** multiple of **Gentiles** who are Christians growing **spiritually**, are praying for God's help. God hears their prayers and sends **The Seven Trumpets** (as in Jericho) to protect them while witnessing **the truth** (Revelation 11:5-6). These two lamb horns will claim they are God's **"kingdom"** on earth and say The Seven Trumpets of God are because of them. They will really **believe it is the truth** because **Satan** is allowed to deceive **"the Christian churches."** Remember "the tares" of Satan are standing along with God's "wheat."

The Roman Empire continues even though the physical Roman

government ended hundreds of years ago (Revelation 13:15-18). These verses prophesy these **two lambs (world Christianity)** "part true" – "part false." **The called-out ones** (God's **churches**) are those who are **fooled by Satan believing they have "the truth" and promote the world to worship** the beast of The Roman Empire as **an image**. But Christ **returns** and destroys this beast which will have ten kings or **the ten world rulers** from **all nations** to fight Him. As in the past, today's Christianity has begun more wars in the name of religion than for any other reason, and will continue to do so until The Return of Jesus. Christianity and its **mixed religion** of **truth, lies, good** and **evil** will continue until Jesus **returns** with God's **kingdom**. Christianity will promote the **image** or the system of The Roman Government until **the end of the time of The Gentiles**!

SUMMARY   It is this beast by the continuance of its **image** or system, which exists until **the end** when Christ defeats and smashes the ten toes or final ten kings of **all** nations in Daniel's great image (Daniel 2). The Seven Christian Churches in Revelation 2 and 3, along with Israel as the other natural olive tree, will be invited to The Wedding Feast of The Groom (Christ). This was fully explained in Chapter 3, 'The Marriage Registry.' Remember, Revelation 18:4 announced that all **Israelites and The Seven Churches** should **"come out of her, my people."** Out of what? Out of Babylon! As long as you believe you are in **the only "true church,"** you **cannot grow spiritually**! Why? Because **everyone is in Babylon** and everyone is to come out of her! Satan has mixed his "tares" (false doctrines) with "the wheat" (Christians). All Christians and Israel, God's **two witnesses**, are commanded to come out of this Babylonian **system**.

ONLY GOD'S WORD, <u>THE BIBLE</u> HAS GOD'S TRUTH, AND IS THE ONLY MEANS TO SPIRITUAL GROWTH.

CHAPTER 5

MARK OF THE BEAST

Much has been biblically written about this Mark of The Beast and the need for all Christianity, including all of humanity, to avoid receiving it. Why? God is going to vent out His wrath upon all who possess it. Is it a literal mark? To zero in on the identity of this mark, everything from one's social security number in the U.S.A. to the United Nations has been identified as The Mark of The Beast. On it goes with continuing speculation. Read the biblical truth, and how you have been deceived by Satan.

The Book of Revelation seems so mysterious. However, once **its purpose** and storyline is understood, The Great Book reveals a great blessing to the entire world.

The Apostle John is told to seal this **Book of Prophecy**. He is told that in the future he must prophecy to all the world what is in The Book (Revelation 10:4). However, he is also told to eat The Book, which would be **sweet** in his mouth, but **bitter** when it reaches his stomach. Why? (Revelation 10:8-11)

John finds it is **sweet** in his mouth because Christ is coming to restore God's **kingdom**, which makes it feel very **sweet** as it is tasted (Revelation 11:15). But, it is also God's **time of wrath** upon the unrepentant world

(Verse 18).   Obviously, this is **the bitterness** to come in John's stomach. Who is to receive the wrath of God's anger and who will be SAVED from God's wrath?

This is the terrifying **mark of the beast**.   Biblically, a Satanic **mark** is to be placed upon the people who follow Satan's way in <u>The Book of Revelation</u> (Revelation 16:2).   God pours out His vial of wrath at the end-time (Christ's **return**), upon all the world who possess **this mark**.

Many in the Christian world try to define this mark.   At all costs, this **mark** is to be avoided by Christians, as well as Israel, God's people (Revelation 18:4).   What is The Mark of The Beast?   Let <u>The Scriptures</u> do the interpreting, and not dreamed-up thoughts of mankind.

<u>AT THE BEGINNING</u>   What is the genesis of this **mark**?   When did it begin?   Has this **mark** been around and no one really is aware of it? Remember, this **mark** is Satanic.   It is the devil's system, which manifests itself at **the end-time** as prevailing throughout the entire known world, just before The Return of The Messiah or Christ.

<u>A STAMP</u>   There are those who believe it is a physical symbol such as the social security number or a Cain "**mark**."   Why?   Because Revelation 13:16-18 states no one will be able to buy or sell during that time.   Making a living will be difficult and that alone will make life difficult.   Will it be a physical sign or stamp on a person which will be the only way to allow them to make a living? For a true **biblical definition**, the Greek word "charagma," signifies "a scratch" or "etching."   It is like a sculptured figure.   This word correlates to "charax," "a stake," that is, "a military mound for protection in a siege or attack." It is "a figure" or "resemblance of something," like an "idol" or "eikon." **It is not a physical mark placed or carried by anyone**. It resembles another image, but what image or likeness is it? It is those who worship the image of the beast (Revelations 14:11). Whose image is it? It is **the dragon** or Satan, who gives power to this beast (Revelation 13:4). This image of the beast is of Satan, the devil. Obviously, those with **the mark of the beast**, worship Satan and his system. What is Satan's system that the world worships and follows? The answers were given 6,000 years ago in The Garden of Eden.

WHERE THE MARK STARTED   After Adam and Eve disobeyed God by eating The Tree of Good and Evil God said they would die. What did Satan, as the dragon and the serpent (snake), say the benefit of eating the forbidden fruit would give Adam and Eve?

Satan said, **"God knows that in the day ye eat thereof, and ye shall be as gods, knowing good and evil"** (Genesis 3:5). There it is. Satan said to follow his advice, eat the fruit, and you will be your **own god**. You will be totally free, and you will decide for yourself what is **right** or **wrong**. Wow!

Satan's system never includes God or His Holy Spirit (The Tree of Life). Just as Satan is **the god of this world** with his own ideas of right and wrong, allowing each to do what seems right in his own eyes. That is Satan's system. Total liberty or freedom to do any combination of **good** and **bad**, but without **"the true"** God **involved**. It is Satan's form of democracy without God. Paul said God is the only way to real liberty or total freedom (Romans 8:21). Without God, you have bondage. When you become one of **God's "children**," you then are delivered from Satanic bondage.

True Democracy or freedom can only come to pass when God is involved! This is a dichotomy, Satan's way, is **without God**. Satan or each individual is then his master or own little god. God's way is liberty or freedom with only **One God,** The Father. That is why God is opposed to idolatry because without God, there can be no **life**, only **death**. Satan is the god of the dead, and **"the true"** God is The God of The Living. Life can only come from **life** and only The True God has **life**. When you have more than The **"one true"** God, determining right from wrong, you will find it only causes confusion or Babylon. Satan's system was spawned in The Garden of Eden, and since Satan is **the god of this world**, this system mushrooms and infects the entire world before Christ's **return**. This Satanic system, **prophetically** and **scripturally proved**, becomes **The Mark of The Beast**.

INHERITANCE VERSES GLOBILIZATION   The world today is divided between two groups – the developed nations and the undeveloped nations. The **haves** and **have nots**. Why is it so? Partly, God had fulfilled His **promise** and truly blessed the nations of The Abrahamic Covenant (Genesis 12:3).

The world governments, especially the top six developed economies, come together to resolve the economic disparity. Their solution is globalization or free trade! The answer is a point of economics – stimulating free trade among all the nations. However, each nation protects its personal economic security in any and all trade agreements.

Many times this causes a hostility if one nation can't compete with another. This human system, by human reason, is based upon competition. One outdoing the other!

When God is involved, competition is not the motivator for a healthy world economy, because **inheritance** is God's answer. Each nation is given, by God, their territorial right to freely develop and benefit their nation, and not compete with each other. Moses said, **"When the Most High divided the nations their inheritance, when he separated the sons of Adam, he set the bounds of the people according to the number of the children of Israel"** (Deuteronomy 32:8).

Instead of wars, people fighting people, breaking God's **inheritance**, a world of confusion has developed with horrendous human problems between nations. What is the answer?

Satan is the god of this world; his system, each nation competing against the other, each deciding right from wrong with one dominating over the other, free trade, **with competition** has been the answer to the world's problems. God's **institution** of **inheritance**, giving everyone a fair share is ignored. Competition with free trade puts each nation against the other. What are **the end-time** results?

TRUE LIBERTY   God and His "way" are for everyone to be free and have true liberty. Paul said the entire **CREATION** is waiting for this "redemption" or "liberty" (Romans 8:22-23). **Democracy** is God's **way**, but only when God is the standard (Romans 8:21). On the other hand, Satan's "way" totally rejects God as the standard and espouses each person to be his or her "own god." Satan is the one who wants the whole world to look to him and ignore **the true God**. Satan, himself wants to be **the savior** of the world (Matthew 4:9). Satan wants to be the one worshipped instead of Jesus, The Christ.

MYSTICAL NUMBERS   The apocalyptic <u>Book of Revelation</u> speaks of a mystical beast coming out of the sea. This beast has seven heads and ten horns. The beast was like a leopard, and his feet were as the feet of a bear, and his mouth that of a lion; and the dragon gave him his power and his seat along with great authority. Who is this beast and who is the dragon?

The dragon is the **old serpent** (Garden of Eden), called the devil and Satan (Revelations 12:9). The dragon who gives power to this beast is the same Satan who deceived Adam and Eve. Satan has since **deceived** the whole world. Do you get it? The entire human society is deceived. It means the world doesn't even realize they are all **fooled** by what is happening right before their eyes.

As Christians, you, being in the world, may believe **good** will win over **evil**. But **the truth** is, the world is completely in a state of confusion or Babylon mixing **good** with **evil**. All can, are and will be deceived. Satan or the dragon is mad at God's people and is at war with **"the church"** (Revelation 12:17). This dragon, Satan, is sponsoring this beast and thereby, fighting against God's people. Who is this beast? THE SEVEN HEADS are SEVEN MOUNTAINS and THE SEVEN KINGS are OVER THESE MOUNTAINS OR GOVERNMENTS (Revelation 17:9-10). The sea from which the beast with seven heads and ten horns ORIGINATES

IS THE WORLD (Verse 15).   Specifically, this sea refers to THE
MEDITERRANEAN SEA and THE KINGDOMS SURROUNDING IT.
The WATERS ARE THE NATIONS OF THE WORLD, which the
dragon – Satan – controls. They are an enemy of God's people – Israel
and will **make war against them**.

Another beast, which comes out of the earth or from the world, has two
horns like a **lamb**, but speaks deceit because his words are from the
dragon or Satan (Revelation 13:11). This beast, out of the earth, rides the
beast which came out of the water. **Out of the earth** means **human**, or of
human origin just as Adam was made from the earth. **This beast looks
like a Christ, but speaks the words of Satan**. This is a **man-made
religion**, not of God. This is **the anti-Christ**, the false worldly religious
leader who supports the beast with seven kings or seven governments. All
these are an enemy of God's people. THESE HORNS, LIKE A LAMB,
ARE THE FALSE PROPHETS (REVELATION 16:13). THIS IS THE
ANTI-CHRIST.

This false religious leader gives "life" or 'belief' to **the image** of the beast
with the seven heads. Notice this **anti-Christ** supports an **image** of the
beast. What is that image? If you do not worship the image, you will be
killed (Revelation 13:15).   "Image" in the Greek is "eikon" or
"representation." The world must worship what the beast, with the seven
heads, stands for. The world will be just like this beast who is directed by
Satan, the dragon and worshipped as a God; and if they do not, they will
be killed.

THIS ANTI-CHRIST MAKES THE WORLD ACCEPT THIS IMAGE

AND PLACES A **MARK** IN THEIR RIGHT **HAND** OR IN THEIR **FOREHEAD** AND NO ONE CAN CONTINUE IN BUSINESS TO EITHER BUY OR SELL.

Generally, the right hand relates to work and making a living and the forehead is one's mind and how they think. What is this **mark of the beast**?

666   In Revelation 13:16-18, this image of the beast, and the accepted way of human life, must worship this worldly system of commerce and government. The proto-type was Tyre, The Phoenician government of world trade or globalization. Satan ruled this system with The Prince of Tyre just as it will be again before **The Return of Christ**. In both cases, it is Satan's, the dragon's, form of government and business (Isaiah 14 and Ezekiel 28).

By worshipping this image the world is not only deceived, but they believe it is God's **approved government** with His Son, Jesus, ruling, as King of Kings. **In truth,** it is **the anti-Christ, "the man of sin"** revealed in II Thessalonians 2.

The world will love this false government, which claims to be God's **government** – The True Kingdom of God. They will worship it. Do you understand the impact of this prophecy? Those, who are alive at the time of this event, will **believe** it is of God. They will worship it. This is a real **warning** to those who only want to do **the true God's "will."** What is the sign? How will you know **the truth**? This **anti-Christ** will cause **all the world** to receive a mark in their hand or forehead (Revelation 13:16).

World trade will not be able to function without this mark. If you want to benefit from this system, you must either have this **mark** or **image** and/or the **number** of his **name** (Revelations 13:17-18). What is the number of his name?

If you have wisdom, you will understand what the number of the name means (Verse 18). What is that number? The number is 666! By understanding the number, the wise will define, exactly what this number represents. Since God's **Word** is wisdom, let God's **Word** define what 666 means.

According to Revelation 13:18, the number, 666 is the number of a **man** or **humanity**. Why is 666 the number of a man? The answer is in Genesis 1. Man was created the sixth day of the week (Verses 26 and 31). That is man's day or the number of man. Why then three sixes or 666?

In Matthew 12:38, the **"scribes"** and Pharisees asked Christ to show them a **sign** that He was of **God** and not of **Satan**. That is the exact point of the mark of the beast. In Greek, the word is "semeion," "a sign which distinguishes" or "a mark." That is exactly the point. How does one tell the difference between the real Jesus and Savior (Matthew 18:11) and the **false savior** and **anti-Christ**? Jesus will tell you. Only an evil generation seeks a sign or mark to reveal who **"the real savior"** is (Matthew 12:39-40). The only physical sign is that The Messiah will be in the grave only three days and three nights. The number **"three" biblically,** delineates the completion or fulfillment for **salvation**. Three constitutes completion, fulfillment or **perfection**. 666 is humanity's way of determining **the restoration** to God's government. Six represents man's or human reasoning, and the three sixes denote humanity's way of determining **salvation** through Christ.

The mystical number, 666, according to <u>The Bible</u> interpreting itself is a totally human idea as each person decides **right** from **wrong** for himself. Each decides what is **the truth** or how to achieve **salvation** in **paradise**. This is exactly what Satan, the dragon, in Genesis 3 told Adam and Eve they would be able to do if they ate of the fruit of The Tree of Good and Evil. This is **Satan's system of government**. It is Satan's rule as **the god of this world** for all humanity. Only those who follow God's "**will**," **without a physical sign**, will worship and follow "**the true**" God. Human reasoning leads to following Satan and his government. The beast, with the false prophet, will claim this Satanic system is literally God's government on earth, but it is not The Kingdom of God, but **the kingdom of Satan**.

The mark of the beast is not a mark placed upon someone, but **a way** of **belief** or a **faith**. Those with **the mark** will refuse to repent (Revelation 16:9). The mark in the forehead is the mind or what one believes and worships (Revelation 17:13). In the right hand is how they work and lead their lives. It is Satan's way of **living** instead of **The One True God's Way of Living**. The **mark of the beast** is not some imprint, but **A WAY OF LIFE**. Satan's way of life and the whole world will be **deceived** just as Adam and Eve were first deceived.

Jesus said, "**I am the way, the truth, and the life: no man cometh unto the Father, but by me**" (John 14:6). The only way to The True God is by the real Christ or The Messiah. The **mark of the beast** leads to an **anti-**

Christ or a counterfeit **false savior**. Before Jesus returns, the entire world will follow a false savior, Satan, **the god of this world**.

<u>SEVEN</u> God's number for The True Savior and to achieve SALVATION is "**seven**." Genesis 2:2 and Hebrews 4 reveal God's **rest** or **paradise** with The Tree of Life is The Seventh Day Rest.

Those who receive God's **seal** will be protected from The Wrath of God (Revelation 9:4). This word "seal" in Greek is "sphragis," meaning "a **mark** of privacy" or "genuineness." This is God's **true government**. This is God's **mark** or **seal**. It sets Christians apart from those with Satan's **mark of the beast**. Christians will be protected from **the end-time** punishment of God. Ephesians 1:13 reveals this Seal of God is God's Holy Spirit which leads you into all **truth** (John 17:17). True Christians will know the difference between **the deception** of **the mark of the beast** because they will be **sealed** with God's Holy Spirit which leads them to understand the **deceptive mark of the beast**.

WRATH OF GOD Those deceived who are still UNREPENTANT, but are blessed with all the riches of globalization of a free trade democracy, WITHOUT THE ONE TRUE GOD, as a standard of right and wrong, will receive God's **winepress** and His "**wrath**" (Revelation 18:3-4).

Revelation 16:15 proclaims **blessed are those who do not defile their GARMENTS OF RIGHTEOUSNESS**. Don't be deceived or fooled, as the world accepts Satan's **mark of the beast** (Revelation 19:18). At that time, the world will look good and prosperous, but in reality, **in the end** will reap the vengeance of God "**Almighty**."

YOU ARE GODS   In Genesis 3, Satan said to Eve she will be her "own god" (free to decide), to tell **right** from **wrong** by herself. Eve became Satan's "mother of all living." Satan was truly the god of this world with his government of rulership. The **true** God, who only gives LIFE, was totally bypassed by Satan's image or mark. This image was completely made by Satan through humanity's own ideas of right and wrong. **The real true** God in **heaven** had absolutely nothing to do with it. Notice how long this beast-like system remains in the world.

THE PROPHECY   Daniel, God's Prophet, reveals to Nebuchadnezzar, The King of Babylon, a historical prophecy starting with Nebuchadnezzar's reign in Babylon until Christ, The Messiah, **returns** and establishes God's own **"kingdom"** and form of **government**. Remember, until Jesus **returns**, these historical events are all of Satan and his government when he first began his deceit in The Garden of Eden. These are all **Gentile "kingdoms"** ruled by Satan, until Satan is overthrown and Christ takes over God's **true government**. Daniel 2 relates this historical prophecy in the form of an image, mark or idol.

Daniel begins interpreting a dream Nebuchadnezzar had of this great image or idol (Daniel 2:28). Daniel states that it is God, The Father in **heaven** who reveals these secrets to the king. Daniel states the dream which the king had has to do with historical events from Daniel's time until **the end-time** when God's **government** WILL BE ESTABLISHED FOREVER. All these Gentile Kingdoms will end or be **"fulfilled."** The word **"Gentile"** means it came from "human ideas," alone, without The True Almighty God. These Gentile **"kingdoms"** are all in Satan's image as started in The Garden of Eden. This giant image or idol had a **head of gold**, arms of silver, belly and thighs of brass, his legs of iron, his feet part of iron and part of clay (Daniel 2:31-33).

Now for a surprising event which takes place. A stone cut out without hands or human origin breaks the image's feet and the entire image collapses and is blown into pieces by the winds of the earth. The stone that smashes the image on the feet replaces The Gentile **system** and becomes **the true government of God** upon the earth **forever**. This covers the entire history from the government of Babylon under Nebuchadnezzar until The Return of The Messiah (Daniel 2:34-35).

These are **"the four kingdoms"** which exists till God's **"kingdom"** takes over (Daniel 2:36-45). In history, these kingdoms are known as The Babylonian, Medo-Persian, Greco-Macedonian and The Roman Empire. Then, Christ begins His **reign**. What is significant is that only these four governments rule the earth until Jesus **returns** with God's **"kingdom."** How can this be? You will soon see Rome's government **never ends till Christ returns**.

Nebuchadnezzar reveals another dream, which includes a large tree where the birds, along with the whole world, receive their sustenance. The tree is chopped down and only its stump remains. The King asks Daniel to interpret (Daniel 4). Daniel states this **"tree"** is Babylon, The King's Empire, which he rules and everyone is taken care of by **the tree** (Daniel 4:1-16). This tree, ruler or king, is cut down and no longer rules Babylon. Why? Nebuchadnezzar was vain enough to take all the credit himself. He felt, he, personally, was responsible for his **"kingdom"** and gained by his own power and not realizing God was responsible for putting him there (Daniel 4:27). Daniel told Nebuchadnezzar to repent and understand how he came to be a king.

The reason for this dream was to teach Nebuchadnezzar it was only God in **heaven** who rules over all and puts into power even the basest of men. In essence, He said, "Nebuchadnezzar, humble yourself and don't worship this great image or idol in spite of your being the head of it" (Daniel 4). Because of his ego, he had to lose his mind and roamed as a beast in the wilderness until he acknowledged that God in **heaven** and only through Him do kings rise and fall according to God's **purpose**. Nebuchadnezzar wandered for seven years as a wild man, and then finally repented and was restored to his kingdom.

When Nebuchadnezzar's rule was past and his grandson, Belshazzar, ruled Babylon, he became **big headed** and acted as if he were God, so in that day, God simply removed Belshazzar as king (Daniel 5).

GOD RULES These **"four kingdoms"** had power as long as the rulers didn't claim to be God or take credit for themselves to rule their kingdoms. Even though these were Gentile **governments**, without God, they were picked and allowed to rule only by God's permission – just as God allows Satan to do what he wants for a short time.

The **mark of the beast** was totally of human origin, from humanity's imagination as led by Satan, the dragon. This **image of the beast** was the same image in Daniel 2. The **mark of the beast** is this Gentile image in Daniel. One flows from the other.

You have seen how this image or **mark of the beast** started in The Garden of Eden with Adam and Eve and continues right through history until Christ's **return**. From **"the kingdom of Babylon"** until **"the fourth kingdom,"** – "The Roman Government" will stay as humanity's system on this earth till The Return of Jesus. This **mark of the beast**, a totally human system, without God, rules until The Messiah's **return**. This fearful **mark**, especially for God's people (Israel and Christianity) is to be avoided at all costs by God's people because if they don't they will be killed. CHRIST SAID, **"YOU ARE IN THE WORLD, BUT NOT OF IT"** (John 17:15-16). God said the wise shall know who and what **the mark of the beast** is, so you cannot and will not be deceived. How do you avoid this **mark of the beast**?

<u>GOLD – SILVER – BRASS – IRON</u> Nebuchadnezzar's great image had a head of **gold**; arms and chest of **silver**; stomach and thighs of **brass** and lastly the legs and feet of **iron** and **clay** (Daniel 2). Then Daniel states, Nebuchadnezzar is the head of gold, and the rest (of the kingdom) become less and less inferior compared to the head of gold – why? Nebuchadnezzar was tried and tested. He was the head of gold because like gold, he was **refined**. What was the reason God tested and tried Nebuchadnezzar? Nebuchadnezzar made a great image of his dream and passed a decree that everyone should **worship** this image and have **no other god** (Daniel 3:11). **The king** excluded The True, Most High God from **his kingdom.** What was the outcome?

Daniel tells the king to repent and humble himself to **"the true"** God who gave him his throne (Daniel 4:27). Because he didn't, God took away

Nebuchadnezzar's kingdom for seven years and he lived in the wilderness as a beast. After seven years, the king came back to his senses and praised God. Only then did God restore his kingship. Then Nebuchadnezzar said it is The Most High God in **heaven** who places men in their position of kingship (Daniel 4:34-35). God's **"kingdom"** is the only lasting, ruling **"kingdom,"** which will rule forever. Nebuchadnezzar, as a Gentile King, repented and accepted **"the true"** God in **heaven** as **"the ruler"** of all. He finally understood only God sets up the basest of men in rulership.

Nebuchadnezzar became a head of gold because he was tried and refined and finally humbled himself before The True, Most High God. That is what made Nebuchadnezzar the best Gentile King of this **great image**. God humbled him, and therefore, he was a superior king over the others, who followed. Now, you are ready to really understand the **mark of the beast** and why God gives a man's number of 666.

Each king, who followed the one before, started to think of himself as a **god**. They credited themselves and did not give God any of the credit. That is the key to the **mark of the beast**. The beasts believe they are **god** and do not need The Most High God to direct them to rule their kingdom. They claim they are **The Kingdom of God** on earth. This is **the mark of the beast** or image of the beast!

Belshazzar, the grandson of Nebuchadnezzar, got carried away with himself (Daniel 5). Belshazzar even desecrated The Holy **things** taken from **the temple** in Jerusalem (Daniel 5:3-4). While he is feasting with his lords and being intoxicated, a finger starts writing on a wall and decrees – that very night – he would lose Babylon with the invasion of

The Medes and Persians. That night he did, indeed, lose his rulership. This is the critical point of **the mark of the beast**. Whenever a ruler, over any empire, decrees himself as a god, without the humility of giving credit to Almighty God in **heaven**, their rulership and kingship will be removed. Only God establishes God's "**kingdom**" on earth by His Son, Jesus (Daniel 2:39).

BACK TO THE GARDEN   This **mark** or **image** of this type of king, which claims to be God's "**kingdom**" on earth, is doomed and under God's curse and eventual destruction. This was the image Satan portrayed to Eve in Genesis 3. Each of the subsequent kings in Nebuchadnezzar image became worse and worse until "**the fourth kingdom**," Rome, which was and is the worst. This kingdom deteriorated to the cheapest form of metal – **iron**. It has mighty strength (militarily), but has the least value. It was a kingdom completely devised from human imagination and reason. In fact, Julius Caesar was the first in The Roman government to call himself Caesar or "sar" in the Hebrew. The Russians called their Caesars, "Tsar," from word in the Hebrew, "sar" which stands for "prince of princes" or "head ruler." No one higher. They claim to sit in God's **throne**.

This **mark of the beast**, which started with Eve, a type of mother-Babylon, procreates the human family, which degenerates in **the end-time** to a complete and total government devised as a self-produced human government with its religion based entirely upon **the commandments of men**. This world government will be a system led by Satan, a false prophet (**anti-Christ**), and the ten kings who control the entire world based upon man's democracy without including The Most High God. It will be exceedingly rich and prosperous and all who **worship** this **image** or **mark of the beast** will prosper and succeed. Everyone will be free to decide for themselves which gods to worship – this image, which is the **mark of the beast** or THE TRUE GOD ALMIGHTY IN HEAVEN AND HIS SON, JESUS.

Notice, the world worships the **image** of the beast. The Roman Empire lasted only about six hundred years and then died. That was the end of the seventh head with one to go, the eighth and final head which is of the seventh (Revelation 17:11). The Roman Empire's **image** or the eighth head of the beast will include **all** the **nations** of the **world**. The world will love it because of the prosperity it will bring.

Since The Roman Empire ended, it is the **"image"** or **"eikon"** (idol), from The Greek which remains. It is **"the system."** Its human form of government and human religious system exists until the eighth head appears. Christ will destroy this final government as Daniel 2 prophesies. How do you tell the difference between those with this mark and those sealed by God's angels?

Simply, "666" is a governmental system claiming to be God's government. As 666 denotes, it will be a democracy based upon a combination of world religions all designed by **human imagination** and accepted as the church of one's choice. It will be filled with either keeping The Letter of The Law, to know right from wrong or just plain designed commandments of men. What is the difference between those with the **mark of the beast** and those with the Seal of God – His Holy Spirit?

Those with the **mark of the beast** will be piously religious, but it **will not change human nature!** Everyone is **still carnal** and will **die**. Those sealed by God "**will**" actually have their very heart and mind changed to only follow "**the will**" of The Most High God. There it is – plain and simple.

A GREAT DECEPTION God's angel warns God's people to come out of her – Babylon – which has made **all the world** drunk or deceived by her teaching. Christians will be deceived, as well as Israel (Revelation 18:4). Basically, this is referring to the 144,000 from The Tribes of Israel and the innumerable multitude – among The Gentiles (Revelation 7:3-14).

Obviously, the **mark of the beast** is not some symbol or literal mark. If the **mark of the beast** was some physical emblem or sign, it would be very apparent to the true believers of God Almighty. The **mark of the beast** is a totally human system of government and religion. It is truly a **number** of a **man** or from **humanity's imagination**. Its "**god**" is **Satan** and not God, The Father in **heaven**. The **mark of the beast** makes **man** his own god, as well as, deciding right from wrong on his own. Notice what God reveals about this **end-time**, just before Christ **returns** with The Seven Last Plagues. In II Thessalonians 2:4-11, Paul gives you **the truth**. Paul states because humanity will follow a false governmental and religious system as if it is God's "**kingdom**," God will cause them to be deceived and become delusional (Verse 11). Christians will be deceived and only come to their senses after the great tribulation caused by Satan.

The **mark of the beast** is a worldwide governmental system and religion, which will be tolerant of all religions, ruled by Satan, with the beast and the false prophet or **anti-Christ**. It will be based upon man-made commandments. When did this system start? In The Garden of Eden with Adam and Eve. This system in Daniel's time prevailed as a Gentile system starting with Nebuchadnezzar as the head of gold. It was the best of all future empires. Why? Because Nebuchadnezzar was refined of gold by his seven years in the wilderness as a beast. Because he finally acknowledged The True God as The Most High God, he had the most superior kingdom.

Those following until The Return of Christ are all inferior kingdoms because they made themselves a **god** and only have a **humanly devised government**. The final Roman Empire continues through the beast with seven heads until Jesus **returns** with His armies, and will become King of Kings over The True Kingdom of God.

SATAN'S LIE   Satan's **lie** to **Eve** was that she would **not die** if she ate the fruit of The Tree of Good and Evil. Satan's system, as the god of this world, can only exist as long as humans remain – **human**. Only when humanity becomes SPIRITUAL is Satan's power finished. Satan is the god of the dead. His mark, a totally devised human system of government, economics, and religion can only end in death. The **mark of the beast** is the image or idol of Satan's rule as a human being. Even though this **democratic system** without The Most High God will be global and will, indeed, produce prosperity in the world, it **never changes human nature**! Unless **humans repent**, they cannot become "**spirit beings**" or **inherit eternal life in God's kingdom**. The end result of Satan's government started in The Garden of Eden and finally, at the end time, becomes the world's system of government and religion. This religious system accepts all religions with a false Christ, **the anti-Christ**. This is a system devised by Satan, which will be filled with piety and religious works by human effort which never changes **human nature**!

THE CHOICE IS LEFT TO YOU. THE WISE VIRGINS WILL REMAIN BLAMELESS OR PERFECT. ALL THE REST WILL PARTAKE OF THE WRATH OF GOD UPON CHRIST'S RETURN, WHICH IS GOD'S GREAT WINEPRESS (REVELATION 14:19).

CHAPTER 6

BABYLON AND THE TWO GRAILS

Babylon, The Great Whore. Babylon started at The Tower of Babel, and this Babylonian system will continue to exist until Christ returns. God blames Babylon for all the religious deceptions incorporated in all the churches. Everything from "no God" to God being "a mountain" or "tree" or "some other part of the creation." Christianity, itself, is divided, as well as all the divisions in The Jewish Faith. Who is Babylon, The Great Whore?

To begin, consider the story about a potter. This potter decided to build a sculpture of Himself, a self-portrait. The **potter** is God. God said to the heavenly host, **"Let us make man in our image"** (Genesis 1:26). God wanted to duplicate humanity in His likeness. To accomplish this goal, He told **the angels** they would be His **messengers**. After all, when angels appear, they look like humans (Genesis 18:1-2).

The Apostle Paul clarifies God's **purpose** as a potter. Paul refers to humanity blaming God saying, **"Why hast thou made me thus?"** (Romans 9:18-25). Why did God make humans? Paul said God is **the potter**, and you are the clay, made from dust, and He decides for your own good, how you can have honor or dishonor in God's **eyes**. Some humans become enemies of God and others are chosen by God to be His own. God is **the one** who decides how He is making you in His **image**. God is **the potter**; humans are but clay.

Paul said those humans who are against God are, unknowingly, fulfilling **God's plan** (Verse 22). God is willing to endure grief, but is also willing to show His wrath to make **His power known**. God endures this life process by suffering Himself to finally have His wrath (anger with grief), fitted or set in proper order to ruin or destroy those who are evil. God decides who needs a severe spanking. Why? So, you will eventually seek only God, **the true** God, who can give you LIFE (I Timothy 2:4). It is God's "**will**" that everyone be SAVED, but only, in His Order according to one's growth (I Corinthian 15). God vents His wrath upon those who refuse to REPENT. How does God deal with the vessels of dishonor?

RETURN OF CHRIST   The 144,000 **saints** are with God on Mt Zion, by The City of David (Revelation 14:1-4). Who are these 144,000? God is ready to bring curses upon the earth, but holds them back until His **servants** are **sealed** (Revelation 7:3). Who are God's **servants**? These 144,000 are of The Twelve Tribes of Israel who came out of **the great tribulation** from Israel (Revelation 7:4-15). Only 144,000 Israelites are converted to Christ at that time. Then, a **great multitude** from all nations will also be converted by going through **the great tribulation** just before Christ **returns** (Verses 9-10).

The 144,000 in Revelation 14 are 12,000 from each of The Tribes of Israel who will meet Jesus **in the clouds** and stand on Mt. Zion. This depicts Christ's **return** to the earth with all the angels and His **saints** or **bride**.

This is **the first resurrection** (John 5) or the **early spring barley harvest**. (Read Chapter 7, 'The Mystery Harvest.') Next is **the late ingathering harvest** or **wheat harvest** and finally, **the fall grape harvest** or God's **wrath**.

GOD'S JUDGMENT   An **angel** tells John that **the wheat harvest** consists of those who will go into God's **"kingdom,"** and later comes **a third harvest**, which is **a grape harvest**, upon whom God unleashes **His wrath** (Revelation 14:15-20). This harvest is God's **winepress** which takes place outside a particular city (Verse 20). What city is this?

BABYLON, THE GREAT An **angel** cries out that the hour of God's **judgment** has come. At this point, the **angel** announces everyone should repent and worship **the true** God (Revelation 14:7-11). Then another **angel** shouts, **"Babylon is fallen, is fallen, that great city, because she made all nations drink of the wine of the wrath of her fornication"** (Revelation 14:8). This great city made everyone **drunk** or **deceived** about **the true** God and His **ways**. This great city **deceives the whole world** with her idolatrous religious ideas.

All those with **the mark of the beast** will receive God's **wrath** or **seven last plagues** and be thrown into The Lake of Fire if they do not **repent** (Verse 9-11). Where is this great city of Babylon?

BABYLON AND THE GRAIL   Check The Scriptures to prove which is really this great city (who is a whore). Some say it refers to Rome or even The Catholic Church. Others say **the harlots** are The Protestant Churches. Some say it is New York City and on and on it goes. What do

The Scriptures say? God is about to make judgment concerning this **whore** (Revelation 17:1-2). This woman has committed fornication with the inhabitants of the earth and its kings and rulers by making them drunk with the wine she gives to the world (Verse 2). You will see the drunkenness is caused by the world's acceptance of the various religious beliefs which are not of God but from the imagination of human thinking and reasonings.

This wine deceives the inhabitants of the world along with the rulers. They become like a **drunkard**. They no longer know "**right**" from "**wrong**." (Chapter 5, 'Mark of The Beast' will explain further). This world believes a lie. This woman, who becomes luxuriously wealthy, also has a golden cup in her hand full of **abominations** and **filthiness** created from all her fornication (Revelation 17:4).

Then, in her forehead (or mind), she has a name written. It states, **"Mystery, Babylon, The Great, The Mother of Harlots and Abominations, of the earth"** (Revelation 17:5). Now, you have some **biblical insight**. This Babylon is a **great city** (Revelation 14:7-11). In what way is this city great? You know it's a city, but it's more than just a city – it's a **great city**. Why? This city is great because it has a cup of wine which deceives or makes **all the world**, its rulers or kings drunk. The world worships this **city** putting their faith in it and truly wants to follow it. They cannot tell "**right**" from "**wrong**." Why? It is God who calls her a whore or a mother of harlots. The Great city of Babylon causes confusion of what is really **the truth** about God Almighty.

BABEL AND THE TOWER   When you go back in history, you find the original Babylon became Babel or **"confusion"** by God diversifying the languages of the world. Why did He divide the earth and its people? God said if He left them with **one** language, they would create a multitude of **dreamed-up ideas**, **false thinkings** and **varied imaginations** about Him. They already, out of their own ideas, built a **tower** to **heaven** as their way to worship God. God **never** told them to build the tower to worship Him. He divided them by diverse languages so a variety of religions about God would be curtailed just as in Babel. Now, in **the end-time**, the world comes together religiously to worship **the true** God by everyone picking **the church** of his/her choice. Everyone is doing what is **right** in his/her own eyes. This **new Babylon** is a **great city**, where many nations worship their individual God according to the religion of their choice without having **the truth** of **The Real God Almighty, and His Son, Jesus**. The world is all made drunk from the wine of this cup or grail.

NEW BABYLON   This **end-time** city not only causes **confusion,** but is, also, a **mystery**. No one who is of this world can really understand **the truth** about this city. In fact, until later, no one seems to even know what or where this city is. She is called great, because she is worshipped by the world and the world makes her rich. This city is a mother or one who spawns or accepts daughters who are harlots. Who is this mother who teaches religious confusion and her daughters are harlots just as she is? Because of her false religious teachings, this great city causes martyrdom to those who are God's **true saints** or **righteous ones** who do not worship her. This **great city** reigns over the entire world (Revelation 17:18).

In Greek, the word for "fornication" refers to **"idolatry,"** **"the worship of** false gods" or "**a false religion**." "Abominations" and "filthiness" refer to "every unclean thing, **which is a lie**." This is the exact opposite of what is **the truth**. She claims to be what she isn't. This is quite a woman. Who is she? Now, for a great surprise!

THE WHORE AND HARLOTS This great city of Babylon, worshipped by the world, is **not** Rome, The Catholic Church, The Protestants or harlots, or even New York City. Also, it is not The United Nations as some believe. Ezekiel, The Prophet, discloses who this **whore** is. God tells Ezekiel to tell **Jerusalem** of **her abominations** (Ezekiel 16:1-2). Babylon is the city filled with **abominations**. Here God calls Jerusalem a woman filled with **abominations**.

Jerusalem started as a Gentile City of The Amorites and Hittites (Verses 4-5). No one was interested in her. God found her covered in blood (i.e., wine which symbolize pagan teachings) (Verse 6). God said she became a city that has LIFE and not death. God made **a marriage covenant** with her to become His Bride. God courted her and was preparing her for The Wedding Feast by making her prosperous (Verses 9-16). She became extremely wealthy in King David's and Solomon's Day and then what happened? Because of Jerusalem's great wealth, she started to commit idolatry and became a whore (Ezekiel 16:17-23). She made agreements with other nations but **not** with **the true God.** This is Jerusalem, not any other city. She even started to follow pagan customs by burning their children in fire, in a place known as The Valley of Gehenna or "hell."

The Book of Revelation states the time period will be after **the two woes** with **the third woe** (Verse 23). This **third woe** occurs at **the seventh**

trumpet when Christ **returns** and unleashes **the seven last plagues**, or the **wrath** of **God** upon mankind and the earth.

Ezekiel accuses Jerusalem of accepting all the religions of the world with their high places or churches of worship. God calls Jerusalem – Egypt, the mother of idol worship (Ezekiel 16:24-27). Jerusalem is worshipped as the center of the world's religious beliefs.

The term "Philistine," is the modern day Palestine or Palistinians. The **daughters** of The Philistines, which are today's modern day Palestinians, hate Jerusalem and The Jews for this very reason (Verse 27). They hate Jerusalem because of The Jews who have allowed all religions to venerate and have differing **Holy places** in that city. Palestinians are Muslims and have no use for The Jewish **religion** or any belief other than their own of Islam. There you have it. The Mosque of Omar is there. It is **biblically** very clear, this great city of Babylon is where everyone in the world, worships – **Jerusalem**.

God states Jerusalem is a wife committing adultery and buying off her lovers – the world, to keep her prosperous and peaceful (Ezekiel 16:31-35). God's **wrath** is poured out against His unfaithful wife by having her lovers, who made her prosperous, turn and devour her (Verse 37-46). All nations of the world shall turn against Jerusalem and make her naked. They turn on her because she proves not to be God's **"kingdom"** on **earth,** and **they (the beast)** are deceived (Revelation 17:15-18). Why? When Jesus **returns, the beast, the false governments** of the world turn on her because they are inundated when God unleashes his **seven last plagues** upon them. They know they were deceived about **the true**

Christ.   There you have it.   Who is this **great city** of Babylon? **Jerusalem** in **the end-time**! THE FALSE NEW JERUSALEM!

THE HARLOTS   Babylon is, also, called **the mother of harlots**. Who are these harlots? In The Book of Hosea, God tells Hosea to marry a whore whose name is Gomer. "Gomer" in Hebrew means "finality" or "completion." Gomer represents Jerusalem, which is God's **bride**. Hosea marries Gomer and bares him a legitimate son, Jezreel. In the beginning, God accepted Jerusalem as His, even though her birth was of pagan origin. He regarded her as His. To learn how she corrupted herself, read all of Hosea. After Jezreel's birth, which was legitimate, she bore a daughter, Lo-ruhamah, which in Hebrew means, **"I will no more have mercy**." Who is Lo-ruhamah? Hosea said this daughter represents Israel. Lo-ruhamah is not of Hosea's seed, but his wife's – while playing the whore.

Then, Gomer commits adultery again and bares Lo-ammi who represents Judah. Lo-ammi, in Hebrew means, **"you are not my people**." Israel and Judah are both rejected by God. What is the reason? At the **end-time**, both Israel and Judah will be united as one nation under God (Hosea 1:10-11). In the first chapter of Hosea, you cover all the history, from The Ten Tribes of Israel going into captivity under Assyria and later Judah going into captivity under Babylon. Both, Israel and Judah finally **unite,** and become God's people (Hosea 2:23). Israel and Judah ultimately accept **the true God**.

Hosea 2:4 reveals how Jerusalem's children become whores or harlots. In Hosea 4:11, The Prophet states Israel plays a whore because she drinks **wine**, especially **new wine**, which causes **real drunkenness**. Israel is called the harlot (Verse 15). Why would Israel be called a **harlot**? She drinks wine which is sour because they play the harlot (Verse 18). Her rulers, in Hosea 4:17, pray to idols or commit fornication. In duality, you now know Jerusalem is the whore whom God married and her children, Israel and Judah, are the harlots.

Babylon, that great center of all the major religions of the world is **Jerusalem**, the mother of **all** harlots. The harlots are Israel and Judah who accept all these other idolatrous, human-made religions by agreements made by their rulers. **Babylon**, or the end-time **Jerusalem**, becomes a **great world city,** and is **worshipped** as the **world's religious** center of all major beliefs in the world. There you have it.

INNOCENT BLOOD   Now you know, Babylon, **the great whore** is **the city** – Jerusalem, at **the end-time**. Israel has made pacts with all the nations and rulers of the world. Trade agreements worldwide, or globalization, produce prosperities for the entire world. Each having its religion accepted by contracts with the rulers of Israel who play the harlot. Peace, peace when there is no peace. At last, Israel is accepted as a legitimate state in the world. A variety of church edifices of all religions fill this international world City of Babylon (the end-time Jerusalem). Israel, as a nation at last, does have peace.

A **temple** is built with **the anti-Christ** proclaiming to be The Messiah. This **temple**, however, **is not sanctified** by God. The whore claims God's **"kingdom"** is already on earth. The world actually rejects **true** **christianity** and those who are **faithful** to **the true God**. In fact, they go through condemnation and persecution. Revelation 18:6 reveals **true**

Christians will be martyred. They know the real Jesus will descend from the east as lightening with great thunder.

Matthew 24:23-25 warns Christians this will be a time when false Christs and false prophets will arise and would even deceive **true Christians**, if possible. But, it will **not** be possible because they will be witnessing **the return** of **the true Messiah**. Revelation 11 states they will witness **the truth for three and a half years of the tribulation**. This is the reason they will be killed. John continues and declares God's **two witnesses** will be killed (Revelation 11:8). Where? John reveals God now looks upon this great city (end-time Jerusalem), **spiritually**, as **Sodom** and **Egypt**. Completely saturated **spiritually** with sin or every abomination and filthiness (just as Revelation 17:5 states). What city does The Bible clearly say Babylon, the whore, is? Notice, the last part of Revelation 11:8 plainly tells you, **"where also our Lord was crucified."** There is no doubt. Babylon, the great whore, where our Lord was crucified, is spiritually dead. Jerusalem with an **anti-Christ** in **a temple** or **a tabernacle**, and all other human religious edifices and churches worshipping this great city as their **seat of origin**. Those who worship this city and the beast despise **the truth of God**. They follow **a false Christ, an anti-Christ** instead of **the true Messiah**, and God's **saints** are martyred! The world will believe The Messiah is in Jerusalem. The Messiah came secretly.

Revelation 18:24 states this Babylon or spiritually-dead Jerusalem was found with the **blood** of **Prophets** and of **saints**, and all that were slain upon the earth. Religion has caused more wars and deaths than any other cause. Notice, however, The Old Testament Prophets were killed in Jerusalem. Neither Rome, New York nor The United Nations qualifies. Babylon, the great city, is none other than the end-time Jerusalem. God calls this end-time Jerusalem Sodom and Egypt, "**spiritually**" where **the true Messiah** was crucified.

THE GRAILS   Jesus enjoined all Christians to drink His cup of wine, which represented His **blood** for the remission of sins (Matthew 26:27-28). An **angel** descends from heaven who is so powerful the entire earth is filled with an extremely bright light (Revelation 18:1-8). The **angel** cries out that Jerusalem/Babylon becomes the world center of every demon and foul spirit. God causes the destruction of the city because **all nations** have drunk the wine from Babylon's cup, which causes those with **the mark of the beast** to be deceived with her false teaching about the real Messiah and God's "**true kingdom**."

A voice declares, "**Come out of her, my people, that ye be not partakers of her sins, and that ye receive not of her plagues**" (Verse 4). These are those Christians who come through The Great Tribulation with The 144,000 Israelites. God decries Babylon, because she made everyone drink of her false, deceptive **cup** about Christ and God's "**kingdom**." They are to be paid back **double** for all her false teachings (Verse 6). God's **wrath** is about to be released upon everyone who has the **mark of the beast**. You will come to see that Christ's cup and Babylon's cup refers to God's **wrath**, which ends with The Lake of Fire. THERE ARE **TWO GRAILS**. Babylon loves her prosperity and the worship she receives. Because she believes herself to be "**God's kingdom**" on "**earth**," she torments everyone who does not follow and worship her (Revelation 18:7).

This Queen, **Babylon**, states in her heart she **sits** a **queen** and is **no widow** and will **not know sorrow**. This queen does not require the **death** or sacrifice of **the true** Christ, for she has no husband. This whore claims she has **no husband** and was **not widowed** by Christ's death since she is God's **kingdom** on earth. She truly sits a queen without the need of any husband as king. She claims she will never die. God's **wrath – the seven last plagues** – ending with The Lake of Fire brings **judgment** to the world! (Verse 8).

CHRIST'S CUP   The patriarch, Jacob knew about the coming Messiah, and prophesied about Christ drinking from His **cup of wine**. Jacob said, in **the last days**, Jesus would come **"Binding his foal unto the vine, and his ass's colt unto the choice vine; he washed his garments in wine, and his clothes in the blood of grapes:"** (Genesis 49:11-12). Jesus Christ, The Savior took upon Himself, **the wrath of God, God's winepress** for each and every Christian who drinks of that cup.

Jesus was given gall to drink (Matthew 27:34). Gall was **mixed with wine** to give those crucified a drug to alleviate the pain of crucifixion. Once Christ tasted it, He would not drink any more. Why?

Jesus, The Christ, wanted to feel the **pain** of his death and **crucifixion**, so He took upon Himself God's **wrath** for each and every Christian. Just as He spilled His **blood** to show His **love** for you, He took the **stripes**, as well, for your healing and thereby, going to hell for you. Jesus would not drink the wine given Him. Jesus, The Christ, The Savior paid fully for the penalty of all of your sins. The **whore's cup** and **Christ's cup** represent the **same thing** – God's **wrath**! Jerusalem's fornication teaches an **idolatrous god**. Satan's cup, Babylon, was now to pay the full penalty of God's **wrath** in The Lake of Fire as God's final spanking.

These are the two grails. Babylon and all the world's human religions are still looking for and seeking **the holy grail** of Christ. The crusaders sought it; archeologists seek it, and in the fictional account of The DaVinci Code, they attempt to find **the true cup** of Christ. Babylon, the great whore, never will be able to drink of that cup because at **the end-time**, Jerusalem will be asking the world to drink of her cup, filled with **false teachings** about God's **"kingdom"** which says she is The Kingdom of God, but it will fail. ONLY THE TRUE MESSIAH, JESUS, THE CHRIST, CAN BRING GOD'S ACTUAL KINGDOM TO REIGN ON THIS EARTH.

CHAPTER 7

THE MYSTERY HARVEST

Most Christian denominations believe there are two harvests representing those who are "saved." There is The Spring Harvest in Jerusalem, which was basically a harvest of barley. The Great Fall Harvest, known as the "ingathering," was a "wheat harvest." Surprisingly, there are three harvests. There is a Barley Spring Harvest; then in the fall, The Wheat Harvest and ultimately, The Grape Harvest. Read the wonderful account, this mystery harvest which reveals everyone is finally saved.

Paul said The Sabbaths and Holy Days are a **shadow** or a **prophecy** of things to come (Colossians 2:16-17). Each Christian **church**, which accepts The Holy Days, determine on their own what part to incorporate into their creed. Each denomination has their belief of faith tied directly to which Holy Days they believe or accept.

Catholic, Protestants, Greek and Russian Orthodox pretty much accept the death of Christ as their Passover. Jesus is **the sacrificed lamb**, and by the drinking of the wine and eating the bread shows the remembrance of His death. Today, most call it Communion because it represents the body and blood of Christ – your Passover. Also, these groups accept Pentecost as the receiving of The Holy Spirit or the genesis of The Church of God. From here on, the rest of God's Holy Days are not followed but corrupted with pagan days such as Easter, Christmas, Halloween, etc. This restricts **the shadow** or **prophecy of things to come** for these groups. Some Evangelicals and **independents** understand other Holy Days such as The Feast of Trumpets as The Seventh Trump commemorating **the return of Christ**. The Worldwide Church of God and The Seventh Day Church of God, among others, accept **almost** all of God's Holy Days – Passover, Unleavened Bread, Pentecost, Trumpets, Atonement, Tabernacles and The Last Great Day. Those of The Jewish Faith, also, accept all The Holy Days.

Amazingly, although thinking they keep all The Holy Days, they do not include **all** THE HOLY DAYS. One of the major Holy Days, which lasts for a year is barely known or voiced by **any group**. This is **The Jubilee Year**, which is a Holy time of God's, occurring every fifty years. What is the mystery? What does The Jubilee represent? Leviticus 25 covers this Holy time. Jubilee also signifies a **shadow of things to come**. IT IS A JUBILEE OR FEAST WHERE EVERYONE IS RELEASED FROM THEIR DEBTS AND RETURNED TO THEIR FAMILY INHERITANCE. Only **The Gentiles** (those without God), are **not released**, but are kept in slavery forever. Why?

TIME OF RELEASE   The Jubilee is a **great festive period**. It lasts for an entire year. It is a time of rejoicing and all debtors are forgiven their debts without penalty. It is a **time of release** and every family is to return to their **family inheritance**. It is truly a period of rejoicing and feasting. It is the genesis of **the horn of plenty**. When a family goes into debt and sells its land and properties, the buyer can only retain that land and property until The Jubilee Year. Once The Jubilee arrives, all debts are forgiven and the debtors have their property back **free and clear**.

An exception would be when a family member redeems the land back by paying the debt off, which would include a premium and then the land goes back to the family. The Book of Ruth is a good example of **redemption** by Boaz. **The inheritance** is returned before The Jubilee, free and clear. Only The Gentiles, **those without God**, are not released from **debt** and **must make full restitution**. Read and study Leviticus 25 thoroughly to validate these facts. Remember, all The Holy Days of God are a **shadow** or a **prophecy** of things to come. Biblically, The Jubilee represents The Final Harvest, which God calls a **mystery**.

GOD'S MYSTERY Paul said **the saints** and **the faithful** Christians in Ephesus have the privilege of knowing a mystery, which had never before been revealed (Ephesians 1:9). It reveals a very wondrous **prophecy**. In Christ, **all things** (everyone – the world) in **heaven** and the earth ARE GOING TO BE SAVED (Ephesians 1:10). Jesus said everyone who confesses Christ before men, in like manner, THE CHRIST, Himself, will confess as High Priest (Melchizedec) before **the angels** (Luke 12:8). Every single person who confesses The Christ will receive **salvation** (Romans 10:9-10). Paul clearly defines who is SAVED. He states every knee will bow and confess Christ, in **heaven**, on the **earth**, and those under the earth (the dead) will be SAVED (Philippians 2:9-11). God thought of everything in His **plan** and will SAVE EVERY SINGLE PERSON. But, how does all this come to pass?

PARABLE OF THE SOWER AND THE SEED   Jesus speaks of **the**

parable when a farmer sows seed in his field and at harvest time, finds beautiful wheat, but some wheat plants had only blades without fruit. There were tares or weeds keeping those blades from maturing into wheat (Matthew 13). What happened? The landowner tells his servants that an enemy had seeded the tares along with the seeds of his wheat (Matthew 13:27-30). He allows them both to grow together; then, at harvest time, he tells them to take out the tares and burn them, and gather the wheat into his barn.

But wait! In this **parable** when the tares are burned, the wheat is still there – the same seed God planted, which had blades, but, without wheat or fruit. What does the owner do with them since these seeds did not bare fruit? Christ reveals two more parables. One is a grain of mustard seed that grows into the greatest among herbs and all the birds lodge in it. Nothing is lost (Matthew 13:31-32). His **second parable** relates that a woman took some leaven and hid in it three measures of meal till the **whole** was leavened. It became a loaf of wheat bread. Again, nothing is lost – everything is used. Jesus is saying ALL WILL BE SAVED, even the blades will bear wheat, which finally became bread and everything will be **saved**. How does God and His Son accomplish this? The answer is revealed in The Jubilee Year and THE MYSTERY HARVEST.

If a brother mismanages or some of his plans don't work out, making him poor – in debt – and he has to sell his **inheritance**, then a kin (relative) can REDEEM **the inheritance** before The Jubilee (Leviticus 25:25). Likewise, the debtor, himself, when he recoups some funds, may, also, **redeem** his land. The Book of Ruth shows a kin, Boaz, taking steps to recoup Naomi's land.   This lineage is King David's forefather, and likewise Christ, David's seed, REDEEMS all of humanity by **His blood** or the giving of **His life**. This is the reason Pentecost (count fifty from Unleavened Bread – means becoming sinless), is fifty days after The Feast of Unleavened Bread. Christ **redeemed "the church"** before The Jubilee and gave **the inheritance** to them, which is GOD'S HOLY SPIRIT.

John 5:25-27 reveals this is THE FIRST RESURRECTION and James 1:18 calls them **THE FIRSTFRUITS**. What harvest is this? This Firstfruits Harvest is in **the spring** (Exodus 23:16-19). **The fall harvest** is at the end of the year, which is The Great Harvest known as **The Feast of Ingathering**. This harvest comes in **the fall** (Verse 16). You have two harvests, **spring** and **fall**. Ruth 1:22 shows Naomi and Ruth coming back to Naomi's home in **the spring** called **the barely harvest**. This **barley harvest** represents **"the church" REDEEMED** by Christ before The Jubilee Year.

The large wheat harvest is in **the fall** or **time of ingathering**. This is the completion of the year's farming and includes only **two harvests**, THE SPRING BARLEY HARVEST and THE LATE WHEAT HARVEST. Notice, Matthew 13 only refers to **the wheat harvest** or The Jubilee when everyone is returned to their **inheritance**. So far, there are only two harvests. What is **the third harvest**? It's a **mystery**. This is a **"hidden harvest" which has literally been hidden from the world**. Notice, it is only **"the church saints"** and **"the faithful"** who understand what this THIRD HARVEST is as God's **Word** reveals it.

GENTILE'S SLAVES FOREVER   God states if a brother is sold into slavery because of debt, during The Jubilee, that debtor must be freed and returned to his **inheritance** (Leviticus 25:39-43). No usury can be charged and one cannot treat the brother as if the owner is a dictator. He is still a brother and should be set free during The Jubilee Year.

In "**the church,**" they are to be **spiritual Israelites** – as a brother (Romans 2). All others are to be **bondsmen** or **slaves** for life (Leviticus 25:44-46). These are the **unconverted**. These are **the heathen** or **pagans**. Why? Remember, pagans are those without **the true God**. What happens to the pagans? How are they **saved** when God refers to being ALL AND IN ALL **in everyone** (I Corinthians 15).

THE WRATH OF GOD   Prophecy in The Bible reveals the answer to the mystery of THE THIRD HARVEST. THE SEVENTH ANGEL or THE SEVENTH TRUMPET begins to sound (Revelation 11:15). Paul said this is the time of THE FIRST RESURRECTION at **the sound** of **the trumpet**. This is **Christ's return** and "**the resurrected saints" meet Jesus in the clouds** (I Thessalonians 4:16-17). It is at The Seventh Trump, The First Harvest, when all the kingdoms of this world become God's "**kingdom**" with Christ as King of Kings (Revelation 11:15).

One hundred forty-four thousand (144,000) Israelites are resurrected and follow Christ (Revelation 14:1-4). They are called THE FIRSTFRUITS and are in The First Resurrection. This event is summarized when the one hundred and forty-four thousand (144,000) – The Tribes of Israel **along** with **an innumerable multitude** from **all** nations are given God's **seal** or **inheritance** of The Holy Spirit (Revelation 7:1-14). Who are they? These are those who will be coming out of "**the great tribulation yet to** come" (Revelation 14). **They are God's "first fruits" or of The First Barley Harvest**, along with those who make this harvest **in the last three and a half years of tribulation BEFORE** Christ **returns**. This completes **The Barley Harvest**.

Those who do not repent and instead follow Satan with **his mark** will have God's **wrath** poured out upon them (Revelation 14:10). This **wrath** of God is compared to **wine** and called God's **cup of indignation** ending in The Lake of Fire. In the Greek, "indignation" carries the meaning of "anger with grief." Read all of Hebrews 12. This is God's **final spanking**; it has the power to do everything it takes to SAVE you. God's **wrath** is portrayed as a **cup of wine**. What did Jesus say about wine?

<u>**CHRIST, THE VINE**</u>   **Jesus** said He is the **vine** (John 15:1-6). **"Vines"** refer to **"grapes."** Christ said unless you are attached to Jesus who is the vine and **bear much fruit**, you will be gathered (in harvest time) and thrown into The Fire or Gehenna – The Lake of Fire (Revelation 14). Christ revealed when you drink His **cup** of **wine**, your sins are forgiven (Matthew 26:27-28). Jesus is the vine and by drinking from His **cup**, The Passover **"cup of wine,"** you are forgiven your sins. This is His **blood**. Christ had gone into God's **winepress of wrath for you** when you drink His **cup**. Why?

Christ states if you merely drink **His cup of wine** BUT are not **bearing much fruit**, you will **still** be thrown into The Lake of Fire. Jesus said to gather up the **tares** (weeds) and burn them (Matthew 13:30). So, the wheat is left after the tares are burned. No wheat is lost. How does God **save** everyone? The wheat, all of it, is put into the barn.

WINEPRESS OF GOD'S WRATH   The time of **the seventh trump** announces The First Resurrection with Christ's **return** to earth along with His armies (Revelation 11:15). There can be **NO SECRET RAPTURE** when Christ, with **the saints** and **the angels**, unleashes **the wrath** of God which comprises **the seven last plagues.** Christ standing on Mt. Zion with the 144,000 (and an innumerable number), sing a new song about their REDEMPTION (Jubilee) (Revelation 14:1). Another angel cries out, **"Babylon is fallen, is fallen, that great city, because she made all nations** [the world] **drink of the wine of the wrath of her fornication"** (Verse 8). These are those who never drank of Christ's **cup of wine**; meaning they **never repented**.

Revelation 14:9-10, **"the third angel followed them saying with a loud voice,"** [those who] **"worship the beast and his image, and receive his mark in his forehead, or in his hand"** [and his image] **"shall drink of the wine of the wrath of God."** [Notice the outcome] **"he shall be tormented with fire and brimstone in the presence of the Holy Angels, and in the presence of the Lamb."** This is NO SECRET RAPTURE as **the entire world witnesses this spectacular event**. Christ with His **saints** and **angels** pour out THE LAST SEVEN PLAGUES or THE WRATH OF GOD, which finally concludes with The Lake of Fire (hell). Then **blessed** are **the saints** who have patience and who **"keep the commandments of God and the faith of Jesus"** (Verse 12). Then came the outpouring of THE SEVEN LAST PLAGUES and WRATH OF GOD (Revelation 15 and 16).

TWO MORE HARVESTS   John prophesies that those who die in

Christ will go to their rest until their **resurrection**. **"Another angel came out of the temple crying with a loud voice to him that sat on the cloud, Thrust in thy sickle, and reap: for the time is come for thee to reap; for the harvest of the earth is ripe"** (Revelation 14:15). This angelic announcement speaks of another harvest (Revelations 14:13-20).

THE WHEAT HARVEST   In Revelation 14:14 one **who looks like** The Son of Man having on his head a golden crown (king), and in his hand, a sharp sickle. Remember, this is during **the seventh trump**. Christ resurrects those in **The First Resurrection** (barley harvest) and **unleashes The Seven Last Plagues** while standing where the 144,000 is standing on Mt. Zion – David's **throne**.

Another **angel** came out of **the temple**. For this **harvest**, this **angel** comes out of **the temple** and does what? The **angel** cries out to The Son of Man and states, **"Thrust in thy sickle, and reap: for the time is come for thee to reap; for the harvest of the earth is ripe"** (Verse 15). This is **the ingathering**, or **Fall Harvest of Wheat**. You have **two harvests, The Barley in The Spring**, and now, **The Great Fall Harvest of Wheat**.

THE MYSTERY HARVEST   What is this mystery **third harvest**? Another **angel** came out of **the altar** (Verse 18). In **the wheat harvest**, the **angel** comes out of **the temple**, but this **third angel** comes out of **the altar**. Why? This angel has power or control over fire (Verse 18). This is God's **wrath** finalizing in The Lake of Fire or hell (Gehenna). What is this **angel** going to do? This **angel** cries to him who had the sharp sickle, saying, **"Thrust in thy sharp sickle, and gather the clusters of the vine of the earth; for her grapes are fully ripe"** (Verse 18). This is a Third

Harvest – **The Grape Harvest**. This is **THE MYSTERY HARVEST** mentioned in Ephesians 1:9-10. It is **a grape harvest**. Why?

THE WINEPRESS   **"And the angel thrust in his sickle into the earth, and gathered the vine of the earth, and cast it into the great winepress of the wrath of God"** (Revelation 14:19). God is going to make wine from **this harvest** or **spilled blood**. **The seven vials of God** ending by those who are **not** in The Book of Life being thrown into The Lake of Fire or **the final hell**. Those in God's **final harvest – the grape harvest**, are thrown into Gehenna to be burned (Chapters 15 to 20). That is just what Jesus said: **"Let both grow together** [wheat and tares] **until the harvest: and in the time of harvest** [wheat and grape] **I will say to the reapers** [plural]**, Gather ye together first the tares, and bind them in bundles to burn them: but gather the wheat into my barn"** (Matthew 13:30). Why the tares first?

THE TARES   Jesus details the process of these two harvests (wheat and grapes). Christ reveals, **"³⁸The field is the world; the good seed are the children of the kingdom; but the tares** [weeds] **are the children of the wicked one;"** [Satan] (Matthew 13:37-43). Satan sowed the tares. What are **the tares**? The tares are Satan's deceptive teachings which have to be burned (I Corinthians 3:13-15). Jesus said the same in Matthew 13. The **false teachings** or **lies** have to be burned **(first)** before **The Grape Harvest**. Then what happens? The grapes are ready to be harvested after **the carnality** or **false thinking** is burned away (Revelation 14:18). All false ideas or carnal teachings will suffer loss (I Corinthian 3:14-15). How? By fire! However, all persons who had followed Satan will eventually be **SAVED**. There you have it. There are THREE HARVESTS – **The Barley (Spring), The Wheat (Fall),** and **finally, The Mystery Harvest**, which is The Lake of Fire. God has arranged to SAVE everyone. For the complete **process of salvation** of those in **The Grape Harvest**, read the last third of the book – God's Work.

THE GRAPE HARVEST Does Revelation disclose this grape harvest? Yes! Continuing with the context in Revelation 14, you find Revelation 15 follows with **the seven last plagues**. God's winepress is ready to unfold. The **seven last plagues** are **the wrath of God** (Revelation 15:1). Then all of a sudden in Verse 2 John sees **"a sea of glass."** What is this **sea of glass?** John states this sea, a picture of the world, is **mingled** with fire. Who is in this glass **mingled** with fire? Clearly, it states all those who have finally repented and gained victory over **the beast** and **his mark**. However, to do so they have to come out of **the sea of glass, which is on fire** or The Lake of Fire (as you will **soon prove**).

Those, who overcome the beast and his mark, **sing two songs**. First, it mentions **'The Song of Moses'** and, also, **'The Song of The Lamb'** (Revelation 15:3). Amazingly, The Bible has 'The Song of Moses.' This song is for the whole world, and the entire earth will hear it. This song is a prophecy about Israel and how they strayed from God and God's **way** (Deuteronomy 32:1). God abhorred what Israel had become. God warns what Israel's **end** would be. God is angry, and the unrepentant Israelites go into **The Lake of Fire** (Deuteronomy 32:19-22). Their **vine** (grapes) is like Sodom and Gomorrah, and their grapes are **grapes of gall** – bitter and wild (Verse 32). Their vine is the poison of dragons and a poisonous snake (Satan) (Verse 33). This is 'The Song of Moses.' Those who come out of The Grape Harvest (God's **wrath**) come out of The Lake of Fire – REPENTED. These are The Israelites.

'The Lamb's Song' is about those left, The Gentiles, who repent and sing, **"Great and marvelous are thy works, Lord God Almighty; just and true are thy ways, thou King of saints."** This Grape Harvest includes everyone **ever** born (Revelation 15:3). **"Who shall not fear thee, O Lord, and glorify thy name? For thou only art holy: for all nations shall come and worship before thee; for thy judgments are made manifest"** (Revelation 15:4). Compare this with Ephesians 1:10 and Philippians 2:9-11.

In the Greek, the word for "nations" is not "cosmos," "the world," but, "ethnos," which means "all the races of the world." NO ONE LEFT OUT. God and His Son will not lose any of you – even when you are duped into following the worldly ways of Satan. EVENTUALLY, EVERYONE WILL BE SAVED.

CHAPTER 8

THE MIND OF CHRIST

God's "kingdom" with the rewards are based upon only one thing – your "spiritual growth." Salvation is a free gift, unearned and totally free, which will be given to you. <u>The Book of Revelation</u> is the uncovering or revelation of what rewards you will receive by your works. Those who have Christ "in them" (Colossians 1:27) are growing spiritually. The degree of Christ's "mind" in you determines your spiritual growth. The mind of Christ must dwell "in you" in order for you to achieve the rewards God has for you.

Too many Christian groups equate **the mind of Christ** with doctrinal beliefs. They use The Apostle Paul's statement in Philippians 2:5 as a wedge to make everyone in God's **church spiritually believing the same set of doctrines. The mind of Christ** has become a **tool** for too many churches to control God's people.

<u>**PARABLE OF THE TEN TALENTS**</u>   Jesus compares The Kingdom of God to those who receive talents or money from an owner who goes on a trip to a far country for a long period of time (Matthew 25:14-30). His servants are given differing amounts of money. Some receive five talents, some two talents and another one talent. When the owner returns, the one he had given five talents had earned five more talents. The one with two had earned two more talents. The one who only received one talent was

afraid because he believed his owner was a hard man and he feared him. Instead of investing the one talent, he buried it in the ground. He was too afraid to earn more in case he would lose the only one talent he was given. The owner praised the one with five and the one with two talents. He praised both of them because they put their talents to work and increased or doubled what they were given. So the owner promoted those two over all he had.

The one who buried his one talent because of his fear merely dug up the money and returned his one talent without any interest. His master was furious. He took away the one talent he was given, and gave it to the one with ten talents. The servant was fired and removed him to outer darkness. The owner or master demanded growth on his money. Unless a Christian grows **spiritually** and **continually**, the master will reject that servant.

The first point for you to understand is that not every Christian is at the same place of **spiritual understanding**. Secondly, the person with only one talent was afraid to grow. Many times a person thinks he has **all** the necessary or **required truth**. BIG MISTAKE. I remember a young man who grew up in a church from a little boy into his 30's. The **headquarter's church** eventually split into hundreds of different groups. Instead of studying The Bible and praying, he accepted the group that was closest to the one he grew up in. When questioned, he remarked, "I'm too tired to go to all that work trying to decipher which split group was closer to **the truth**." In other words, he was satisfied at the level he found himself. It was a comfort to him to hear all the same sermons, doctrines and works he was familiar with. He literally did not want to investigate if there was another level of growth he could attain to.

To be fair to this young man, he had personal trials – going through a divorce. His wife only married him to be able to come to The United States. He had changed careers and then he was in a car accident that didn't allow him to drive for long periods. He had to move to be near his office. But, all is not lost. When his life settles, he will begin to grow in the knowledge of Jesus Christ as **new truth** hits him in the face.

When one feels they have **the truth**, it hinders future personal growth. The need for **spiritual growth** of thirty, forty and fifty times becomes a secondary reality. When you feel you have enough **truth** or literally satisfied with the knowledge you have, you may find Jesus expects much more dynamic growth from you than you may expect from yourself (Matthew 25:29-30).

JERUSALEM CONFERENCE The Apostles were a good example of having different levels of **spiritual understanding** between themselves. The Pharisees (who believed in Christ), kept complaining, asking why the converted Gentiles are not circumcised and not keeping The Law of Moses. So, a conference had to be held with The Jerusalem Church, which included Church Elders and Apostles. The Pharisees, also, felt those Gentiles who weren't circumcised and not keeping The Law were also **not** in **the church** (Acts 15:1-24). The "**church teaching**" believed only Israelites should be in "**the church.**" This created quite a disagreement and caused arguments. If Gentiles could be part of The Commonwealth of Israel without being circumcised and not needing to keep The Law of Moses, it was not the accepted **"church doctrine"** of the time. But notice, **"the church"** accepted The Pharisees' disagreement even though the believing Pharisees and their followers were only a **sect** in **"the church."** "Sect," the Greek, means **"a heretic."** Even though they were heretics, **"the church"** did not demand their excommunication. In fact, they held a conference in reference to the various opinions of all The Apostles, Elders and The Jerusalem Church in general. The reason the problem was settled peaceably was due to their listening to God's Holy Spirit by having **the mind of Christ**.

According to James, the outcome came about because The Apostles, The Elders and the entire Jerusalem Church agreed that ONLY ISRAELITE CHRISTIANS had to be circumcised and keep The Law of Moses. Why? Because **the temple** was **still there** with **"the shekinah"** and to be able to enter **"the temple," one had to be circumcised**. This existed until **the temple** was destroyed in 70 A.D. and The Old Covenant **ceased** and only The New Covenant existed after that time (Hebrews 8:13). It was decreed The Gentiles would receive The Holy Spirit without the need of circumcision or keeping The Law of Moses. This was NEW SPIRITUAL GROWTH and **A CHANGE OF CHURCH DOCTRINE**. They all had to grow by accepting the NEW TRUTH (Acts 15:24). In fact, some of Paul's ministers who served with Paul were part of the circumcision party (Colossians 4:11). But, realize, none of them were **at the same spiritual level**, yet still had **the mind** of Christ.

FAITH AND SIN Romans 14 is a great chapter proving THE DIFFERENT LEVELS of **spiritual growth** and understanding God allows to comprise **"the church."** Paul covers those who are weak; or those who understood very little **spiritually**, or even those who felt they knew what was **the whole truth** and felt they needed nothing more. It turned out some **weak** Christians believed they had to be vegetarians. Others believed they could eat anything. Then, there were others saying you must keep a specific day to please God; so, Paul admonished them to let each person be fully persuaded in their own mind and their own **spiritual level of growth**. Paul was teaching an extremely important **spiritual lesson**.

The Apostle explains how you must stop judging one another **spiritually** (Romans 14:7-13). Paul contends you, as Christians, must never **offend anyone**. The point of this chapter is to prove Paul was referring to **the mind of Christ**. Paul summarizes, **"...for whatsoever is not of faith or personal belief is sin"** (Romans 14:23).   Paul tells you at whatever **spiritual level** of belief or **faith** you are at, you **must** do what you believe God wants you to do! Your Christian duty is to try **not to offend anyone**. You, as Christians, must only be ready to answer with the hope that is in you when someone asks what and why you believe as you do (I Peter 3:15).

Peter asks what attitude you should have if someone asks you for **an answer** of your **faith**. Peter states you should answer in humility, being careful not to offend the one seeking or asking you. Peter, as well as Paul, refers to **the mind of Christ**. Both Apostles state as a Christian in God's **church**, you, as well as **everyone** else, may be at **a different level** of **spiritual understanding** and **truth**. It all depends upon whether you are **spiritually growing** or not and whether you are getting more of the mind of Christ.

A HERETIC   The Pharisees in **the church** were considered a **sect** or **heretic**. In the Greek, a "heretic" or "haritikos" is defined as "a separating tendency."   That is why in Acts 15, The Pharisees were called **a sect** instead of defined as **schismatics**.   Even though they had a doctrine or belief, they were not **schismatic** or **divisive**.   In other words, they were **never** trying to cause a **split** in "**the church**." On the other hand, Paul said that a heretic, known to be subverted, sinning and self-condemned, after being admonished twice, should be rejected (Titus 3:10).   (Two strikes, and you're out.) Why?   Because it was a matter of trying **to split "the church**."

The Pharisees who were considered a **sect** or **heretical** weren't causing a split in "**the church**."   They had a different understanding.   Once "**the church**" decided Gentiles did not have to be circumcised or keep The Law of Moses, The Pharisees could remain in "**the church**."   That is why Paul accepted his fellow minister, Justus, as his co-worker (Colossians 4:11).   Justus believed Gentiles should be circumcised and should keep The Law of Moses; but Justus never caused any **schisms.**

THE BODY OR CHURCH   The Apostle Paul makes it extremely clear how "**church members**" in The Body of Christ should relate to each other (I Corinthians 12:22-27). Paul said those members who are the most **feeble** or **weak** must be given **more honor** because **they lack** the **spiritual knowledge** others had.   Paul relates this in Romans 14.   The difference is this: **"That there should be no schism, or split in "the church" but that the members should have the same care for each**

other" (Verse 25).   **Now**, for **the mind of Christ**. It matters not if everyone is believing exactly the same, doctrinally, because it is Christ and God's Holy Spirit, only, which brings you and everyone else to **the truth**.

DIVISIONS AND SPLITS   What causes a schism in **"the body?"** Simply those trying to force their beliefs upon others.   That is why **"churches"** split and divide. That is not **the mind of Christ**. Christians can be at varying levels of **spiritual understanding** and still be part of **the body**.   The weaker Christians, who **only** have **the milk** of **the word**, cannot swallow a large piece of **meat** or **the truth**. You need to grow at a pace God knows you are able to digest and grow as Christ leads you. You, as Christians, need to be careful that you do not offend the weaker ones in **the body**, but give honor and respect to everyone. Paul confirms this in I Corinthians 12.

What causes all the different denominations, groups and **"churches?"** Simply the **act of incorporation**. A letter of incorporation merely defines people as **a creed of belief** which does not allow **spiritual growth**. That is what Paul was against in II Corinthians 3. When you do not allow fellow-Christians to be at their own specific or different levels of **spiritual truth**, you are following Satan who wants to stop you and other Christians from growing by God's Holy Spirit (as wise virgins) (Matthew 25). Your responsibility before God is to be ready to help those who are ready to seek your help by not offending anyone. Now, to prove what is **the mind of Christ**.

NO WRITTEN LETTER   In II Corinthians 3:1-2 Paul said, **"[1] Do we**

begin   again   to commend ourselves? or need we, as some other,
epistles [letters] of commendation to you, or letters of commendation
from you? ²Ye are our epistle written in our hearts [New Covenant],
known and read of all men: ³Forasmuch as ye are manifestly declared
to be the epistle of Christ..."

What is an **"incorporated church?"** An **"incorporated church"** is a
group of people, who come together based upon a legal letter or epistle.
Paul said **true Christians do not need a legal letter**. This legal letter is
sent to a state as a declaration which states any number of members
belong to that particular group. But Paul said just the opposite of what a
true Christian needs to do. A stated letter or epistle limits your **spiritual
growth**. How? Everyone in that **letter of incorporation** must be at **the
same level of belief** or are not considered part of that group. Paul warned
against such actions should they decide for themselves which minister
they wanted to follow.

In I Corinthians 3:1 Paul states The Corinthian Church was carnal, and
they were only babes, **spiritually.** He then explained why they were
carnal (Verse 3). They had splits and divisions among them by choosing
the minister they liked or **"the church"** of their choice (I Corinthians 3).
Paul states all ministers are **Christians** if they are based upon Jesus, The
Christ. He relates that all ministers' teachings will be tested, ultimately, in
The Lake of Fire. Ministers need to be extremely **careful** in all their
teachings. If their preaching is false, it will **all** burn. Why? Christians are
at **different levels** of **spiritual understanding**; so **ministers** and fellow
christians must all have **the mind of Christ**.

CHRIST'S MIND   **The True Church of God** is not any incorporated group, but a **spiritual group** with God's Holy Spirit leading Christians who are at different levels of **faith** and **growth**. It is not an incorporated group by any letter or certificate but is totally a **spiritual body** with Christ in them (Colossians 1:27). Each and every member can be growing in the grace and knowledge of Christ at different levels of understanding. So, what does it mean to have **the mind of Christ**? Read Philippines 2. Paul said if there be any comfort or fellowship (church group), it is by God's **spirit** with bowels of mercies. There it is. BOWELS OF MERCY is what keeps God's "**church**," as "**a body**," in fellowship. NOTHING ABOUT CREEDS OR DOCTRINES. Jesus said everyone will know you are His Disciples because **you have love for one another** (John 13:35). No doctrine or creed is needed.

Paul said you are to be like-minded. How? By creeds and doctrines? No! By being of one accord and of **one mind**. He said every man should look not to his own good, but what is good for others (Philippians 2:2-4). "**[5]Let this mind be in you, which was also in Christ Jesus...**" What **mind**? (Philippians 2:5). Even though Jesus was The Son of God, He became your servant (Verses 6 and 7). That is **the mind of Christ**, to not cause splits or divisions or starting different church groups. **The mind of Christ** never causes splits or schisms over creeds or any doctrines. If Christ be "**in you**," you are at a different level of **faith** from others in "**the church**." Jesus said some of you have two talents, five or even ten talents. Your job is to increase the amount of talents God has given you.

KNOWING THE TRUTH   Christians have God's **love** (I John 5:16).

As long as you love God and your neighbor, you would not be a sinner by even having THE THOUGHT OF BREAKING THE TEN COMMANDMENTS. You are Christ's "**Epistle**," and it is written in your hearts. As long as you have **the mind of Christ**, being a servant, you won't have any splits or differing groups.

<u>SPIRITUAL GROWTH</u>   Any inspired preaching by a **minister** of **the word** must be tested (I Corinthians 14:29-31). Each member, as an individual Christian, is to check all <u>Scriptures</u> the way The Bereans did. The Greek, in this case, is "diakrino" or "to try and separate." Just as The Bereans had to prove to themselves from <u>The Bible</u>, whether these things be so or true, so should you (Acts 17:11). You do not **all** have the same amount of **spiritual knowledge.** You will not have schisms or splits in the body of Christ if you have **the mind of Christ** – serving others! Why did they search <u>The Scriptures</u>? Unless one continually studies <u>The Bible</u>, your level of **spiritual growth** will be limited or eventually stunted. Faith increases by The Word of God (Romans 10:17). The more one studies, the more one increases in **faith** and **spiritual growth**. As long as you have **the mind** of Christ, always attempting to serve others, you will always be of "**one body**" – **the** "**body**" of Christ! When everyone finally becomes **perfect**, as God is **perfect** and as Jesus admonished, you will eventually come to have the same amount of **spiritual understanding** and will truly know God as your only guide to SALVATION (I Corinthians 13:12).

CHAPTER 9

WHAT IS SIN?

Most Christian's want to avoid sin. Trouble is each Christian's denomination has its own "version of sin." Anyone who sins, and then when they repent, their sin is forgiven. The less you sin, the better your life will be. Your spiritual growth continues to achieve your reward in God's "kingdom." Amazingly, sin for a Christian has a greater requirement than you might realize. You will discover what the definition of Christian "sin" is and a greater understanding about God and His "kingdom."

God's **"Word"** declares, **"Sin is the transgression of the Law"** (I John 3:4). Pretty clear, or so it seems. For many Christian groups, it is the verse which defines sin according to <u>The Bible</u>. To commit murder is a sin. To steal is a sin. To covet a neighbor's goods is a sin. God's Laws define sin. Humans transgressing these Laws are sinning.

<u>**MISSING THE MARK**</u>   More specifically, the question is, what does it **mean** to sin? In <u>The Bible</u>, the Greek word for "sin" has many **shades** of meanings. However, sin mainly conveys the meaning of "missing the mark." The question, which should be asked, is missing **what** mark? You will discover sin **varies** in **the mark** that is missed.

A mark is a target toward a goal one tries to achieve. "Missing the mark" or "sinning" can be different depending upon which group is doing the defining. What type of people are missing the mark when, indeed, they are obeying God's Law? Always remember, sin is the transgression of The Law.

USING THE LAW LAWFULLY Surprisingly, God's Law **was not given to everyone** as a legal requirement! Wait, don't jump to conclusions. You must **scripturally prove** how God determines how one keeps God's Law for **the purpose God had always intended**. The Apostle Paul said, many are busy teaching God's Law, but do not have a **complete understanding** of what **purpose**, initially, God had in giving His Law (I Timothy 1:7). God has a **specific reason** for giving His Holy Law to achieve a certain **mark** or **goal**. **Missing the mark** or sinning against God's Law means one has come short of **fulfilling His Law** as God had intended. To claim to be a teacher of The Law and not know God's reason for The Law is **missing the mark** or **sinning** by misleading many individuals.

PURPOSE OF THE LAW Paul states if one uses The Law as God **intends** then The Law is good (I Timothy 1:8). By using or keeping The Law for the **wrong purpose**, is missing the mark. Only using God's Law as He intended makes The Law "good." A person must use **The Law lawfully**, the way God intends; otherwise, he or she will be sinning.

Paul makes an amazing statement in I Timothy 1:9-10, **"⁹Knowing this, that the law is not made for a righteous man, but for the lawless and disobedient, for the ungodly and for sinners, for unholy and profane,**

for murderers of fathers and murderers of mothers, for manslayers, **[10]For whoremongers, for them that defile themselves with mankind, for menstealers, for liars, for perjured persons, and if there be any other thing that is contrary to sound doctrine;"** Wow! There it is. It can't be any simpler. God's Law was not intended for **Christians or repentant, converted people**. Christians must have a different definition for **sin** or **missing the mark**.

UNREPENTANT ISRAEL   Paul said The Abrahamic Covenant came 430 years before The Law was given (Galatians 3:17). Abraham knew God's Laws, but it wasn't until **430 years** later that The Law was ratified with Israel for a very special reason (Genesis 26:5). At the time of Moses and Israel at Mt Sinai, God made The Law – **a covenant** or a **contract** with Israel. Only then, did The Law become **legally binding**. Remember, The Law not only had **blessings** but **cursings** to it. The Law now demanded **judgments** or **sentences** in a Court of Law in **the tabernacle** and **the temple** (I Kings 8:32). Israel ratified or agreed to keep every jot and tittle of it (Deuteronomy 30:19). Did you ever wonder why God enforced The Law with Israel as a legal requirement?

NO LAW, NO SIN   Even though God's Laws were known prior to God's **covenant** with Israel, God's Law was not legally binding. What was the difference? In Romans 5:13, Paul said until The Law was legally binding upon Israel as <u>The Old Covenant</u> – sin or transgression of The Law **wasn't imputed** or **legally** binding upon humanity because there was no Law with **judgments** or **cursings**. Notice Genesis 26:5; there were no **judgments** at the time of Abraham. If one kept The Law, he or she would live a good human existence as Paul said in Galatians 3:12. He said if a man keeps The Law, he shall live in them. His life experiences will be great. However, if he didn't follow The Letter of The Law, there would not be a penalty or curse, but there would be consequences when they made bad choices – breaking any **commandment** or **statute**. Why did God institute **The Letter of The Law** as a binding, legal contract? In Galatians 3:19, Paul was inspired by God when he said The Law **was added** as a legal requirement for sin (I John 3:4), because after God gave The Ten Commandments, orally, Israel broke them. After they sinned, God added **the statutes** and **the judgments**, which made The Law a legal requirement for Israel (Malachi 4:4).

Notice, the same thing was mentioned in Deuteronomy 5:22 when God gave The Ten Commandments, He **added no more**. Only when they sinned He added to The Ten Commandments – The Statutes and Judgments (Deuteronomy 5:31-33). Because of Israel's sin, God made The **Letter** (written) Law legally binding in "a **court** of Law." Sin or transgression of The Law was now **missing the mark** in keeping The Law. This legal contract was now binding upon Israel once they entered **the promised land**, and it lasted **only** until The Messiah or Christ came (Galatians 3:19). When Christ did come, The Law once again would have no legal binding, and there would not be the necessity for any **judgments** or **cursing** for **Christians** (Galatians 3:13).

When Christ came, the new Priesthood of Melchizedec removed the curses of The Law. The Law was changed under this **new administration**, which only gave **life** and **not death**. Keeping The Letter of The Law gave a **blessed human existence**, but **never promised salvation** (Deuteronomy 30:15-16). That is all keeping The Letter of The Law could ever do, which is the very reason Abraham kept them – to have a decent life (Genesis 26:5). Then, why did God **bind The Law** as a legal entity? In Genesis 26:5, there were no Holy Days. They did not begin until Exodus 16 with The Sabbath, which had started The Holy Days. These were all **shadows** for Israel.

In Deuteronomy 5:29, God answers, by saying if only there was such a **heart** in them, that they would fear me and keep My **"commandments,"** **always**. Israel just couldn't keep The Commandments because they were **unconverted** and **unrepentant and had a carnal heart**. That is why God made <u>The Old Covenant</u> of legally keeping The Letter of The Law with Israel. They were unrighteous, just as Paul said in I Timothy 1:7-10. The Law, in The Letter, to be used lawfully applies only to **unrighteous, unconverted, unrepentant** people. Therefore, I John 3:4 does not apply to Christians! The Law, in reference to sin or **missing the mark** of **the righteousness** of The Law is meaningless for **salvation**. The Law can never justify, or make you **righteous**; nor could anyone ever expect **salvation**. Keeping The Letter of The Law only gives a good human existence.

THE VAIL   After Israel sinned and Moses was returning the second time from Mt. Sinai, his face was shining and the people were afraid and began to worry. Whenever Moses spoke to Israel, he put a vail covering his face. When he would go back and speak to God, Moses would remove the vail. What was the reason for this? (Exodus 34:29-35). Paul gives you the answer in II Corinthian 3:6-16. Paul revealed Moses wore the vail because the people were afraid to hear God speaking to them. They knew Moses had spoken to God when his face was shinning so brilliantly. They just did not understand God's message. In II Corinthian 3:13 and 14, Paul said Israel just did not understand God's reason for The Law. They couldn't understand The Old Testament or The Torah Law, which would have led them to Christ. The Law as a **legal contract** was to teach them they couldn't keep it, and could only make them realize they had to repent (Galatians 3:24). They were carnal and weak in the flesh, and all God wanted was for them to have a change of heart (Deuteronomy 5:29).

Instead, Israel thought The Law would make them **"righteous."** Even if The Law with its sacrifices made them acceptable to God, The Law could never make them **"righteous."** The Law only reminded them that they were, indeed, sinners. The Law became their **"righteousness"** (Deuteronomy 6:25) instead of relying on God's **"righteousness"** to lead them to **"perfection"** (Matthew 5:48) and be Holy as God is Holy (Ephesians 1:4).

Sin is the transgression of The Law (I John 3:4) for **carnal, unconverted, stiff necked** people. They could never, however, completely keep The Law. They, then, became transgressors of The Legal Law (James 2:10). They sinned and **missed the mark** in trying to keep God's Law **perfectly**. They had a wrong heart. Keeping The Law in The Letter could never and would never change their hearts. They could not become **righteous** or Holy as God by keeping The Law. **Sin**, as the **transgression of The Law**, legally only applies to carnal, unconverted, unrighteous people as Paul said in I Timothy 1:7-10. The definition of **sin for a Christian** is far more **demanding** than the transgression of The Law.

THE OFFENSE   Once Jesus removed **the curse** of The Law with His **sacrifice**, The Law only became a way of living a good human existence. The Law has no dominion over **Christians** in The Letter (Romans 7:4-6). Sin now becomes a **spiritual matter** and not a **legal problem**. It changes the definition of what **sin is** for a Christian or a **repentant person**. The Apostle Paul goes back to the beginning of creation referring to Adam in The Garden of Eden. Paul states sin entered the world by **one man** – Adam. Since all have sinned, death passed upon all mankind (Romans 5:12-21).

In Romans 5:13, Paul makes an amazing statement concerning **sin**. Paul states that **sin** was **in** the **world** even though there was **no Law**. In Genesis 26:5, Abraham already knew God's Laws before The Law became a **legal covenant** with Israel. What did Paul mean? Simply, Paul went on and said **sin is not** imputed where there is **no** Law. One cannot **miss the mark** if there are no legal demands of a Law. Since The Law was not a legal requirement by God for 430 years after Abraham, **sin** had no law saying it was, indeed, "**a sin**." There was **no legal requirement** to not **miss any mark**.

Adam's sin had nothing to do with a Law. Although Adam did not break any legal Law, his sin was still an **offense**. It caused an **injury to God**. Romans 5:14 states Adam's sin was a different similitude than legally breaking a Law or The Law. Adam's transgression against God was eating of The Tree of Knowledge. Adam's sin had nothing to do with The Law. Therefore, in I John 3:4, the transgression of The Law, was not Adam's sin. Adam's sin was not against God's Law. Adams's sin and transgression was against God's command when he ate of The Tree of Good and Evil. The meaning of sin can change in relationship to the goal God wants you to achieve. In this case, sin is called an offense and not a sin against a Law. Sin, in Adam's case, had a completely different definition than the transgression of The Law. The word **sin** does not have a static definition. How plain, sin can vary within God's **purpose** and **plan**. God only wanted Adam to eat of The Tree of Life, God's Holy Spirit, without any Law.

The Law had no legal requirement at that time from Adam to Moses, even if The Law was known. The definition of sin had to do with an **offense** rather than the breaking of a Law. If no Law, there is no sin of The Law. It is still an **offense** to God as it **injures God** or His **creation** as well as mankind. That is why **The Great Commandment** is to LOVE God with all your heart, mind and body and to LOVE your neighbor as yourself. Ultimately, any **offense** or **injury**, physically, mentally or **spiritually**, causes God an **injury**. Any **unrighteous act is missing God's mark**. It is still a sin in God's eyes without the transgression of The Law.

CHRISTIAN SIN   What is **a sin** for Christians? Missing the mark or sinning for a **Christian is a lot more demanding** than I John 3:4, or the transgression of The Law. Notice, Christ's comment when He said He did not come to destroy The Law, but to fulfill it (Matthew 5:17-18). In fact, Christ continued and said that not one jot or tittle of The Law would pass till **all be fulfilled** or completed. The Greek word for **"fulfilled"** is **"teleroo,"** which is **"completion of everything."** When The Law states it is to be "fulfilled," in the Greek, it does not mean "to do," or "keep" but "**to finish since it is full**." The Greek word "to do" or "to keep" is "poeio," not "pleroo." Jesus made an astonishing statement in Matthew 5:20. "**For I say unto you, that except your** [Christian] **righteousness shall exceed the righteousness of the scribes and Pharisees, ye shall in no case enter into the kingdom of God**." Christ puts **sin** on a much deeper level than I John 3:4. What does Jesus mean by being more **righteous** than **the scribes** and Pharisees? The wages of sin in transgressing The Law brings death. CHRISTIAN SINNING KEEPS ONE OUT OF GOD'S KINGDOM.

The answer, **scripturally**, is given by Christ in the rest of Matthew 5, and culminating in Matthew 5:48. Jesus said, "**The Law and The Ten Commandments, must now be written in your hearts**." If you do not steal, The Law states you are **righteous** (I John 3:4). To be in God's "**kingdom**" (**salvation**), Jesus reveals you can't even think it in **your** mind **to steal**. If one doesn't steal, he doesn't break The Law. Why the difference? Because as Paul stated in I Timothy 1:7-10, The Law is made only for **unrighteous** or **carnal people**. Carnal humans can only keep The Law in The Letter. The definition of sin for a Christian is a matter of **mind** and **heart** because The Christian is not carnal but has repented. The goal is **spiritual**, not of the flesh, but of **the mind and heart**. For **Christians**, one cannot by human effort, ever please God (Romans 8:8). Therefore, I John 3:4 does not apply. It is completely a **spiritual matter**, and that is why the real target or goal is Matthew 5:48: "**Be ye therefore perfect, even as your Father which is in heaven is perfect**." That is your **Savior's definition** of being **more righteous** than "**the scribes**" or Pharisees. Christians must become **PERFECT**.

The word "**perfect**" in the Greek is defined as "**blameless**." When you strive to be **perfect** or **blameless**, you do not **miss any mark** or **sin**. They have hit the goal of **righteousness**. They have committed no offense to God or His **creation**. This is exactly as Adam's offense when sin or missing the mark of The Law was not legally enforced even though known. The Law doesn't change nature or make one **perfect**. Now, you **know** what **real Godly righteousness is**. Read **the biblical definition** of sin for a **Christian**. "**All unrighteousness is sin: and there is a sin not unto death**" (I John 5:17). Committing **any offense**, which **injures God, His creation**, or **mankind**, in any way, whether in **mind, heart** or **physically**, is **missing the mark** or sinning. To offend someone in any possible way, should not even come into your thoughts, because even thinking about it, is **a sin**. God's goal is that you become **Holy** or **perfect**, **blameless**, with God being **all and in all** (Ephesians 1:4; I Corinthians 15:28). Transgressing The Law for a **Christian** is almost meaningless compared to **Christians** never even **thinking of sinning** let alone **literally sinning** (I John 3:4). Committing an **offense** keeps you **out of God's "kingdom**." How does God make this come to pass?

THE AIM OF THE COMMANDMENTS   Everything God does is to give you every chance to become **perfect** and Holy as God, by and through His Son, Jesus. "**The end** [or aim] **of "the commandment" is charity** [or LOVE]" (I Timothy 1:5). The Ten Commandments were given to bring you to LOVE God and your neighbor from your very **heart**. Paul continues, "**out of a pure heart, and of a good conscience, and of faith unfeigned**" (I Timothy 1:5). This is far more than not sinning against The Letter of The Law. The Law never expected or demanded or could ever lead you to **perfection**.

The word "pure" in the Greek is a "catharsis" or "uncorrupt heart" or "good desires." "Good," in the Greek is "beneficial" or a "profitable conscience." Finally, FAITH that never **loses trust** in God and His Son, Jesus. Remember, what is not of **faith** is **a sin** or **missing the mark**. This is a total change from a carnal (beast-like) nature to a Holy, Godly **nature**. This change is much, much more demanding than merely following **only** The Letter of The Law. In Verse 6, Paul said some have turned aside from **the real purpose** of God's **plan** for you to become **perfect**, and instead try to use The Letter of The Law to make you **perfect** or **righteous**. These people are ignorant of God's **purpose** for His Holy Law. The Law cannot make anyone **righteous**. It is meant for carnal people to change from having a stony heart to acquiring a heart of flesh and come to Christ (II Corinthians 3:1-5). The Law is for carnal people so they can, eventually, **repent** and be able to come to Christ.

<u>GOD ALL IN ALL</u> Paul said if you LOVE God, you begin to understand God does everything for your good (Romans 8:28). Paul states when you LOVE your neighbor, it fulfills (pleroo) or completes God's Law (Romans 13:8). LOVE is the vehicle God uses and **not** The Letter of The Law, **to complete** or **fulfill** The Law (Romans 13:10). LOVE is God's tool to make you **perfect** (Colossians 3:14). It is simply God's Law shed abroad in your heart by God's LOVE (Romans 5:5). It is just what Christ said in Matthew 5:48. Finally, when Christ puts down all enemies, God will be **all and in all** (I Corinthians 15:28). Remember, GOD IS LOVE. Christian **sin** will no longer **miss the mark**. All **unrighteousness**

is sin, but God and all His Family and **creation** will be in LOVE, and there will be **no hurt** or any offense in His "**kingdom**."

<u>**GOD'S RIGHTEOUSNESS**</u> Christian sin is defined as "**all unrighteousness**." Any offense or injury to God or His **creation** is **missing the mark of God's "righteousness**. How does God make you **righteous** as He is **righteous** and **perfect**? As expected, God gives His "**righteousness**" by His own **free choice**. It is a decision you, too, have to make. That is why **repentance** is required. **Repentance** is your free choice to seek only God's "**will**" or His **Word**. How does God do it?

Once you have REPENTED, your mind and heart will desire and only want to think, do and be, just as your Father and His Son, Jesus. What does God do at this point? When you have REPENTED and, by free choice have opened your minds, which only God can open – which is an unmerited **gift** from Him. Romans 5:5 Paul said, God sheds His LOVE in your hearts by His Holy Spirit. God's Holy Spirit leads you to TRUTH or reality. No more carnal deception. You, now, have hearts (desires) and minds (pneuma) open to be taught **the truth** by God (John 17:17). WHAT TRUTH?

The truth is about God and His **creation**, which includes all mankind. God's Holy Spirit manifests God's **agape** type of LOVE. LOVE, so strong, that the ONE giving that "love" gives all that God is: All His "**glory**," riches and **righteousness**. God's **righteousness** is God's LOVE or **agapé**. **Ultimate giving** was "**the life**" His Son, Jesus, gave. This is the **mark or goal of God's righteousness**. This Glory of God is all His **goodness** and **riches** in Christ. Anything less is **missing the mark** or

Christian sin (I John 5:17).

When God reveals His LOVE for you through His Holy Spirit, you grow in that **LOVE** as you discover more and more of His Holiness and **goodness**. Your "**love**" for God and His **creation** will escalate as you grow in Christ's **riches** until you achieve the stature and maturity of Christ (John 13:34-35). When you eventually receive a **spirit body** and your heart and mind is also **spiritual**, you will then be Holy, **perfect** or **blameless** as God, The Father. No Law or conditions will apply. You will, then, have complete liberty or freedom. Absolutely no restrictions or conditions (Romans 8). You will LOVE God and everyone He has created, **with all your heart and mind**. You will not commit any sin or offense because God's Law will be written in your heart and mind. You will be total **agapé** – LOVE as GOD IS LOVE. THEN, WITH YOUR SPIRITUAL BODIES, YOU WILL BE PERFECT, AND HAVE ACHIEVED THE MARK OF PERFECTION.

<u>LOVE VERSES HUMAN IMAGINATION</u> The Apostle Paul issues a warning for all Christians in II Corinthians 10:4-5. He said Christians must fight the war against carnality or beast-like – human imaginations. What is human imagination? Paul continues and reveals that any human **thought** against God's **thoughts** must subject itself to Christ's **mind**. Paul relates Christians have warfare to fight your human mind or reasoning whenever it is contrary to God's thoughts. Why? In Matthew 15:19, Jesus said out of your hearts or desires, proceed evil thoughts. Just before the world flooded in Noah's time, He said humanity had come to the place that every thought in mankind's **imagination**

produced nothing but **evil thoughts**.   What is wrong with human imagination?

HUMAN IMAGINATION   In Hebrew, in <u>The Old Testament</u>, the word for "human imagination" is "yester."   This word connotes "things framed."   It compares to a potter, who as an artist, framing whatever he chooses within his mind.   This is what in contemporary art is known as **abstract art**. It has no restrictions, no discipline or standard. The abstract artist sets his own limits or standards. He is totally free to draw whatever he wants. The point is this type of artist determines his own **reality** or being TRUE to himself of what he desires to produce. God said that a human's heart (desire and thoughts) following his own imaginations is evil from his youth up (Genesis 8:21). Why? From your birth, as long as you do not seek God's **"thoughts,"** your imagination (given enough time), ends in evil. Why?

HUMAN I.Q. The higher one's human intelligence or I.Q., the more ability for one to abstract or imagine reality or **truth** from his own point of view. In science, it is called a Human Paradigm or point of view. In higher education, it is known as **abstract reasoning** or thinking **outside of the box**. There are no standards, no restrictions or limitations except what the individual decides on his/her own what is right or true. In the time of **the judges**, Israel decided by themselves, **"what was right in THEIR own eyes"** (Judges 21:25). That is why God said it is those who are humble or poor, with limited thinking options, who grasp and understand **the truth** or reality. It is far easier when one does not have as many options to come to **repentance** as a child.

When babes are born, they are totally neutral. They know neither good nor evil. They are teachable. They are humble, ask questions and seek **truth**, which is why Jesus said you must become like a little child (Mark 10:15). But, deep within you, yourself, is the real culprit. It is your flesh, trying to survive at any cost, which is an issue. Besides your flesh, the heart, your motivations and your desires corrupt your thought processes as to manufacture any solution (good or bad) for survival. The desires of the heart are at the root of your problem.

God made you this way for a very **good reason**. Since God is Holy and is making you Holy, you must become as He is. And, eventually, with God as "**your coach**," you will be **all and in all** with God, The Father (I Corinthians 15:28). Since God has total **free choice**, He can be whatever He chooses to be. God in His **perfection** wants to make you exactly the same way. One difference between God and humanity is **GOD IS THE ONLY STANDARD!** Anything less is not God or Holy or **perfect**. Only God has **life** to give. Even by human effort keeping **the righteousness** of The Letter of The Law doesn't do it because it requires human effort to keep it and your **human effort** is too weak in the flesh (Galatians 4:9). You need God's "**righteousness**" in your heart and mind (Hebrews 10:16). Remember, Einstein's sentiment: "I only want God's **thoughts**; the rest are details." How do you get God's "**thoughts**?"

GOD'S THOUGHTS   Christ said in John 17:17, **"Thy Word is Truth."** God's thoughts are **reality** or absolutely **the truth**. In Greek, the word for "truth" is "aletheia" or "verity," "certainty" or "absolute." That is why Jesus said in Matthew 4:4, **"Man shall live by every Word of God!"**

There it is. How does God put His **Word** in your hearts and mind?

A STANDARD   By now, you have proven **human reason** or **imagination** has no limits or standards to determine **right** from **wrong**. That is why God gave Israel The Letter of The Law as its standard of **righteousness**. However, keeping The Letter of The Law does not change anyone's carnal nature. Only God can do that. How does God bring it to pass? Once you know your imagination has no standards or limits for **judgment**; God tells you, through Christ, to use "**righteous judgment**." How do you use "**righteous judgment**?"

In I Corinthians 10:5, Paul states Christians are to cast down every **imagination**. Here the Greek word is "logismos" or "what is humanly logical." Human logic, continually, comes up with a host of solutions to any problem. The Bible refers to it as Babylon or confusion. Many differing languages, along with different cultures, cause many not to understand a standard of "**right**" and "**wrong**" when conversing in these languages or cultures. God, therefore, has created a standard, even with all the diversity of nationalities; and all will be united in harmony by this **one standard**.

With all the creative diversity, God has arranged for His family or His "**kingdom**" to have a FUTURE THAT HAS NO END. A future that entails discovering God and all His **riches** and **goodness**. These riches come through His Son, Jesus, as God's **firstborn**. God states, The Firstborn Son is the beginning of His (God's) strength (Deuteronomy 20:17). Since His Son is the beginning of God's strength, you, also, as His family of Sons, add **your strength with The Son, Jesus** and all the **riches** in Christ.   The creative reality is truly unlimited with **innumerable dimensions**, which at present, are only known by Christ and Your Father. How glorious and beyond human comprehension (I Corinthians 13:9-10). Now for THE STANDARD, which grants you to have His Laws written in your heart and mind. Paul said humans, at present, even with God's **Word**, can only know in part (I Corinthians 13:9).   It is a discovery process, which evolves into a **set standard** or schoolmaster. What is it? You **already know it**, but how does God guarantee you will have His **righteousness** or Holy **goodness**?

Paul reveals an amazing reality when he said, "While in this childhood state, you learn **piece by piece**." Then when you are **perfect** (Matthew 5:48), what you know, in part, will be done away – how? Paul reveals **agapé LOVE** is the greatest **gift** from God. Why? Because God is **"love"** or completely giving and charitable (I Corinthians 13:11-13). God's **"love"** is perfected in you by His **Word** (I John 2:5). LOVE IS THE STANDARD that is missing from the carnal, unconverted minds and hearts. That is why Israel, being carnal, needed The Letter of The Law. Its imagination or human thoughts could only come to evil, when contrary to God's **Word**.

LOVE – "agapé love" is **total giving, even at the cost of one's life**. That is why The Great Commandment is to **love** God with all your heart, mind and body, and **love** your neighbor as yourself, which makes you **perfect** or Holy as God. Why? Because God is **love** and that is what you are to become when He sheds His **love** abroad in your heart by His Holy Spirit (Romans 5:5). That is THE MISSING STANDARD. Once **perfect**, and you have God's **love**, you will not sin; in fact, you cannot sin (I John 5:18). That is **the standard** of **righteous judgment**, which God will add to your heart. How simple, how clear. This takes absolute **faith** in the heavenly Father.

When God's **love** takes over your **logic** or **thinking** process, all your creative choices become free to do whatever you wish. Total liberty and freedom. No Laws, no restrictions, no conditions. Through Christ, the whole **creation**, in His "**kingdom family**," will create unbelievable riches and goodness because then God will be **ALL AND IN ALL**. THE UNPARDONABLE SIN IS TO REJECT GOD, HIMSELF, which is His **love** given by His Holy Spirit. **That is the sin unto death** (I John 5:16). When you have GOD'S LOVE, it will never enter your heart or mind to break any "**commandment**" or to cause any offense or injury to anyone, let alone God.

THE CHOSEN AND THE FAITHFUL   In Ephesians 1, Paul said The Christians at Ephesus, are **chosen** and **faithful**. The **chosen** are THE SAINTS (Holy) who will be The Bride of Christ. The **faithful** (God fearers) will be The Guests at The Wedding Feast with Jesus as The Groom. As amazing as it seems, even those of The Jewish **faith** know The Letter of The Law does not make one "**righteous**." In The Jewish religion to be **righteous**, one has to be a "**hassidim**" or a "**righteous one**." To be a **God** "**fearer**," one has to be "tsedaq" or "faithful." The word "faithful," in Hebrew is, "tsedaq," and comes from Melchisedec or "**the faithful ones**."

Whether in The Old Testament (The Scriptures) or The New Testament,

you must become Holy or **perfect** as God. To fool yourself and not have
the love (agapé) of God by His Holy Spirit is a **lack of faith**. One is not
even a "God fearer" or "**tsedaq**," let alone becoming **righteous** as God or
a "**hassidim**." Christian sin is I John 5:17, **"all unrighteousness is
sin."**   You must become Holy and **perfect** as your Heavenly Father,
Almighty God. Anything else is not having God's "**righteousness**."
Christians cannot be guilty of any offense to God or His Creation. YOU
EITHER HAVE THE LOVE OF GOD (AGAPĖ) SHED ABROAD IN
YOUR HEARTS OR YOU HAVE **MISSED THE MARK AND ARE
SINNERS**.

CHAPTER 10

GOD'S REQUIREMENTS FOR CHRISTIAN SALVATION

Your salvation will now be covered. Since everyone will be saved by Grace, what are the requirements and rewards for Christians? Those who do not meet the requirements will go in The Lake of Fire or "hell."

To avoid The Lake of Fire and to be able to receive the greater rewards of God's "kingdom," <u>The Bible</u> clearly reveals what each and every one of you must strive to become. You will finally know, biblically, who can and will achieve Christian salvation.

Many Christians, striving for **salvation**, fall into two extreme groups. One group believes all you have to do is believe in Jesus Christ. You must believe in your heart and accept Jesus, as God's first begotten Son. In addition, you must know, for a certainty, Jesus' **sacrifice** paid for your sins, so you can be **saved**. This view can be termed the **extreme liberals.**

The second group consists of **super conservatives**, who believe a Christian must keep The Letter of The Law. The only **works** annulled are the offerings and sacrifices. Since Jesus was your sacrificial lamb, a Christian is not required to offer sacrifices. The rest of The Letter of The Law is incumbent upon Christians as a requirement for **salvation**. Which group is right? **Scripturally**, you will find both are **right** and both are

wrong.

GOD'S PURPOSE   What is the problem? Why are there such diverse ideas among Christians as to the requirements for **salvation**? The basic difficulty is they do not understand God's **purpose**. Once you know why God created the universe and all mankind, you will have a better foundational understanding to learn what Christians are required to do to be **saved**.

The following is a list of accepted beliefs by many Christian groups for **salvation**. They are accepted as God's **purpose** for humanity by many differing Christian groups. THEY SEEM SIMILAR, YET ALL DIFFER IN SOME RESPECT.

WHAT IS GOD'S PURPOSE FOR HUMANITY?

1   Is God building a **"kingdom?"**

2   Is God building a **"family kingdom?"**

3   Is God creating sons and daughters to be in His **"kingdom?"**

4   Will God's **"kingdom"** be in **heaven**?

5   Will God's **"kingdom"** be on earth?

6   Is God's **"kingdom"** a physical **"kingdom?"**

7   Is God's **"kingdom"** a **"spiritual kingdom**?"

You must **biblically prove**, EXACTLY, according to God's **Word**, what

God's **purpose** really is.   Surprisingly, God's real **purpose** is **none** of those previously mentioned.

God is creating a "**kingdom**," composed of "**spirit beings**" who will be His "**family**." This family will be on a new earth with God, The Father and His Son, Jesus. This is the **message** of The Gospel. It is God's newsletter – **the good news** for **His "family kingdom"** on **the new earth**. However, this is not God's **full or complete purpose**. The Scriptures prove God's real **purpose** is to help all mankind. This will be the beginning of your understanding to know what you, as a Christian, will be required to do to receive **salvation**.

ALL IN ALL   God will reveal His entire **purpose** to you if you read all of Ephesians I. From Verses 1-8, Paul states from the very beginning, before any physical creation, God PLANNED for you to be one of His Sons.   God foreknew and preplanned all this.   Then, Paul made an amazing statement: **"[9]Having made known unto us the mystery of His will, according to his good pleasure which he hath purposed in himself. [10]that in the dispensation of the fullness of times** [end time] **he might gather together in one all things in Christ both which are in heaven, and which are on earth; even in him."** Do you understand the **magnitude** of Paul's statement? God is going to **SAVE EVERYONE**. This is an amazing revelation.

God, through Christ, intends to **save** His entire **creation**. That is why The Apostle Paul said God's entire **creation** is **groaning** and waiting to become His Sons in Christ (Romans 8:21-22). Paul states this is a **mystery**! This mystery is why so many Christian groups differ in their understanding. Not everyone has **spiritually grown** to understand this puzzle or mystery. Paul does give the details of how Christ will **save** everyone (I Corinthians 15).

I CORINTHIANS 15   This is known as 'The Resurrection Chapter.' Some believed the resurrection had already past while others believe there is no resurrection. Paul states Jesus was the first to be resurrected and Christians will be resurrected, later – every man in his own order (I Corinthians 15:20-28). Paul said just as all of Adam's children died, they all will be **saved**; but God has a specific order or time table for each of you and all who have ever lived.

Paul said **the end-time** comes when Jesus defeats all of His Father's, enemies (Verse 24). The last enemy is death. Death will be abolished. Once death is finished, all the authority given to Christ, by God, is returned to God by Jesus. Why? Read Verse 28! Jesus gives all authority back to God, The Father, so **God may be all and in all.** Scripturally, at the end, God's **purpose** is for Him to be **"in everyone."** Everyone in heaven and earth will be **in Christ**. God **saves** everyone, so God can be **all and in all** (Ephesians 1). **This is God's biblical truth and purpose**. God is not only building a **"family kingdom of sons,"** but He is going to be personally **"in"** everyone. God's **purpose** is to make everyone Holy with God, Himself, dwelling in everyone by His Holy Spirit. God will actually be **all and in all!** This has been God's **plan** or His **complete purpose.** Since God's ultimate **purpose** is to be **all and in all,** how is God accomplishing this work of His? Jesus said, **"This is the work of God, that ye believe on him whom he has sent"** (John 6:29). This is exactly what Paul wrote in Ephesians 1. Paul said at **the end-time**, God had predetermined that everyone in heaven and earth, will come to God, The Father. God will eventually be **all and in all!**

ONLY BELIEVE   One group, "**the liberals,**" believe you don't have to do anything but just **believe** in order to have **salvation**. Just believe in Christ. That is all that is required. Jesus said, **"He that believeth on the Son hath everlasting life; and he that believeth not the Son shall not see life; but the wrath of God abideth on him"** (John 6:47). There you have it. All a Christian has to do is **believe**. Nothing else is required.

The Work of God is to believe on Him whom He has sent. Whatever Christ states, you should believe Him. Prove, according to His **Word**, what Jesus is teaching you. Paul said in these **last-days** God has spoken to you by His Son (Hebrews 1:2). In times past, God spoke by The Prophets (Hebrews 1:1). Now, God, The Father, speaks to you by His Son. Christ will tell you **exactly** what you need to do. In Matthew 4:4, Jesus said, **"It is written, Man shall not live by bread alone, but by every word that proceedeth out of the mouth of God."** So, just believing in Christ's name is **not enough**. Much more is required. What is required? God speaks through and by His Son, Jesus. You are to believe in everything Christ states. Jesus, The Christ, said you are to live by every Word of God. Jesus is speaking God's **Word**. Christ said, **"Verily, verily, I say unto you, He that heareth my word, and believeth on him that sent me, hath everlasting life, and shall not come into condemnation; but is passed from death until life** [Just to believe in Jesus is not enough]**"** (John 5:24). One has to **"hear and understand every word"** that Jesus tells you. Christ has the only answer. What did Jesus say is required to pass from death to **life** or **salvation**? The liberal view of Christianity is not enough. You must believe **Jesus' Words**, which tell you what is required for **salvation**; and, **biblically**, you must test the ultra-conservative view of what a Christian must do for **salvation**.

THE LETTER OF THE LAW   The conservative Christian group, on the very far right, believes you must keep or do **The Letter of The Law**. The Torah or The Law includes Genesis, Exodus, Leviticus, Numbers and Deuteronomy. Only the offerings and sacrifices are **not** to be kept. Why? Because Jesus was your **"sacrificial lamb."** That is true, but is that all Christ came to do? Did Jesus come merely to keep The Law, fulfill and complete The Law? The "Letter of The Law" in Greek means "gramma," or "what is written." It is The First Five Books of The Old Testament. These ultra-conservatives justified their belief by the following **scriptures**:

1   Matthew 5:17: Jesus said He did not come to destroy The Law, but fulfill it. Those advocating their agenda reiterate, "See, Jesus did not destroy The Law but came to keep it."

2   Book of Acts: Those advocating keeping The Letter of The Law always tell you to read The Book of Acts. The Apostles kept The Holy Days. Therefore, you must keep The Letter of The Law.

3   Genesis 26:5: Since The Law was not written or enforced until 430 years after Abraham, why did Abraham tithe and keep God's **commandments, charges** and **statutes**. The Law, therefore, was

enforce before Moses. Therefore, Christians are required to keep The Law.

4   Exodus 18:16: Before The Ten Commandments were given at Mt. Sinai, Moses was already teaching The Israelites all of God's **statutes**. The Law was known before Israel made **the covenant** with God to keep The Letter of The Law.

5   Matthew 23:3,23: Jesus said The Pharisees sit in Moses' seat, and therefore, do all they say. In Verse 23 Christ said to keep The Law.

There you have it. Biblically proving, The Law was known and kept by Abraham before God gave it to Moses and Israel. Also, Moses taught **the statutes** before they came to Mt. Sinai. Jesus, also, said you are to keep The Law since The Pharisees sit in Moses' seat. Christians are, therefore, required to keep The Letter of The Law. In addition, I John 3:4 states: **"sin is the transgression of the law."** Unless you keep The Letter of The Law, how are Christians to know what sin is? This seems very logical and understandable as to why so many Christians believe they are required to keep The Letter of The Law.

AN AGENDA   Before you **scripturally prove the truth**, it is helpful to be in a Godly state of mind or have **the mind of Christ**. In Philippians 2, to have Christ's **mind**: (1) You must take on the attitude of a servant and not as a master of **the truth**. (2) You must be willing to be teachable, as little children (Mark 10:14). (3) You, also, must realize mankind can only know in part. No one knows **the whole truth**. God reveals to each as

Christ directs His **"body"** or **"the church"** (I Corinthians 13:12). (4) **You, as well as all other Christians, are** at a **different level of faith** or **belief** and must respect each other's level or position of belief. Read all of Romans 14. Finally, Jesus said He speaks in mysteries about **God's Work** (Matthew 13:11-12). However, those who diligently seek God (Acts 2) will have God's puzzle opened to their understanding. The **truth** is **one flawless, beautiful story**. Each **morsel** of **truth fits perfectly**. If one piece of your understanding doesn't fit, you are not rightly dividing The Word as Paul told Timothy (II Timothy 2:15). Keep praying and searching for **the truth** of God's **Word**.

As is evident in searching **the truth** in The Bible, you must not hold to a **personal agenda**. A **personal agenda** is when a person, studies The Bible and approaches The Word of God, to prove what they already know or presently believe is **the truth**! But a servant, as a little child, wanting their Father's direction, studies The Bible to learn whatever it reveals even if it may contradict one's present belief. Do not allow your human mind to have its own imaginations. Instead, seek God's **"will"** and His **Word** as revealed by His Son. Increase your **talents** to **two, five** and **ten** as Christ admonished (Matthew 25). Don't hide your one talent in the ground.

WORD DEFINITIONS You are, now, almost ready to prove what God requires for Christians' **salvation**:

Your quest is to resolve what Christians must do to be **saved**. No other consideration is at stake, neither prophecy, or whether having a happy human existence, or attempting to prove your personal beliefs, etc. **Salvation is the issue**, nothing else. Many discussions, by differing Christian groups over their faith are meaningless, as they do not stick or follow through to what is **required for salvation**. This is the only discussion. Nothing else. Your only quest should be to find out what you have to do to be **saved**!

THE APOSTLE PAUL'S ANSWER   The Book of Galatians deals personally with **salvation** and exactly what you must do, especially in regards to the keeping of The Letter of The Law and **circumcision**. Paul answers the claims by the ultra conservatives who demand **the keeping** of The Letter of The Law as a requirement for **salvation.**

DEFINITIONS   To address Paul's clear explanation of "**the works**" and **deeds** of The Law **with circumcision**, requires you to define certain Greek meanings of words translated into English. Words such as **righteousness, perfect, justified, faith, works, deeds,** and others. As you study The Bible and read these terms, you may have been viewing their meanings in a very **general** or **generic** way. Yet, in reality, in Greek, these terms signify **precise**, and very **defined meanings**. You must attempt to come to a common **understanding** of these words.

1   **"Perfection:"**   Commonly, you would **think** the meaning is to be "**without mistakes**." The Greek, carries the definition of "**being without blame in a court of law**." It signified "**being in court**" and "**being innocent**." You are, therefore, **blameless** (whether guilty or not), according to your **repentance**.

2   **"Righteousness:"** Normally, you would believe "**righteousness**"

would mean "**to do something perfectly**" or "**never making a mistake**." The Greek conveys "what is legally – **just** – whether mistakes have been made or not."

3   **"Justified:"** The Greek, in this case, is closer to its generic understanding so "one had a right to do what they did, whether right or wrong." "To be 'justified' is not to be held legally responsible." "One is innocent, even though guilty."

4   **"Faith:"** "Your point of view" or "how you choose to believe" or "what you believe" and "whether **wrong** or **right**, is **not** the issue."

5   **"Works"** and **"deeds:"** Both English terms come from a Greek word, "ergon," which means "any human effort" or "work."

You will find all these words have to do with either **being on trial** or **going to court** (before God and Christ) to determine if one is committing a crime against God and/or is guilty of sin against **His standard of righteousness**. God's **court** revolves around the **mercy seat** in God's **temple**. **The true temple** is in heaven and this **mercy seat** is occupied by God, The Father, and Jesus, The Christ or Melchizedec.

On earth, **the temple**, when in existence, is God's **throne** or **mercy seat**. It is an exact duplicate of **the true temple** in heaven. However, this **mercy seat**, on earth, only had God's presence, occasionally, when God's "**Glory**" or "**shekinah**" was there. Inside this **mercy seat**, are two tables of stone or The Ark of The Covenant. In each case, in **heaven** or on **earth**, both relate to receiving mercy for a person's crimes or sins before God. You must **biblically prove**, what is **the purpose of the**

mercy seat? The final definition is to understand why **God even had a temple on earth** and continues to have **one in heaven**.

When you read all of I Kings 8, you'll find Solomon's dedication prayer for **the temple** he built on earth. **The purpose** of **the temple** is where God judges His people, Israel, whether they are guilty or innocent regarding His Laws (I Kings 8:32). Clearly, THE TEMPLE'S PURPOSE IS TO HAVE A PLACE TO WORSHIP GOD AND A PLACE TO RECEIVE MERCY OR FORGIVENESS OF ONE'S SINS OR CRIMES. **The temple** on earth and, also, the one in heaven are **God's court houses** where people are indicted and are tried as to their guilt or innocence. **The temples** are **God's courts** – one for The Israelites and one for The Gentiles. All the questions about The Law revolve around God's **courts** and whether one is going to receive **mercy** for their crimes or found innocent, regardless of **guilt** or innocence.

The temple on earth has to do with one's guilt or innocence **while living this human existence**. **The court** or **temple** in heaven has to do with the final White Throne Judgment. Either way, **both temples** have mediators or attorneys for the defense as The Levitical Priesthood or The Melchizedec Priesthood. Now, to the question of the requirements of The Law upon **"the Christian community."**

<u>**THE TEMPLE COURT**</u>   Without understanding **the purpose** of **the temple**, which is a **courthouse**, where Israelites go to worship God, and ask for mercy – there is no possibility of finding out how The Law of Moses, or <u>The Torah,</u> applies to Christians. Since it is God's **purpose** to be **all and in all,** those who are **saved** become Holy as God is Holy.   This

is a family relationship (Hebrews 12:10). God chastises people **but only to bring them to the truth** (Hebrews 12:11). When Israel sinned by building the golden calf, God would no longer lead them into "**the promised land.**" From that point on, God had an **angel** lead them and judge them. This **angel**, as God's **judge**, would give **no mercy** (Exodus 23:20-21). This necessitated **the tabernacle**, a **courthouse**, where God would **try** them for committing crimes against His Laws administered by Moses.

Originally, God, at Mt. Horeb or Sinai, **verbally** gave them The Ten Commandments only **AND ADDED NO MORE** (Deuteronomy 5:22). At this point, The Law of Moses only **included The Ten Commandments**. All God wanted from Israel at this juncture, was for Israel to keep His Ten Commandments in **their hearts**; and He wanted nothing more. Notice, The Ten Commandments are in **the mercy seat**. One's guilt or innocence is based upon The Ten Commandments alone. **The Letter of The Law** only **reminded** them they are **still sinners**. Keeping The Letter of The Law did not give mercy.

Once Israel sinned and because Moses pleaded not to have God **slay them**, God instituted a legal system of **works** and **deeds**. God made them pay penalties such as animal sacrifices or, if a heinous crime, they were put to death. This was the only way Israel could be God's **witness**. This court system with its legal demands was intended to bring Israel to repentance or to Christ, The Messiah. The Law of Moses not only included The Ten Commandments, but, now, the added **statutes** and **judgments** and became **the judicial system** in **the tabernacle** (Malachi 4:4). It was Israel's chance to plead for mercy or acceptance by works.

The Levitical Priesthood were their intermediaries or defense attorneys, enabling them to settle out of court, by offering sacrifices, which was their reminder they had sinned.

THE MERCY SEAT **The tabernacle** or God's **court** for Israel was based upon the principle of receiving mercy or **settling** out of court (I Kings 8:32). God's angel, however, offered no mercy (Exodus 23:20-21). How could an Israelite, who was guilty of breaking God's Law, get mercy? Only by having access to **the mercy seat**. No one, however, could go into The Holy of Holies except The High Priest and only once a year on The Day of Atonement. Even, The High Priest couldn't have direct contact to **the mercy seat** because the two angelic cherubs guarded it just as they protected The Tree of Life in The Garden of Eden. No one could have contact with "the ark" to receive mercy. Until Christ came, the way into The Holy of Holies wasn't possible. Mercy only came after Christ died.

In "the ark" only the two tables of stone containing The Ten Commandments were there – nothing else. **The mercy seat** was placed right over this "**ark.**" The only way **mercy** could be obtained in God's **court** was by keeping The Ten Commandments. However, these **ten commandments** were written in stone because Israel was carnal and had a stony heart or were not repentant (II Corinthians 3:3). This is why The Israelites could never receive mercy from God, as long as they kept The Ten Commandments in The Letter, but without **a right heart**. (Read Chapter 9, 'What is Sin'). **The court**, therefore, always required **"an eye for an eye"** or **"a tooth for a tooth"** – and absolutely **no** mercy!

The reason God does not give **salvation** or grace to those keeping The Letter of The Law is because they had and still have a wrong heart. The Apostle Paul said by keeping The Letter of The Law you would only receive death. Paul stated The Letter kills, but keeping The Law in **"the spirit"** gives **life** (II Corinthians 3:6). This is why **the angel** gave no mercy. You must keep **the commandments spiritually**. Keeping The Ten Commandments, in The Letter only, is not good enough! Only by keeping The Ten Commandments, **with a right heart**, gets mercy! Keeping The Letter of The Law only allowed a good human existence, but **no salvation**!

God told Israel in Deuteronomy 5: **"[29]O that there were such an heart in them, that they would fear me, and keep all my commandments always, that it might be well with them, and with their children for ever!"** That includes **eternal life** or **salvation**. That is the only way to receive **mercy** from God and be **saved**. Nothing else is required. After God gave Israel The Ten Commandments, He **added nothing more**. Pretty plain and, as usual, simple to understand. That is all God ever demanded for **salvation**.

<u>GOD'S COURT OF LAW</u> First, you need to understand God's legal terms in His **court** or **temple**. In too many cases, you could make a giant mistake, especially when the conservatives try to defend themselves in **court** without an attorney or mediator who understands The Law and its legal meaning. If you go before God for **"mercy"** it is wise to be knowledgeable about the rules of conduct in God's **court**. Just as you have defined certain terms for **righteousness**, you must understand **the**

legal definitions, to know when asking God to forgive you – in His **court** or **temple**.

1 **"Holy:"** The Greek word is "hagios." The definitions are "blameless," "purified" or "without blemish" or "spot." "To be Holy" is "not to have a **spec** of uncleanness or sin." "Totally pure." Absolutely PERFECT, without a spec of error or being wrong. A little leaven leveneth the whole lump. Not a spec, only completely Holy (I Corinthian 15:6).

2 **"Sin:"** The Greek word is "hamartia," meaning "an offence" or "to miss the mark." One has caused "an offence" to someone or something, and therefore, "missed the mark" or "sinned."

3 **"Offence:"** The Greek word is "paraptoma," meaning "a slip," "lapse" or "deviation" – "an error." To cause an offence to someone or **something** is "to make a slip" or "error towards that person or thing." It is "causing an injury" or "some sort of harm."

4 **"Transgression:"** The Greek word is "parabasis." The definition is a "violation" or "breaking of The Law," **That is, a Law which is legally binding in a court of Law**.

5 **"Debt:"** The word in Greek is "opheilema," translating to "something owed" or "due."

6 **"Perfect:"** The Greek word is "telios," and can mean "fully mature" or "be complete" or "full age." It does not mean "to do" or "keep" or "be without mistakes."

7   **"Mercy:"** The Greek word is "elchos," meaning "compassion" or "tender hearted."

What happens in **court**?

<u>CHRISTIAN COURT</u> In I Peter 4:17, Peter said judgment or a Christian's trial is now in this present, human life. (Romans 5 discusses this entire subject). Paul said Christians are justified or legally innocent in God's eyes because of **faith** (Verse 1). You can, therefore, have peace with God with Jesus Christ as your Mediator and Defense Attorney. Notice, no law requirement or debt or sentence needs to be paid. You are made **legally righteous** by **faith**, and God is not offended by you **when you repent**. God sees no error or guilt in you. You have **atonement** or **acceptance** and have received mercy from God (Verse 11).

Now, to learn the history of sin. Sin, or **missing the mark** or **to be accepted** was due to Adam by his sin or **offense** to God. He was, therefore, **guilty**. Adam did **not break God's Laws**, but **disobeyed** God, and therefore, **spiritually** broke **The Fifth Commandment**. Adam had a choice between The Tree of Life and The Tree of Knowledge. His sin was **not** a **breaking** of The **Letter** of The **Law** as there was no legal requirement of The Law. It was because Adam **spiritually** broke The Fifth Commandment, he sinned or **"missed the mark."** Without Christ's sacrifice, Adam received the penalty of **death**. Death passed on through Adam and Eve's progeny even though everyone since then had sinned and deserved death. In Romans 5:13, Paul said, when there is **no Law**, **sin** or **missing the mark**, is **not imputed** – there is no Law. Adam did not break The Letter of The Law because **it did not exist.** He broke it **spiritually**,

only. So, **sin, missing the mark** or causing an **offence**, is not a **transgression** and has no **debt, penalty** or anything **owed**. Amazingly, one can sin and not be **guilty** before God's **court** unless a Law is in force. Throughout history, it is the same in most nations. Without a Law, sin doesn't carry a penalty. God certainly had a wonderful **plan**. Since the world is carnal, nations require laws in order for their citizens to live in a somewhat **civilized society**. Since humans aren't Holy, there has to be Laws. Laws are only required for carnal, unrepentant people, so they can finally **repent** and come to Christ.

Paul called Adam's sin an **offenses** and his **transgression** or **debt** of **death** was not caused by breaking any Letter of a Law in any **court**. Romans 5:15 states you have a **free gift** or **grace** by Jesus, The Christ. As Christians, to commit an **offense** is sin, without any Letter of The Law (I John 5:17). **Righteousness** or what is legally **just** for a Christian is Christ "in you" (Verse 17). His **"righteousness"** or being **"just"** is **His free gift** or **grace** given to everyone (Verse 18).

The Letter of The Law was put in force as a legal requirement to receive mercy so you could understand you are **guilty** of **sin**; and therefore, are **transgressors** and do **owe a debt**! (Verse 20). That is what **repentance** is all about. Israel was **carnal** and never **repented**. The Law, legally, in The Letter, could only produce **death.** Once a Christian repents and has God's Holy Spirit, that Christian is dead to any of the **legal** requirements of The Letter of The Law. Once you have God's Holy Spirit, any and every **offense** is sin. That is what Romans 7 is all about. Read it. Once you die with Christ, you no longer have any legal demands levied by The

Letter of The Law in God's **court**. This is the reason there is no White Throne Judgment in God's **heavenly temple** or **court for Christians**. Now, for Christian's, **grace** (a gift) reigns through **righteousness** or being legally **just** by Jesus. How plain and clear. The Letter of The Law with its legal requirements no longer applies to Christians, even when you sin, **as long as you repent**.

GALATIANS   Paul clears up the legal claim of The Old Covenant requiring the keeping of The Letter of The Law as having any hold or requirement upon Christians. He was so disturbed about this problem of circumcision and The Letter of The Law that Paul personally wrote his **epistle** in his own hand (Galatians 6:11). Paul absolutely wanted Christians to know there are NO LEGAL REQUIREMENTS, whereby God expects Christians to keep The Letter of The Law, in order to be **saved** or to be **righteous**.

Galatians 3 spells out God's **requirements** very clearly for Christianity in regard to **salvation** and **righteousness** (being blameless). Paul said The Galatians were **fools** not to believe **the truth** concerning **salvation** (Verse 1). He said, **"Did you Galatians receive God's Holy Spirit by faith or by keeping The Law?"** (Verse 2). This is the whole point. Once you are begotten with God's **Holy Spirit**, you are **then** a **Son** and have **the inheritance**. God literally writes HIS Law in your heart and mind. You will see this is the vital point about keeping or **not** keeping The Letter of **The Law**. You are now an **heir** and no longer need The Law. To fully comprehend this, read Galatians 4. Then, in Galatians 3:3 Paul said, **"Are you so foolish?"** You became a Son of God by **"the spirit."** Do you, now, think you are going to become **perfect** or **blameless by the flesh**, trying by your own human effort, to be **righteous** or trying to be accounted "**just**?" "**He therefore that ministereth to you in the Spirit, and worketh miracles among you, doeth he it by the works of the law, or by the hearing of faith**" (Verse 5)? Paul, now, brings in Abraham. He reveals Abraham **believed God** and that is what **made Abraham righteous** or "legally **just**" and "**acceptable**" by God. It was Abraham's **faith** that was **counted** as **righteousness** (Verse 6).

Abraham kept God's **commandments, charges and statutes** (Genesis 26:5). None of which made Abraham **righteous**, but he did have **faith**. The Apostle Paul said the same thing about himself in Philippians 3:6. He said he kept The Law blamelessly, just as Abraham did. Paul said all his **law keeping** was regarded as a loss (Verse 7). Keeping The Letter of The Law was **all for nothing** if by keeping The Law, you expect **salvation**. The Law only produced a good, decent human life. Once you are **spiritual**, with God's Holy Spirit, you are no longer in the flesh and need no human laws.

Paul continued by saying of his **own righteousness**, which is of The Law, did not give him God's **righteousness** to be **just** or **acceptable** to Him. Only **faith** in Christ accomplishes this (Philippians 3:9). As long as Paul relied on becoming **righteous** by the works of his human effort to keep The Law, it did not please God. Paul said all human effort (in the flesh) never pleases God (Romans 8:8). Only by **faith**, in Christ, do you **become righteous**. That is exactly what made Abraham **righteous**. God must be **all and in all** for you to become like God. The Law and all its works by human effort cannot do it for you, because, in The Letter, these works only apply to carnal human beings who are only starting to come to learn about Christ.

Now, to understand some very **misunderstood** scriptures. What are The Works of The Law? "Works" in Greek is "ergon" or "labor." Therefore, erroneously, many believe the works Paul spoke of were the sacrifices because it took "work" to sacrifice an animal. It is **true**; sacrifice does have to do with "**works**" of The Law, but there is much more to **Works of The Law**. You must let <u>The Bible</u> define The Works of The Law.

Scripturally, Galatians 3:10 reveals **The Works of The Law**: "**[10]For as many as are of the works of the law are under the curse: for it is written, Cursed is every one that continueth not in all things which are written in the Book of The Law to do them.**" What are **the works**? **The works** are everything written in <u>The Book of The Law</u>. **The works** include the entire book or Letter of The Law. Paul clearly explains it. All human efforts to keep The Letter of The Law put you **under the curse** of **The Law**! It is vital you read Galatians 3. The Law never justifies or makes you legally acceptable to God (Verse 11). You can keep all The Laws in The Letter, perfectly, as Abraham and Paul, and you are still guilty of your sins.

Paul said no man is **justified** or **forgiven** of his sins because forgiveness of sins only comes by **faith in Christ**. Just as Abraham and Paul understood it (Verse 12). But, if a person wants to live by or keep The Law, it's okay because it, definitely, will give you a good human existence, but it will never give you **salvation**. That is why keeping The

Letter of The Law never pleases God. God only wants you to be in "**the spirit**." However, keeping The Whole Law will never give you **salvation**. It just is not required for Christians. The person keeping The Letter of The Law can only expect the blessings of a good human existence such as good health, safety, prosperity and a long human existence, but does not please God or give you **salvation**.

Paul relates that Jesus **redeemed** you from the curse of The Law and now the blessings you have, do not come from The Law, but through **the promise** given to Abraham through Christ (Verses 13 and 14). Not the blessings of The Law but only THE BLESSINGS OF SALVATION THROUGH CHRIST. In God's **court** or **temple** the judgment was based upon the blessings and cursings and on how completely you kept The Letter of The Law. In Christ, the cursings are gone, and now the blessings come through Abraham and **the promise** of your **inheritance** of God's Holy Spirit. There you have it. Now, put the entire story together so you know how God becomes **ALL AND IN ALL** "in you" through and by His Son, Jesus, The Christ.

ISRAEL – GOD'S WITNESS   Why did God change The Priesthood from Melchizedec, a Priesthood, which loved **righteousness** and was based totally upon **faith** to The Levitical Priesthood based on human works? It happened after Israel sinned. When they built the golden calf, God instituted The Priesthood of The Levites, under Aaron, as High Priest. In Exodus 32:9, when Israel built the golden calf, God said, **And the Lord said unto Moses, I have seen this people, and, behold, it is a stiffnecked people.**" [They were a carnal people.] **"¹⁰Now therefore let**

me alone, that my wrath may wax hot against them, and that I may consume them, and I will make of thee a great nation." Because of their sins, God was going to put all Israelites to death except The Tribe of Levi. Then Moses interceded as Israel's defense attorney, and said The Egyptians, now will say that God brought Israel out of Egypt to put them to death rather than be God's **chosen people**. Moses brought up an excellent point.

God must keep His **promise** to deliver His people by creating a legal system that allowed them while still being a carnal people, with wrong hearts, and still be His **witness** as His **chosen nation** to the world. A **new agreement** was entered into, between God and His people – **The Old Covenant**, or The Old Testament. It was a system which recognized they were, indeed, **carnal** and **unconverted**. It was legislated by a **court** or **the tabernacle**, which had a new defense attorney, The Levites, to intercede for them. Now, God's Law, also, included, **judgments**, the **curses** or a **sentence**. Israel could still be a **witness to the world** and still pay the penalty of death if and when **capital sin** was committed. For breaking The Ten Commandments, the guilty Israelite would be killed. This kept Israel sinless and still kept them a **righteous** nation to be His **witness**.

This was a perfect solution, to the point Moses made. This Old Covenant was never made with Israel's fathers because they had a **right heart**. They were carnal or still not begotten with God's **spirit**. Therefore, their Priesthood under Melchizedec, was based on **faith** with **no legal requirements** or judgments. This Old Covenant or Old Testament demanded a carnal priesthood, with carnal commandments for human life with only penalties or judgments (Hebrews 7:15). Finally, this **legal court** system, based upon carnal people, would finally lead stiff-necked people to Christ. It was a **just system**, which **continued God's plan perfectly**.

OLD COVENANT RADIFIED   Hebrews 9:16-22 gives the history of The Covenant or contract made with Israel at Sinai.   Paul said, "a **testament**" ("a will" or legal contract), to be in force, **the testator or** "will-giver" has to have died. This Covenant or **"will"** becomes a legal contract in court. **A "will"** has conditions and to understand its benefits, one must keep the stated requirements. The **"will"** is in force when blood or death ratifies the contract. Moses covered all the conditions of The Letter of The Law, and then, took blood from the sacrifices of calves and goats and sprinkled both the book and all the people (Hebrews 9:19-22). Why?

Hebrews 7:15 states this **"commandment"** was a **carnal** one for **carnal** people (I Timothy 1:7-10). The animals signified people who were carnal (beast-like, **sarx**). These unconverted Israelites, with their wrong hearts and with the spilling of animal's blood, acknowledged (when guilty), they were, indeed, still sinners. That is why animal's blood was used. It proved The Israelites were still carnal or beast-like.   Therefore, this **agreement** or **covenant,** never could forgive their sins. It only reminded them that they were still sinners. The Letter of The Law spelled out what conditions, of **"the will,"** they broke.   NO SALVATION OR FORGIVENESS OF SIN WAS EVER PART OF THIS OLD COVENANT WITH ISRAEL.   This **testament** was administered by **Moses** as **Judge** and **The Levites** as **Priests** or **the defense attorneys** for the people. There is no remission of sins without blood. This remission was not forgiveness, only a reminder they were still sinners (Hebrews 7:22). One who believes they must keep The Letter of The Law to be forgiven of sin never qualifies for mercy by Christ's **blood**. They are faithless and still guilty.

Just before Moses died and Joshua replaced him as Judge, Moses had restated the conditions, benefits and the curses. These are known as the blessings and cursings of this **<u>Old Covenant</u>**. If they kept the full Letter of **"the commandments, statutes** and **judgments**," they would be blessed in **"the promised land"** with prosperity, a long, healthy, safe life, but never **eternal life or salvation**. This agreement only promised a great, successful human existence. They, however, had to keep every detail of it (Deuteronomy 30:17-20). And, the people all agreed (Deuteronomy 5:32-33 and Deuteronomy 5:27-29). That is why one cannot keep only parts of The Law (James 2:10). One would then be unrighteous according to The Law. This <u>Old Covenant</u> or **"will"** was made only for carnal, unrighteous people who would seek forgiveness in God's **court, the temple** or **tabernacle** (I Timothy 1:7-10). This type of agreement had never been made before with any other group of God's people, such as Abraham or Adam and Eve. The Melchizedec Priesthood was different than The Levitical Priesthood. With Melchizedec, one could obtain God's **blessing** of **righteousness** without The Law. Righteousness, with Melchizedec, came by **faith – no legal Law**. Christians cannot **offend anyone** – whether a neighbor, a co-worker or God.

God had instituted many **covenants** with mankind. With The Priesthood of Melchizedec, one could receive **righteousness by faith** without any Works of The Law (Galatians 3:6 and Hebrews 11:8-10). The Levitical Priesthood could only **point** to forgiveness and **salvation** (Galatians 3:24). The Levitical Priesthood could not forgive sin or give **salvation**. Animal sacrifices were made when they broke any of **the statutes**. The reason for the animal sacrifices was always a reminder to them they were still carnal or beast-like. The Holy Days, also, were **shadows** to be kept, to remind them they needed The Messiah, Christ, to fulfill God's **plan** of **salvation**. These **shadows** only prophesied things to come, which was The Christ (Colossians 2:16-17). WITHOUT GOD'S COURT, THE HOLY DAYS DO NOT HAVE TO BE KEPT. Holy Days have nothing to do with sin; they only represent a **shadow** of Christ. Once Jesus came and fulfilled **salvation** for Christians, they were **redeemed,** and received their **inheritance** (Ephesians 1). All these legal works and deeds no longer were necessary because **in Christ**, they are fulfilled. The Chapter on 'The Covenants' in God's Puzzle Solved goes into further detail.

CHOICE   Have you ever wondered why God did not put Cain to death for murdering Able? Very simply, there was no **legal law** to condemn Cain. Nevertheless, he was banished from God's presence. Paul said sin is **not imputed** when there is **no** Law (Romans 5). The legal requirement of The Law did not happen until Israel made that **covenant** with God at Mt. Sinai. The Greek word for "impute" is "ellogeo." Its full meaning refers to "put on account." Paul is telling you when there is **no written** or **Letter of The Law in force, you can sin**, but **not be held accountable for the crime**. Again, it is exactly what is done in **court** today, such as committing a crime, but there is no law against it. One may commit an offense (do injury), and they have **sinned** or **missed the mark**, by **not** doing **righteousness**, but it is **not a transgression** because there is **no law**. Therefore, there is **no debt** to pay. That is why God did not kill Cain for murdering Able. There was no **legal Law** enforce. Adam and Eve knew God's **commandments** and **statutes**, but as yet, they were not made into a legal Law. Adam and Eve had a **covenant of choice, "life"** or **"death."** There was no Law as a **legal requirement** to make it a transgression with a debt. The only **condition** for Adam and Eve to have **salvation** was to eat of The Tree of Life and not of The Tree of Knowledge. The Law, as yet, was not legally necessary. It is that simple.

GENESIS 26:5 Now, you can deal with the reasons Abraham kept God's **commandments**, **charges** and **statutes**. You will clearly understand why Abraham tithed to Melchizedec, and kept **the commandments** and **statutes**, which at this juncture, did **not** make Abraham **righteous** – only **faith** did. The question to ask is why Genesis 26:5 makes no mention of **judgments**. Before The Levitical Priesthood, Abraham, who was **blessed** by Melchizedec – The King of Righteousness – considered Abraham **righteous** only because of his **faith** and not by keeping God's **commandments** or **statutes**. Remember, Moses taught The Israelites, before they came to Mt. Sinai, to keep God's **statutes**, but again **no judgments** were given. Why? Simply because **judgments** are only enforced when Laws are **legally required**, The **judgments** in Hebrew require **a sentence** or **penalty for breaking The Law**. Up to this point, in Abraham's time, in Adam and Eve's time or in Israel's time before they received <u>The Old Covenant</u> or <u>Old Testament</u>, there was **no Law legally** required. Therefore, **no judgments** or **transgressions** or

debts. Only after God imposed His **courthouse** and **the tabernacle**, did **the commandments** and **statutes** become a **written** Law with legal demands. **No judgments** up to this point. Once The Covenant was enforced by blood sacrifices, it was in force with **all the judgments** or curses. Now, they had a choice of a good human existence in **the promised land** or they would be left with a curse. That was The New Law, The Letter or legal requirement of blessings and cursings (Deuteronomy 30). Why? Because they sinned and were carnal, with a **wrong heart**, He gave them over to Moloch and the pagan star, Remphan. They were carnal and had a carnal way with carnal commandments (Hebrews 7:15), to come to Christ and eventually REPENT. Otherwise, there was **no mercy** or forgiveness.

<u>**NO INHERITANCE**</u>   Why did Abraham tithe to Melchizedec and keep **the commandments** and **statutes**? Because Abraham knew **"the promised seed,"** Christ, would come **in the future** and so, as yet, he had not received **the inheritance** of **God's Holy Spirit** (Hebrews 11). Abraham continued to offer **sacrifices**, because he knew he was still **carnal** and only received grace or **righteousness by faith**. Abraham had a right heart, but no begettal of God's Holy Spirit. He was not, as yet, a Begotten Son of God. He gave tithes to Melchizedec because he had **no inheritance**, and therefore, still had to offer animal sacrifices. He **knew** he **was carnal** and until Christ gave The Holy Spirit, Abraham was unconverted, although he had a right heart.

Now for a surprise. The Hebrew word for "statute" in Genesis 26:5 is different than the Hebrew word for "statute" under <u>The Old Covenant</u>

made with Israel. The word for "statute" in Genesis 26:5 and Exodus 18 are the same, but not after God made **the covenant** with Israel.

In Genesis 26:5 and Exodus 18, the Hebrew word for "statute" is "chaqaq." This word is in the **feminine**, which means "customs," "ordinances" or "statutes." As a feminine derivation, it carries the meaning of "preservation" or "prosperity." In the feminine gender, it is not mandatory, as laws in a court. They are **not a requirement**, but it is a **free-will choice** – not a demand. They promised a good human existence guiding them towards a long life and prosperity. That is why Abraham tithed to Melchizedec, and it was his choice to keep **the commandments** and **statutes**. It **proved** Abraham's **faith** that he trusted only God for his prosperity and a good human existence, without **salvation**. Abraham knew he was still **carnal** and hadn't received **the inheritance** of God's Holy Spirit. That wouldn't happen until Christ came. That is what they shadowed or prophesied. Abraham continued sacrificing because he knew he was still carnal. Abraham was **led** by **God's Spirit** as a **Prophet**, but **not begotten** by God's **Spirit** as a Son.

This is why Jacob made **a proposition** with God. Jacob knew **the commandments** and **statutes** had no legal requirements as a Law. Jacob, like Abraham, knew he was carnal and hadn't received **the inheritance of God's Holy Spirit**. Therefore, since he was under The Melchizedec Priesthood based upon **righteousness by faith**, he promised God, that if He, God would protect and prosper him, Jacob would then tithe. Jacob had a choice, just as Abraham or Cain, as well as, Adam and Eve. They were totally under a different **covenant – no judgments** or **curses**.

DEUTERONOMY 5   That is why God, when He uttered The Ten Commandments, He only wished Israel had a **right heart** to keep His **commandments** and **added nothing more** (Deuteronomy 5:29). Up to this point, God never required any of the fathers to keep the type of **covenant** He would, later, enter into with Israel (Deuteronomy 5:3). After receiving **The Ten Commandments**, they immediately sinned, by building the golden calf; so God instituted The Ten Commandments along with **the statutes** and **judgments**, which made this **"covenant" a point of Law** in **court**. Israel, as God's **witness** to The Nations had to be **righteous** even though they were carnal. He, also, built **the tabernacle** with a new Levitical Priesthood. Why? This Priesthood was a **carnal Priesthood** for **carnal people** with a carnal **commandment** (putting one to death), with **the judgments** or **curses**. This Priesthood couldn't offer blessings, as with Abraham, but only have a mis-trial and settle for animal sacrifices to remind them they were criminals and incorrigible. A capital offense brought death. National Israel was still **righteous**, by The Law, and therefore, God's **witness**.

The Hebrew for "statute" in this case was "choq," not "choqqah." "Choq" is in the masculine and not feminine. "Choq" conveys being "bound" or "necessary." It became a Law and not a choice, as with the fathers. This was totally different. The Covenant with Israel was only meant for unrighteous, carnal people who had **a wrong heart** and were unconverted. That was **the purpose** of The Letter or written Law (I Timothy 1:7-10). It was a legal document in God's **court** to either "bless," if you were innocent or "a curse to condemn you," if you were guilty. **No free choice** as with **the covenant** with The Fathers.

Keeping The Letter of The Law requires one to become responsible for keeping it all just as The Old Covenant demanded. One must **continue sacrificing** even though Christ came. Why? Because one lacks **faith** and doesn't accept Christ's sacrifice as payment for your transgressions and debts. The curses of The Law are enforced. If one **repents** and believes Jesus fulfilled The Law by His **righteousness** in **faith**, you, then, are **inheritors of God's Holy Spirit**, and **Christ "in you," makes you righteous**. **God's righteousness saves; your own righteousness** can only bring **death**. God's **purpose** is to be **all and in all** through Christ. To be under The Letter of The Law is death (II Corinthians 3:6). To be in The Spirit of The Law under The Priesthood of Melchizedec is LIFE. One is in direct opposition to the other. One gives **life**, while the other gives death.

THE PRESENCE OF GOD   Here's a baffling question for you. Once The Apostles and Jewish Christians were baptized and had God's Holy Spirit, why did they keep worshipping in **the temple** and keep The Letter of The Law along with The Holy Days? **The biblical answer** is so simple as Jesus answers this question. Remember, The Work of God is to believe on Him, Jesus, The Christ. When Christ spoke to The Samaritan woman, a Gentile, He told her the day would come when Christians would no longer worship God in this mountain or **the temple** in Jerusalem (John 4). He plainly said that Christians would only worship God in **"Spirit."** From that point, to keep The Letter of The Law, was meaningless for **salvation**. Why? Because, God only wants to be **worshipped in "Spirit."** That leaves **all** human efforts of works or deeds unnecessary, if you want to be **saved**. It is quite clear. Christ said from that point, **only** worshipping God "in **the Spirit**" brings **salvation** or is acceptable to God. When was this to happen?

At the time of the writing of <u>The Book of Hebrews</u>, Paul said this <u>Old Covenant</u> was already decaying (out of use) and would be replaced totally by a <u>New Covenant.</u> When did this happen? In 70 A.D., Titus and his forces completely demolished **the temple** and by so doing, God's **court** was out of existence. Then, how could <u>The Old Covenant</u> exit? It couldn't. What was the use of worshipping God when no **temple** or **court house** was there to be able to give mercy? **The biblical answer is this**. As long as God's **presence** or the "**shekinah**" was there, one could worship with God's presence or "**glory**" and receive mercy. That is why <u>The Old Covenant</u> stayed **in force** as long as God was there. One knew where God was. The Apostles and Jewish Christians continued in <u>The Old Covenant</u> of The Letter of The Law with God still in **the temple**. When The Apostles kept The Holy Days, when God was in **the temple**, **His Name** (presence) was there, also. This will occur again in **the new temple** during The Millennium. With God's presence, the carnal Israelites and unconverted Gentiles will all come to **the temple** in Jerusalem to keep The Feast.

It was decided in Acts 15, The Gentiles did not have to keep the legal burden of The Law because they already received The Holy Spirit and did not have to be circumcised. The Gentiles didn't go into **the temple**. They already worshipped God "**in Spirit**." In 67 A.D., God's "**Spirit**" or "**presence**" **started** to leave **the temple**, and finally, with the destruction in 70 A.D., ended <u>The Old Covenant</u> and all its demands. From this point on, God only wanted to be worshipped **"in Spirit"** just as Christ has explained to you.

KEEPING THE LETTER   Is it a sin to keep God's Laws in The Letter today?   Of course not.   To do good, humanly, is not wrong. Remember, in Galatians, Paul said those who live in God's **commandments** in The Letter **will** have a good life. What is important for Christians to know is The Letter of The Law **is not a requirement** in order to receive **salvation**. It is good not to commit murder, steal, covet, etc. It gives one a good life by eliminating all sorts of problems, such as being free of human worries and needing to pay penalties.   However, keeping The Letter of The Law cannot make you **righteous** or **justified** (perfect or blameless). Only Christ can do that for each of you.

Most of The Works of The Law are impossible to do anyway. You can't keep The Holy Days or tithe lawfully without **the temple**. God made sure of that. To keep The Holy Days according to The Law, God's **presence** must be there.   When **the temple** was destroyed, God's **presence** or **"shekinah"** wasn't there.   One could no longer keep The Holy Days according to The Law because God's **presence** was gone. Some say, because Jesus said, **"where two or three are gathered in His name, He will be there,"** and Christians think God is, also, there – but He isn't. Only His Son, Jesus, is there, and you can hold a fine church service with two or three Christians in attendance.   But, realize God's **presence** wouldn't be there. Jesus said to only worship God, The Father. Without **the temple** and without God's **presence**, you cannot legally obey The Law and keep The Holy Days. Remember, it is not a sin to keep The Holy

Days, but they are no longer binding (only as shadows) for Christians. Christ already fulfilled this part of The Law for Christians. Jesus is The Passover Lamb; Christ has made you unleavened. You, already, have God's Holy Spirit. Christ is your Atonement. Christians have been **redeemed** long before The White Throne Judgment of God, by Christ. These "days," for Christians, have already happened, and are no longer, a shadow of things to come. Christians have already received their **inheritance** of The Holy Spirit.

Remember, God is The Judge. He has, however, given all **judgment** to Christ (I Peter 4:17). Christ, as Melchizedec, is your High Priest or defense attorney, interceding for your sins, and God judges your innocence through Christ's **sacrifice** and His **righteousness**. You are all legally **justified** and **held blameless** or **perfect** before Christ. THE ULTRA-CONSERVATIS, WHO BELIEVE CHRISTIANS MUST KEEP THE LETTER OF THE LAW – SCRIPTURALLY, ARE WRONG. YOU ARE NO LONGER UNDER THE CURSE, AND THEREFORE, FREE FROM THE LETTER OF THE LAW, AS A POINT OF SALVATION. Since **judgments** no longer apply to Christians – Christians are, therefore, sinless because there are no legal demands of The Law, which apply to them (Romans 5). Now, you have proven TRUE CHRISTIANITY is neither to the left (the extreme liberal) nor to the ultra-right, which requires you to keep The Letter of The Law. What's necessary for Christians to be **saved**?

THE COVENANTS   From the time of Adam and Eve until Mt. Sinai with Israel, The Covenant with humanity was a **covenant of free choice**.

No legal requirements were demanded. As Paul said, when there is **no Law**, there is no sin. The Letter or written Law, as a legal document, did not occur until Israel sinned, and Israel, from then on, had to keep every part of The Law or: legally – they were transgressors and guilty of sin. The Law demanded **death** for capital crimes. The **statutes** were **human-relationship ordinances** applying only to **human interrelations** for **God's physical creation**. Nothing in **the statutes** had anything to do with **salvation**. If they were kept, then one would be blessed with a healthy, safe, prosperous and long human existence, but it never brought **salvation**. That is why The Pharisees and Sadducees disagreed about **a resurrection**. The Sadducees knew The Law had **no resurrection**. The only other requirement in **the statutes** was the **shadows** or prophecy about what Christ would do to bring everyone **salvation**. That is why Paul said no one was to judge a Christian about these **shadows** because Jesus already fulfilled this part of The Law for Christians (Colossians 2:16-18). Christ is your Passover Lamb. He has made you unleavened. Jesus has already given The Holy Spirit to you. Christ already atoned you to God, and you no longer pray in a **temple** on earth but have a direct line to God, The Father's temple, in heaven. Christ has **redeemed** you, ahead of The Last Day Jubilee, and therefore, these **shadows** or **types** in Colossians 2:16 (Sabbaths, Holy Days, New Moons, Meal Offerings and Sacrifices), have already been fulfilled in The Law by Jesus.

The "covenant of choice," The Tree of Life, God's Holy Spirit by faith, came through the administration of The Melchizedec Priesthood. This gave **"life"** – God's Holy Spirit, by **faith** and not by **the works** of The Law (Galatians 4). When Abraham offered Isaac, **the covenant of**

promise, there were no conditions or Law required; only **faith** was counted as **righteousness**. That is why Abraham tithed to Melchizedec because he hadn't received **the promise** of God's Holy Spirit. It was to be in the future, at the time of **the new heaven and new earth** or The Jubilee – The Wedding Feast (Hebrews 11).

Abraham kept The Commandments, **charges**, **statutes** and **laws** to have a good human existence with health, safety, prosperity and a long human life. Remember, no **salvation**, only a good human existence. Not keeping them wasn't a sin, because there were **no legal** requirements of The Law in force. Only **faith** mattered for **righteousness**. The **third covenant** was a "**carnal covenant**" with **carnal commandments** by human effort (Hebrews 7:15); because the people, themselves, were carnal (I Timothy 1:7-10); but, they had no **faith** (Hebrews 4). The **carnal commandments** were **all** the **legal** works and deeds, **the statutes** and **the judgments** demanded. This became the legal penalty in God's **court** or **temple**, which would continue so, you, as a **true Christian** could be one of God's people. The **fourth covenant** was the **enactment** of **all** that The Letter of The Law foreshadowed (Hebrews 10:1) along **with** the sacrifices (Malachi 4:4) (Colossians 2:16). This was The New Covenant, which was by promise and was given totally by grace (Matthew 5:14-16). The curse and judgments were abolished. No death or shadows for Christians. Blessings were not from The Law or the keeping of it, but from the **riches in Christ** in **heaven** who is on God's **right hand** as your High Priest – Melchizedec. Once again, The Order of **Melchizedec was reinstated** which was a **Priesthood** of "**righteousness**" by "**faith**" and "**rest**" **in Christ** known as **The Sabbatismose**. No law, no more legal requirements, but once again,

under Melchizedec, **a covenant of free choice based only on faith**.
There's nothing wrong for Christians to keep **"the statutes"** because as
Paul said they allow you to have a good human life (Galatians 4). Under
Melchizedec, however, **only faith** in God, The Father by His Son and
living by every single Word of God as Jesus reveals, is required for
salvation.

God's **Ten Commandments, statutes** and **laws** were known from Adam
and Eve's day until they became a matter of **legal laws** in **God's court** or
temple. It is impossible for people to keep The Letter of The Law
because there is no Levitical Priesthood or **temple court** to enforce them.
When **the temple** was destroyed in 70 A.D., it was the end of The Letter
of The Law, with no courthouse to enforce it. Now, The Letter merely
tells carnal, unconverted people how to live a decent good life on earth.
Many nations have copied some of these Laws for their own civil
societies.

In <u>The Old Testament</u>, Pharaoh, himself, understood the penalties of
adultery. Abimelech, also, knew about adultery. The Hammarabi code
covered many of **the commandments**. The ancient Summerian
civilization, The Akkadians, Babylonians and Egyptians knew **the
commandments**. God's Laws were known since Adam and Eve. Seth's
generations passed on God's Laws. Even Cain spread God's Laws, but
they had a reprobate (carnal) mind (Romans 1). However, since Adam
and Eve did not choose The Tree of Life (God's Holy Spirit), these Laws
could only show how to live a decent life. No sin was imputed
(Romans 5). This is why Adam's sin was called an **offense** and **not a**

transgression. Until The Covenant with Israel, The Law was not a legal requirement (Romans 5). Remember, **"an offense"** in Greek means **"an injury"** or **"harm to God or His creation"** (which includes mankind), but it was not imputed as sin until The Law became a legal Law at Mt. Sinai or Horeb by blood.

CHRISTIAN JEWS AND APOSTLES After The Day of Pentecost when Christians received God's Holy Spirit, what was the first thing The Apostles did? The next day after Christianity began (Pentecost), The Apostles Peter and John went into **the temple** to **pray**. God's **presence** was there. It was nine o'clock in the morning, the hour for prayer. That is the reason The Apostles went into **the temple** – to pray. But Jesus said when you pray, you should say, **"Our Father, who art in Heaven."** Prayer in **the temple** to Christians really wasn't necessary or was it?

CHRIST ANSWERS   Jesus was talking to a Gentile woman, a Samaritan. He told her the day would come when Christians would neither **pray** by The Mount in Samaria or in **Jerusalem** (John 4). He said, **at that time**, God would only want His people to seek or please Him **spiritually**. It would be a time when **the temple** was no longer there. That happened in 70 A.D. by Titus and The Roman Army destroying **the temple** or God's **courthouse**. Seeking God's forgiveness by The Letter of The Law in **the temple** was over. This will be true until **the temple** is restored in Jerusalem by The Messiah, The Christ, and The Letter of The Law will again be in force, when God's **courthouse** will be restored. This will include the entire Letter of The Law **with the sacrifices** to bring those still **carnal** Israelites and the still **carnal** Gentile's world to Christ. The

Apostle Paul said the same thing in Hebrews 8:13, when he revealed <u>The Old Covenant</u> (**the old wine**), was decaying and would vanish. Exactly what Jesus told the Samaritan woman. The **legal letter** of The Law was finished. Why did Apostles continue to pray in **the temple**? They knew the time for <u>The Old Covenant</u> to be annulled, hadn't as yet, taken place (Hebrews 7:18). Paul said this carnal (legal letter) Commandment lasted only until Melchizedec was restored as High Priest (Christ). The "**Old**," would be annulled. That annulment, however, did not transpire until God stopped the worshiping of Him in **the temple** and that did not happen until 70 A.D. **That is why The Apostles**, who were **Jewish** and all **Jewish Christians** kept praying for forgiveness and kept The Letter of The Law including The Holy Days and Sabbaths. Jesus hadn't ended <u>The Old Covenant</u> with Israel. He said until the time would come when **only** by **spiritually worshipping God** would be the only way, which would be acceptable and please God (John 4). Then, <u>The Old Covenant</u> – The Letter of The Law, with all its "legal works" (judgments), **CEASED**.

How did The Apostles know the time to stop worshipping God in **the temple** had not yet occurred? Simply because **God's presence** or the "**shekinah**" or **God's "glory"** was still there. God was still in **the temple.** An Israelite could still pray to God because God was **still there**. Josephus, The Jewish historian recorded God's **presence** or **spirit** did not leave **the temple** until 67 to 70 A.D. That is why Jewish Christians, as Israelites, with The Apostles kept The Letter of The Law and The Holy Days and Sabbaths as a **shadow**. God was still there, and He could be worshipped. That is why Paul in Ephesus said, **"I must, by all means, make The Feast in Jerusalem."** God was still there! He still could be prayed to and receive forgiveness for his sins.

This was the entire debate over Christian Gentiles. The Jewish Christians and converted Pharisees believed The Gentiles needed to be circumcised and must keep The Law of Moses to be able to go into **the temple** and worship God. The Church with The Apostles and Elders decided they did not have to go and be circumcised or keep The Letter of The Law **because** they already had received God's Holy Spirit. Remember, **"the covenant"** God made with Israel **did not** include The Gentiles. The Gentiles became **"spiritual** Israelites" without being circumcised or keeping The Letter of The Law (Romans 2). The Gentiles, with God's Holy Spirit, had God write The Ten Commandments in their hearts (Romans 2). That was all God required of The Gentiles. They could worship God, **spiritually**, as God had initially wanted The Israelites to do from the beginning (Deuteronomy 5:29). Once **the temple** was destroyed, The Law could no longer be wholly or completely kept. If one keeps The Law, it must be kept in its entirety according to The Old Covenant (Matthew 23:23 and James 2:10). Without **the temple**, one **cannot** keep **The Sabbaths** and **Holy Days** according to The Law as Christ had already **fulfilled** these **shadows** for Christians.

GOD'S PRESENCE   The only way you could keep The Law in reference to The Holy Days is by **the temple** existing. Why? Because The Law demands it, but also, God's **presence** would be there. Some Christians believe they can keep God's Holy Days by Christ being in their midst.   They, by their **human thinking**, stretch The Law in their imaginations. They say by Jesus claiming **"where two or three are**

gathered, in "my name," I will be in their midst" or CHRIST WOULD BE THERE IN SPIRIT. That is true. That would constitute **the church** assembling together for a **"church service,"** but that is not **the purpose** of The Holy Days. The Holy Days, according to **The Law, demand** the assembly of **God** to be there where He, **God, puts His "name"** and not merely Christ being in their midst. God's very presence, the "**shekinah**," God's **"glory,"** The Father, must be there. By Jesus being in the midst only constitutes a Church service, not the keeping of God's Holy Days.

During The Millennium, Jesus and His Bride, **the church**, will be in **the temple**, and God, The Holy Father's **presence** as the "**shekinah**" will dwell there, too. Remember, **the temple** is God's **throne** with **the mercy seat** to give you forgiveness for your sins or trespasses. The only place that could happen after **the temple** was destroyed is in **the temple** in **heaven** not on earth. If you wanted to keep God's Holy Days today, you would have to go to **heaven** where **God's mercy seat exists**. No one can keep The Holy Days on earth today, with no **temple** and with no **presence** of God, Almighty. That is why Christ told Christians to pray, **"Our Father who art in Heaven."** This is the reason, **no humans**, including The Jews, who are responsible, are able to know **which days** are **God's Holy Days**. Debates and arguments continue. Even The Jews keep two days for each Holy Day because they do not know which are **the true** Holy Days. When Christ **returns**, this **truth** will be made known, and the worship in **the temple** will be reinstated.

JESUS ANSWERS   Biblically you have proven that **"the extreme liberals"** are not **entirely** correct nor are the extreme conservatives

entirely correct.

Salvation cannot happen without the subsequent steps. First, The Levitical Priesthood does not exist since there is no **temple**. Presently, Christians are administrated under a new Priesthood, The **Order** or lineage of Melchizedec. The Christ or Melchizedec is Jesus who shares God's **throne** of **mercy** or **judgment**. This New Covenant is different from The Old. The New Covenant is **spiritual** because God is a "**Spirit**" and only wants Christians to worship Him in "**Spirit**" (John 4). Praying for mercy is through Christ, who is The High Priest or Intermediary (an attorney) to God. Since God desires you to worship or please Him in "**the Spirit**," He only wants His Laws written in your hearts, **spiritually**. And, that is all God wanted from the beginning with Israel (Deuteronomy 5:29). These only included The Ten Commandments written in your hearts.

The Ten Commandments are all that is in **the ark** of **the covenant**. Once your heart repents, the stone is removed from The Ten Commandments, and God gives Christians access to **the mercy seat**. The Letter of The Law was only placed in the **side** of **the ark**. Keeping The Law could never give you mercy or forgiveness. All the Letter of The Law could do is remind you of sin (Romans 5:20), but never gave mercy for **salvation**. The Letter only provides a person with a wonderfully good, human existence. Since Jesus is God's "**work**" and if you believe in His **Words,** which are The Father's **Words,** you will be **saved**. Christ's answer in Matthew 19:16-25 is very clear. The rich man asks Jesus, "What must I do to **inherit eternal life or be saved**?" What did Christ reply? "**Keep the Commandments**" – period! Nothing else. Please, no human imaginations, like, what He may have meant. Then, the rich man said, **"I have kept them from my youth up. What do I lack?"** The rich man was very clear. He even asked Jesus which **"commandments"** and Christ gave the example of only referring to The Ten Commandments. But, what did he lack? The Greek is "hustereo," or **"to fall short."** What **ingredient** was he **missing**? He only fell short in **one area**. Jesus said, **"If you be perfect** [or without blame] **sell and give all to the poor."** He lacked a **right heart**. He was spiritually covetous. He didn't keep The Ten Commandments in his heart. He kept **The Letter** or **requirements** of The Ten Commandments but not in his **"nature"** or **"heart"** (Romans 2). That is **all** your **Savior** (by His very **Words**) said is necessary to be **saved**. Nothing else!

That is what God from Mt. Sinai said to Israel, as well (Deuteronomy 5:29). The Ten Commandments is all that is required to get into New Jerusalem when God, The Father, is there but with no **temple** because The White Throne Judgment is over. In **the new heaven** and **new earth,** the only requirement, for you to step into the city of New Jerusalem and have the right to eat of The Tree of Life, is to keep God's Ten Commandments (Revelation 22:14). What does God require for Christian **salvation**? Only to keep His Ten Commandments **spiritually, in your heart**.

WHAT IS SIN   What is the definition of sin? (I John 3:4): **"sin is the transgression of The Law."** But, as usual, people read the verse and not the context. The Apostle John said: **"in Jesus, every man has this hope, by purifying himself in The Christ."** Why? Because the transgression of The Law is sin. **The purpose** of The Letter of The Law is to make those who have repented know they had sinned (Romans 5:20).   The Letter of The Law only brings you to Christ (Galatians 3:24) and in Christ, you are sinless.

What The Apostle was saying, is God, by His Son, Jesus, takes away sin and **not by The Letter of The Law**. The Letter only tells you **the need for Christ**, and you are a sinner according to The Law. This **legal Letter of The Law** only brings you to Christ. The Letter only kills or condemns you (II Corinthian 3:6). Keeping or knowing what the legal Letter of The Law and how it discloses what sin is, will not give Christians **salvation**.

<u>CHRISTIAN DEFINITION OF SIN</u>   Now for a secret surprise. Christ said Christian **righteousness** (legally made right) must **exceed the righteousness** of The Pharisees (Matthew 5:20).   What was **the righteousness** of The Pharisees? In Matthew 23, Jesus said The Pharisees sit in Moses' **seat** of **authority**. Whatever they say He said, "The Jews must do." What was their "**righteousness**?" To be circumcised and keep The Letter of The Law of Moses. That was what The Pharisees demanded in Acts 15, which caused The Great Church **debate**. The Christian Jews had to keep The Letter of The Law, but Jesus said Christians must **exceed** the **righteousness** of **The Letter of The Law**. Then Christ spent the rest of Matthew 5, 6 and 7 explaining how to **exceed** the **righteousness** of The Pharisees. Jesus, The Savior, is stating The Letter of The Law is just **not good enough for Christian salvation**.   Does that mean one is not permitted to keep The Letter of The Law? NO. If one decides to keep The Law to be able to live a good human existence, that is okay, but it does not **make a person a Christian, let alone please God** or guarantee

salvation. The flesh can never please God (Romans 8:8). Keeping The Letter of The Law for **salvation** only ends up in **death**. It is not **good enough** for Christians. A **Christian must be perfect** (blameless) before God. That can only happen by **Christ In You** (Colossian 1:27). God must be **all and in all** for you to be Holy like Him. That is **God's requirement for Christian salvation**. Christians cannot commit any offense (injury) to God or humanity. **Sin** for Christians means one rejects God to be **all and in all** in you.

A CHRISTIAN DEFINITION   Since a Christian must **exceed** the **righteousness** of The Law, is there a **biblical definition** of what **sin is for a Christian**? I John 5:17 states, **"All unrighteousness is sin: and there is a sin not unto death."** What is a sin unto death? Those who keep The Letter of The Law only (by the flesh) leads to death (II Corinthian 3:6). A Christian must **exceed the righteousness of The Law** because **that righteousness** can only **produce death**. That is the sin unto **death**.

A Christian can sin and **break** The Letter of The Law (I John 3:4), and, as long as they repent, they are **still saved**. That is what Paul told you in Romans 6:23, **"The wages of sin is death."** Since **no one can keep all The Letter of The Law, "the wages of sin is death."** Paul does tell you how you can keep The Law, **spiritually** and receive **life (commit no unrighteousness**). In Romans 7:21-25, Paul revealed that he, as a human, had two laws reigning in him. In **his flesh** (human effort), he obeyed The Law of sin. As long as Paul tried to keep The Letter of The Law, he sinned and the wages of that sin was death (II Corinthian 3:6). However, with his **mind** or **heart**, he obeyed The Law of God, which was the keeping of The Law, **spiritually** and not in The Letter or written legal works.

In Verse 4, Paul gives the answer how to **exceed the righteousness** of The **Letter** of The Law and keep the Christian definition of sin in I John 5:17. Paul thanked God, that through Jesus Christ, in his flesh (human effort), he served The Law of sin, but in his **mind** or "**pneuma**," he served The Law of God. Human **righteousness** by humans keeping The Letter of The Law doesn't please God (Romans 8:8). Only by having a **right heart or mind** can you keep The Ten Commandments, "**spiritually**," and be **guaranteed** to be **saved**. God is not concerned about your human efforts by The Law or any other human efforts as monks running off to be alone and attempting to be pious. This is all a form of "**will**" worship. Humanly, it seems right and good. But, it doesn't fly. Only with Christ living in you, literally, with God's Holy Spirit, which will make you have **the mind of Christ**. God knows your flesh profits nothing.

In John 6:63, Jesus said "**the Spirit or mind that quickeneth or gives life.**" The flesh or what humans do to please God, profits nothing. All of your human attempts to please God are meaningless. Only God's **Words, "Christ In You**," can change your mind to only think like God or Christ. Only God's **Words** can give **life** or change your mind with "**the Spirit in man**" and God's Holy Spirit. Your human body is nothing. You must lose it.

WHAT GOD REQUIRES By God writing His Law (Ten Commandments) in your hearts and minds, He will forgive all your unrighteousness and sins and remember them no more (Hebrews 8:8-12).

Christians must understand God is not interested in how you keep The Letter of The Law. That has to do with your flesh, which will be gone when this corruptible (flesh) puts on **incorruption** (I Corinthian 15).

If the flesh no longer exists, then sin is gone because you worship God and only in "**Spirit**." It is only "**the Spirit in man**" (the mind and heart) with God's Holy spirit (truth) that is in your heart and mind. You will, only then, have a **spiritual** body (John 3). ALL GOD WANTS IS TO HAVE CHRISTIANS HAVE HIS TEN COMMANDMENTS WRITTEN IN THEIR HEARTS. THEN, GOD WILL BE **ALL AND IN ALL** (I CORINTHIANS 15:28)!

CHAPTER 11

CHRIST'S WILL

The Book of Revelation uncovers important BIBLICAL knowledge! **The Book of Revelation** reveals Christ, Himself, reading His "will." His "will" went into force after His "death" and "resurrection" (Hebrews 8-9). It is time Jesus reads His "will" to you by His angel through writings of The Apostle John.

There are two parts to His "will." Part 1 covers the first ten chapters of The Book of Revelation (Christ's will) and part 2, 'The Little Book' covers the last 12 chapters of The Book of Revelation. This chapter on Christ's "will" concentrates on Chapters 1 to 10 of The Book of Revelation.

Christ has a "**will**," and He, Himself, is the **executor** of His own "**will**." In order to put this "**testament**" or "**will**" in force, He had to die (Hebrews 9:14-20). Once He died He went to share His Father's **throne** as your High Priest, Melchizedec. **Everyone** will **be SAVED**, but each, according to what is written in **the "will**," and will receive a different **personal reward**. Some will be The Bride; others **witnesses** or **ushers** at The Wedding. The rest are Guests who will either live inside New Jerusalem or outside The City of New Jerusalem. Those who live outside **the city** will be close enough to partake of The Glory of God, which lights up the new earth. Those who go through The Lake of Fire are outside **the city** and without God's **"glory."** They will be in **"spiritual darkness**."

THE CHILDREN   When Adam and Eve were in The Garden of Eden or The Garden of Pleasantness, Adam was a type of Christ while Eve represented **the church** as **the mother** of **all living** (or **saved**). Since they did not obey and were put outside of **the garden**, but still in Eden – Land of Pleasantness, they will represent those Guests who receive God's **"glory,"** the "shekinah."

These are The Guests who will **not** live in The City of Jerusalem, just as Adam and Eve, as well as, Cain and Abel could not live in The Garden of Eden.

Once Cain murdered or martyred Abel, he was sent out of Eden into The Land of Nod or Land of Wandering – **the wilderness**. The **saved nations** will walk in **the light** (Glory of God) from New Jerusalem (Revelation 21:24). Those who remain do not walk in **the light** (the children of Cain) will basically, **live in darkness**. The Guests from the nations are the children of Abel who were persecuted or martyred. Where do Cain's children live in God's **"kingdom?"** Remember, The Law is **a shadow of the type** of God's "kingdom." <u>Genesis</u> is a part of The Law.

CAIN'S CHILDREN   In the account of The Wedding Feast, there are **Guests** who are dressed in the wrong garments. They are **not righteous**. These Guests with the wrong clothes are cast out of The Wedding Feast into **outer darkness** where they will weep and gnash their teeth (Matthew 22:11-14). Who are they; where are they, and why are they crying?

Only those who keep **the commandments** will be able to come into **the** city (Revelation 22:14-15). Why? These will be those who will be thrown into The Lake of Fire (Verse 15). Jesus tells you why they will not enter New Jerusalem.

Christ said those who keep God's **"commandments" in their hearts** will be **the greatest** in **God's "kingdom"** (Matthew 5:19). Those in God's **"kingdom"** who teach **"the commandments"** do **not** have to be kept; **will be called the least in God's "kingdom."** There you have it. Those who don't follow or teach The Commandments **will eventually be** in God's **"kingdom,"** BUT MUST FIRST GO INTO THE LAKE OF FIRE. They will not be invited to attend The Wedding Feast by not being written in The Marriage Registry – The Book of Life (Revelation 20:15).

Now, you know why those not allowed in The Wedding Feast are **crying** and **weeping** in the **land** of **darkness**. No light is coming from God's **"glory."** These are **Cain's children** (who will be in the **darkness** or the **wilderness**). They will be on their own without God until they take of **the waters** and **the leaves** from **The Tree of Life**. **Spiritual growth** will always continue in God's **"kingdom"** for those in darkness and also those in "**the light**" from God's **"glory"** (Revelation 22:2).

Everyone has now been covered as to how they will be **saved**, although everyone's reward is different. The parable of the ten talents tells you this aspect. Those who only have one talent, with no continual **spiritual growth**, are thrown into The Lake of Fire. Notice, their reward is exactly as those who can't enter The Wedding Feast. In both cases, they end up in The Land of Nod, wandering without God's **"light"** or **"glory."** They are in **spiritual darkness** and need the healing leaves from The Tree of Life.

They will have no access to The Tree of Life, but only its healing leaves. They are those who followed Cain and need to go through The Lake of Fire (I Corinthian 3). Now to read Christ's **"will"** or **"testimony"** of those who will be written in The Book of Life to be able to attend The Wedding Feast. Cain's children will burst out, the billions who must **grow spiritually** (Ephesians 5:26-27). Their growth from babes in Christ to **spiritual maturity** will take place in God's **"kingdom."**

A PROPHECY In reading Christ's **"will,"** you will see this **"testament"** reveals how those who are in The Book of Life can inherit **salvation** and get the **reward** of attending The Wedding Feast. Christ's **"will"** or **"testimony"** is The Spirit of Prophecy (Revelation 19:10). This Book of Revelation, in the Greek is **"the apocalypse,"** meaning **"the uncovering."** Now, you can uncover Christ's **"will,"** which shows you a prophecy of how God's people inherit their **salvation** and **reward!**

HIS SERVANTS Jesus states The Book of Revelation is His **"testimony"** or **"will"** written to His **servants** (Revelation 1:1). Who are His servants? Revelation 1:11 reveals this **"book"** or **"will"** is for the benefit of **the seven candlesticks** who are The Seven Churches in Revelation 2 and 3 (Revelation 1:20). But, The Seven Churches are only part of the benefactors of Christ's **"will."**

Jesus has **two witnesses** who represent the heirs of Christ (Revelation 11). One **witness** comprises The Seven Churches. Chapter 2 '**Who Is The Church**,' proves the other **witness** is Israel (Revelation 7). These are **the two witnesses** who **grow spiritually** from the **two olive trees** – The Church in The Wilderness (Israel) and The Church of God, composed mostly of Gentiles (Revelation 2, 3 and 14).   These are Christ's **servants** who receive a **reward** in addition to **eternal life** in God's **"kingdom"** (Revelation 21 and 22).   His servants, Israel and The Church of God must come out of Babylon to be able to **inherit** their **reward** (Revelation 18:4).

REVELATION 1   The following is **the "will"** of Christ, **His "testimony,"** to His servants.   Jesus starts by revealing He is making **Kings** and **Priests** of all His servants (Israel and Church of God) (Revelation 1:6).   Then **the angel** states Christ is coming in the clouds, and ultimately, everyone will **see** Jesus even those who actually pierced Him. John found himself on The Isle of Patmos for this prophecy. Everyone who reads, hears and **keeps** this **prophecy** will be blessed and rewarded (Revelation 1:3).   Those who keep this prophecy are Christ's **two witnesses**, which The Book of Revelation reveals.

John was in **"Spirit"** (vision or mind) on The Lord's Day (Revelation 1:10).   What is The Lord's Day? The Book of Joel prophecies The Lord's Day is **the seventh trump** or **the return of Christ**.   That is why John, in **spirit** on The Lord's Day, heard a great voice or a **trumpet**.   This is **the theme** of the **"will"** of Christ (Joel 1).   Go over Chapter 1, **'The Schoolmaster.'** Jesus looks just as God, The Father does (Revelation 1:13-15).   He has **seven stars – the angels** over **the seven candlesticks** who are The Seven Churches listed in Revelation 2 and 3.   Out of His mouth comes a sharp two-edged sword – God's **Word** (Hebrews 4:12). This is the **prophecy** to His **servants**, Israel and The Church of God (Revelation 1:20).

REVELATION 2 AND 3   The first of God's **two witnesses** are "the seven churches" which compose The Church of God beginning with the destruction of **the temple** in 70 A.D. until Christ **returns**. This is when The Old Covenant and The Letter of The Law ceased and only The New Covenant is legally in force. Now, **salvation** is of **grace** and **not** of human works.

The Book of Revelation is written explicitly to **the seven churches** who are to be Christ's **witness** until He **returns**. Understand, they all have different problems and doctrines or beliefs. Analyze each of these **seven churches** to see what Jesus wants each to do. They can receive a specific reward based upon them coming out of Babylon in regard to their specific problem:

1   The Ephesian Church has lost their first love. They stopped worshipping **the one true** God and His Real Son, Jesus (Revelation 2:4). Christ warns them to get back to **the true** God and His Son, Jesus. If not, when He **returns**, He will remove their **candlestick** (Revelation 2:5).

2   The Smyrna Church must remain **faithful** to the works they are doing so they can receive **a crown** of **life** – **salvation**, so they don't go into The Lake of Fire (Revelation 2:9-11).

3   Pergamos has a different problem. They, as a Church of God, are making a business out of **"the church."** They are doing just what Balaam and Balak did. They caused Christians in Pergamos to follow idolatry or fornication. When Christ **returns**, they will be His enemy, and He will fight against them if they don't **repent**.

Those who overcome will be at The Marriage Feast of God as Guests – a new stone (Revelation 2:14-17). Some will be as Bridesmaids as "a stone" or "the wall" in New Jerusalem.

4   Thyatira, as one of God's **"church"** is following Jezebel and her worship of Baal. They are steeped in pagan holidays and worshipping idols. This Church of God will go through **The Great Tribulation** just before **the return** of Jesus. The ones in this **church** will be martyred especially her children – the future generation of this **church** during The Great Tribulation (Revelation 2:20-25).

5   Sardis is a **"church"** "at ease." They believe they have **the truth** and all they want to do is to spend their time doing human works. They believe going to church, being busy keeping Holy Days, giving money and praying is all that is necessary. Changing their human nature is not what they think they should or need to do. To them, Christianity is keeping themselves busy with so-called **church work**. Jesus states they are dead. They will be shocked when Christ **returns**. They are **not growing** in God's Holy Spirit. Only a few are going to make it to attend The Marriage Feast. Most go into The Lake of Fire (Revelation 3:2-6).

6   Philadelphians have a little strength or **truth** but do witness Christ. They will not go into **the tribulation**, but will be in a place of safety while they witness in the wilderness. When Jesus comes, they will be a pillar (Boaz) in God's **"kingdom."** They will be part of The Bride (Revelation 3:7-12).

7   The Laodiceans are the most deceived in Babylon. They believe they are the only **true church**. Satan does not even have to make them follow pagan teaching. They are so sure of **having the truth** they cannot grow **spiritually**. They are **lukewarm** with only the first talent and cannot see the need to grow beyond the **one truth** they have. They are blind and naked, but think they are rich and have God's **truth** (Revelation 3:14-21). Elijah had the same problem. God had to tell him there were seven thousand others who followed **the true** God and, not Baal, besides Elijah (Romans 11:2-4). Besides **the seven churches**, there is more than one group with **the truth**.

What does Jesus tell this Church of His? **"I counsel you to buy of me Gold."** Where? In The Lake of Fire. Those who overcome and start to **spiritually grow** in God's **spirit** will reign with Christ on His **throne**. They can be The Bride of Christ! (Revelation 3:14-22).

They are one of **the two witnesses** of Christ. **The seven churches** are all of Christ's or The True Churches of God – Catholic, Orthodox, all Protestant, Evangelicals and Independents. They are all God's **churches**, but with different creeds, doctrines and faith and **truth**. They are all **the called-out ones** or "**ecclesia**," but they must continue to **grow spiritually** for their rewards. They must come out of Babylon (Revelation 18:4).

CHRIST'S WILL   After Jesus finishes listing His **requirements** to **the seven churches**, there is a pause in reading His "**testimony**." Suddenly, a door was opened in **heaven**, and a loud voice, as a trumpet, shouted, **"I**

will show you things which must be hereafter." John is told from that point on (that is, John's time when on The Isle of Patmos), he was to receive the future events in prophecy. God, The Father, is revealed in all His **glorious splendor**, just as a rainbow in its brightest glory. God is sitting on His **throne** and in His **right hand** is a **sealed book**. No one is worthy to open <u>The Book</u>. This book is Christ's **"will"** or **"revelation."**

A lamb is slain by a beast having **seven horns** and **seven eyes**. Why does Jesus have **seven horns** (Revelation 5:6)? Biblically, **horns** are **governments**. What governments? This is the beast with seven heads in Revelation 13. This is **"the fourth beast"** of Daniel 7, The Roman **government**. This Roman **government** crucified Jesus under Pontius Pilate. How plain. The **seven eyes** roaming the earth are from God's **throne** (Romans 4:5). These **seven eyes** are the **seven angels** or **stars** who watch over **the seven churches**. There, you have it. CHRIST IS WORTHY TO OPEN THE BOOK, WHICH IS IN GOD'S RIGHT HAND WITH THE SEVEN SEALS. Obviously, this book with the **seven seals** is <u>The Book of Revelation</u>, and only Christ, by His death, was worthy to reveal or **uncover** (Apocalypse), **His "will."** He is The Redeemer of Israel, The Church in The Wilderness (Acts 7:38) and The Church of God, **the seven churches** or **candlesticks**. The voice spoke to John, as the book is opened and shows the future in prophecy of what will happen to His **two witnesses – Israel** and **The Christians**. They **both** must come out of **Babylon** (Revelation 18:4). The stage is set. Now, begins the **uncovering** of **world prophecy** until God's **"kingdom"** comes with **the new heaven** and **the new earth**. Just before the opening of the **first seal**, the four beasts around God's **throne** with the twenty-four

elders, fall down before The Lamb, and they had **vials of odours**, which are **the prayers** of **saints** or **the righteous** (hassidim) – **chosen ones**. They were praising Christ that He has **redeemed** His **saints** as they prayed to help them come out of Babylon. The Lamb will have **redeemed** them to be Priests and Kings when He **returns** (Revelation 5:1-10). Their number was ten thousand times ten thousand and thousands of thousands. This is The Bride of Christ! If the analysis is correct, that puts the number about 100,000,000 people. Thousands of thousands. (Very few out of the billions who have been born). Not many will be The Bride (Daniel 7:10). However, there are The Guests, which are invited to The Wedding Feast. Then there are those who come out of The Lake of Fire. ULTIMATELY, EVERYONE IS SAVED! (Revelation 5:13)

THE SEVEN SEALS   **The seven seals** represents all the events from The Roman Empire until The Kingdom of God begins to reign on the earth. **The seven seals** cover the entire time period from The Fourth Beast, The Roman Empire until **the last days** are completed in **the end of days** or **the end-time**!

The first seal is opened, and you find a person sitting on a white horse, who appeared like Christ. He had a crown, and took control by a war. Who is this? Emperor Constantine claimed to be a Christian and in history; he viewed himself as **the thirteenth Apostle**. Constantine claimed The Roman Empire was God's **"kingdom on earth"** and he took over The Christian Church which was divided into two geographical areas, The Western Empire under Rome and The Eastern Empire under Constantinople. The two churches, or two lamb's horns, in Revelation

13:11 was The Roman Christian Church in Rome which became The Catholics and The Eastern Orthodox churches in Greece or Constantinople. They had no choice. Constantine took over **the two churches** of God at The Council of Nicea in 325 A.D.

The second seal continues the time frame. Christ said Herod's **temple** would be totally destroyed, which occurred in 70 A. D. (Matthew 24:1-2). The Christian Churches were taken over by deceit and led by and controlled by Constantine (Matthew 24:4-5). What will be the next event? Little wars and **world wars** are prophesied, which are the **beginning of sorrows**. Then what is **the second seal**? **The red horse** or wars and **world wars** are **the second seal** (Matthew 24:6-8).

Now, for **the third seal**. A **black horse** follows which depicts **famine** and **pestilences** (Matthews 24:7). This roughly begins **the dark ages** to **the time of reformation. The fourth seal** of The Four Horseman of The Apocalypse or "**uncovering**" is a **pale horse**. This pale horse depicts war and famine (Revelation 6:8). Jesus said this was the beginning of sorrows and continues until 1947 – a very significant date (Matthew 24).

Now a **vital seal** is about to open: Each of **the sorrows** continue with wars, famines, and plagues all over the world. The Four Horsemen are only the **beginning** of sorrows. All these sorrows continue in the world until Christ comes and brings **true peace**.

THE FIFTH SEAL This **fifth seal** concerns the martyrdom of those who began to grow as Christians. These are those coming out of Babylon and are martyred. Jesus referred to this event in Matthew 24:9-13. God symbolically speaks of **those being martyred** as **under the altar** denoting a time of **trial** or **sacrifice** (Revelation 6:9-11). An example might be when The Levites sacrificed clean animals (God's people) on the **sacrificial altar**. Those sacrificed are symbolically crying out in prayer (incense or odors), **"How long O Lord do you not judge and avenge your people."** This denotes a long-time period of thousands of years (II Peter 3:8-10).

White robes were allotted to them, and told to wait and rest for a season (thousands of years) until their brothers are also martyred (Verse 11). Who are these future ones who must, also, be sacrificed? This time period starts with all martyrs of Christ from the Day of Pentecost in The New Testament until 1947. Why 1947? This includes all Christian martyrs whether by Genghis Kahn, Catholics against Protestants or Protestants against Catholics, all the way through World War II. Everyone knew about the Jews, but millions of Gentiles were killed also. Their sacrifices are all inclusive until the very important date of the year **1947**. Why? At this specific time (1948), Israel legally became a Nation. From this point on, **the two witnesses**, Israel and Christians, could be martyred in The Great Tribulation. **The fifth seal** of **tribulation** ceases and now, **the sixth seal** could commence the martyrdom of **the two witnesses**.

From this point on, began **our very day** – why? The next seal is **the sixth seal** when a great earthquake occurs (Revelation 6:12). This earthquake is so large it turns the sun black and the moon looks as blood. When is this? This is the prophecy in The Book of Joel. Read all of it. Notice, Joel 2:10 reveals these events usher in Christ's **return**, and a **great earthquake** causes the sun and moon to be darkened.   This is **the sixth seal** (Revelation 6:12).

Where are you, in today's time period, with these seals? Remember, **the fifth seal** ends with Israel being established as a nation. Then the time of **the two witnesses** begins – The Nation of Israel and The Seven Churches – God's "**churches.**" Before Israel became a nation, you would not have had these **two witnesses. The sixth seal**, therefore, initiates the time of this future martyrdom, which may very well be the beginning of the present day with **the terrorists,** who not only hate Israel, but all Christians. When do **the end-days** or **time of the end** begin? Will you be able to tell? Yes!

The end-days begin with **the sixth seal**. When this great earthquake occurs, changing the color of the sun and moon, you will know **the end-days** have begun. BY READING ALL OF THE BOOK OF JOEL, YOU WILL UNDERSTAND. This is the start of **The Day of The Lord** – which is **the very purpose** for **the writing** of The Book of Revelation. When this **sixth seal** is opened, the kings, great men, rich men along with everyone on earth are frightened, and start to believe it is all happening because of God and **the day** of God's **wrath** must be near (Revelation 6:17). An earthquake so large there hasn't been one like it since humanity existed. Wow! The entire world feels this earthquake (Revelation 16:18).

BABYLON'S CHURCHES   God's **church** has called many, but with **seven different types of doctrines and beliefs of faith**. This is why The Apostle Paul said Christians do not need a **legal letter** to tell they are a part of God's **church**. They are not to be **incorporated**. God's **church** is a **spiritual entity** based upon **spiritual growth** in one's **heart**. The physical church you attend does not qualify you as a **called-out one** who can attend The Wedding Feast! **Every Christian is in Babylon** and must **spiritually grow** out of it!

Now, for **the seventh seal**, when Christ opens its meaning – **the end of days** begins. Just before **the seventh seal** is opened, Jesus reveals who is going to have to go into **the great tribulation** to receive their **inheritance** or reward at The Wedding Feast. These are those of Israel and **the seven churches** who have NOT been **growing spiritually**. They have been too complacent in their Jewish **faith** or in their Christian **faith**. The 144,000 Israelites and an innumerable number from **the seven churches** (Revelation 7:1-17) have to be **sealed** or protected by Christ because they have to go through **the great tribulation**, and come to the place they have **grown spiritually** (Revelation 7:14). Then, they are guaranteed to be in God's "**kingdom**" (Revelation 7:14-17).

SEVENTH SEAL   The seventh seal begins the sounding of **the seven trumpets**. You will see this is God, through Christ, starting to bring His **two witnesses** into **God's rest** (Hebrews 4). The **two witnesses** will have grown in **faith** to enter God's **rest** or The Millennium as His Engaged Bride. When **the seventh seal** is opened, there was silence in **heaven** for half an hour. **Seven angels** stood with **seven trumpets**. Then another **angel** stood at **the altar of sacrifice**, with incense – **the prayers of saints.** A very prophetical event for God's people. These **prayers** of **saints** caused the angel to take the **incense** (prayers) with **fire** and toss it to the earth. Then **the seventh angel** began to sound **the first trumpet**. This is the beginning of the great tribulation. **The first four trumpets** and the war to follow are **the prayers** of God's **two witnesses** as they witness during the three and a half years of **The Great Tribulation**. That is how long **the seven-trumpet time-period** lasts (Revelation 8:1-6).

JERICHO Just as Joshua took The Israelites into **"the promised land"** they had to first confront **Jericho**. God had Israel blow **trumpets for seven days**. On **the seventh day**, Israel all shouted with **the seventh trump** and the walls of Jericho **fell**. Then Israel entered **the promised land**. Jesus does exactly the same thing. **The seven trumpets** blow when Christ intervenes in **world affairs** to deliver **His servants**, Israel and The Churches of God, out of **The Great Tribulation** at His **return** at **the seventh trump**, and they are able to **enter the promised land** on Mt. Zion as His Engaged Bride. This is **the barely spring harvest** or **first resurrection** (Joshua 6).

THE FIRST FOUR TRUMPETS During **the first four trumpets**, God directly causes world catastrophes to help His **two witnesses** in **tribulation**. These **trumpets** affect, the earth, the sea, the rivers and the sun and the moon. To more perfectly understand this read all of Revelation 8. With the conclusion of **the four trumpets, the angel** states there are **three woes** (world trouble) or **three more trumpets**, which God causes to come to pass. **Three woes!**

THE THREE WOES **The first woe** (fifth angel) causes smoke as from a furnace to come over the earth. From this smoke will come locusts. What do these locusts do? They have the ability to torment humans, but they will not cause death. This is the **beginning of**

Armageddon and its **battle**.   Read all of Revelation 9. **"Blow the trumpet in Zion."** This is **the fifth trumpet** (Joel 2:1). These locusts are as military horsemen and so shall they run (Revelation 9:9). This is **"The Day of The Lord"** (Joel 2:11), and Jesus directly intervenes on behalf of His people. Pleading **"Come out of her my people"** (Revelation 18:4). Who is God sending against His people (Psalms 83:1-18)?

In Psalms 83:4 there are people who want to keep Israel from **being a nation**, and they hate Christianity. These are **THE TERRORISTS OF TODAY!** THESE ARE TODAY'S TERRORISTS FROM THE ARAB NATIONS (Psalms 83:6-8). Assur, or present day Iraq, will be part of those coming against Jerusalem. These Arab Nations will want to destroy every vestige of <u>The Bible</u> with The Jewish **faith** (Psalms 95:12).

The second woe is **the sixth trumpet**. The **Euphrates River** will be made passable for the armies of The East. Be ready for the nations of the world to come against The King of The North mentioned in Daniel 11:29-45. When the nations of the world see The King of The North, listed in Psalms 83, they realize the **world oil supplies** are at stake. Babylon, The Great Jerusalem, has been a **lie**, **the anti-Christ** sitting there as The **"Messiah"** is a lie. The nations of the world turn against Babylon (Jerusalem), **the whore,** and will come with an army of 200,000,000 (Revelation 9:16) to secure the oil for the prosperity of their world. They meet in conflict in The Valley of Decision or Armageddon (Joel 3:3-16). Now, there is **one more woe**. This is **the seventh trump** or The Return of Christ.

<u>**THE SEVENTH TRUMP**</u>   As the nations of the world assemble to

stop The King of The North (The Arabs, destroying Israel as a nation), they all assemble for the **last woe, the seventh trump**, to **secure** the prosperity of the world. They also are furious for being deceived by The Great Whore, Babylon, or **end-time** Jerusalem (Revelation 17:16-18). Suddenly, **the revelation** STOPS the prophecy of the blowing of **the seventh trump**. A mighty angel, with a loud voice, roars like a lion and seven thunders uttered their voices. At its conclusion, John was ready to write what **the seven utterances stated**. The angel stopped John, and said, **"Seal what those seven voices uttered"** (Revelation 10:1-4). Then, the angel stood on the sea and the earth and said, "The God who created everything is ready to reveal the final prophecy." In the days of **the seventh angel** or **seventh trump, the mystery of God** will be **revealed**. No longer will God keep **the truth only** for His **servants**, but now the entire world will know the real God and His Son, Jesus, The Christ. Just before the sounding of **the seventh trump**, John is stopped from writing. Why?

The voice from **heaven** told John to take a little book from the angel's hand. Why? The angel continued and said, **"Eat this little book. Make it part of you, and in your mouth, it will be sweet and in your belly, it will be bitter."** Whatever is in this book it reveals something that is sweet (**good**), but when it settles in his stomach, it becomes bitter or evil and gut-wrenching. Why is John told not to write what is in the book? The Book of Revelation finally tells you this book will tell a prophecy, by John of the future from Revelation 10 to Revelation 22. THIS PROPHECY WILL NOW BE REVEALED WHEN GOD MAKES **ALL HIS TRUTH** KNOWN TO THE WORLD!

CHAPTER 12

THE LITTLE BOOK

The Little Book The Apostle John is told to eat is both bitter and sweet. The sweet part of **The Little Book** covers The Return of Christ and the establishment of God's "kingdom," revealing the final mystery of God being opened to everyone's understanding.

The bitter part will be for those who carry The Mark of The Beast with its penalties. They will have to go through some very painful experiences of God's "wrath" (His "winepress"). The end result is for everyone to be saved – every man in his order (I Corinthian 15), and each receiving their own personal reward. Christ's "will" is a prophecy, and therefore, ends with a warning to everyone who does not heed the words written in **This Little Book**.

John is told he must "**prophesy**" to the world what is sealed in The Little Book (Revelation 10). How can John, as an elderly man, prophesy to the world? John died not too long after The Book of Revelation was finally completed. Who would do the prophesying? Revelation 11 tells you who is to prophesy to the world and when.

THE TWO WITNESSES An **angel** gave John a rod and told him to measure **the temple** (Revelation 11:1-2). This is very significant –

prophetically speaking. John is told to measure **the whole temple**, along with **the court** of Israel. However, **the court** of The Gentiles is not to be measured. Why not? During this time, John is told great power will be given to God's **two witnesses** to prophesy for three and a half years, clothed in sackcloth (be **repentant**). This is **the biblical answer** of how John will prophesy to the world after he died. How? The **two witnesses** will reveal what was in The Little Book John **ate** and then **sealed**. Now, **the two witnesses will continue** John's prophecy. The sweetness in John's mouth is **the witness** of Christ's **return** with **the seventh trump**. This Little Book becomes bitter in his stomach because Christ with **the saints** and **angels** will be pouring out **the seven last plagues of God's wrath** (winepress). Christ's **return** will "**not**" be in secret.

TWO OLIVE TREES AND CANDLESTICKS Suddenly, **two olive trees** and **two candlesticks** appear. God is describing His **two witnesses**. These **two witnesses** are 144,000 of The Tribes of Israel and the innumerable multitude of The Gentiles (Revelation 7:1-15). How do you know? These are those who came out of **the great tribulation** as **God's witnesses** (Verse 14). That is what Revelation 11:3 states they **will do**. The **two witnesses are not two prophets** or two individuals, but are 144,000 from Israel and an innumerable multitude from The Church of God. The **two prophets** are **two churches** – Israel and Christians. That is why God did not have **the court** of The Gentiles measured. This is the **innumerable multitude** of Christians. There it is. The **two witnesses are two churches**. **Candlesticks**, according to Christ, are **churches** (Revelation 1:20). The entire prophecy of Revelation is written to God's **two churches** – The Church in The Wilderness (Israel) and The Church of

God. Now, who are the olive trees? These two olive trees standing before God's **throne** are **Judah** and **Israel** (Zechariah 4). The Apostle Paul, The Apostle to The Gentiles, writes God rejected them and that only a remnant of Israel (144,000) will be **saved** at this time. The **wild** olive tree is grafted into the **natural** olive tree and will become God's **witnesses** also. So, **the two witnesses** are 144,000 Israelites (a remnant) and **the innumerable** Gentiles – the wild olive tree. These two olive trees, The Church in The Wilderness, are the 144,000 and The Church of God – **the seven candlesticks** (Acts 7:38). Now, you have **the biblical** answer. **The two witnesses**, Israel and Christianity cover Christ's **"will"** or **"revelation."**

These **two witnesses** have power to plague the earth and bring down fire (Revelation 11:5-6). How? The **first four trumpets** are depicting world catastrophes. Remember, Revelation 8:3-5 states the prayers from these **two witnesses** before God's **altar** are their prayers and God then sends the fire from the altar and casts it to the earth. These are **the seven trumpets**, which God releases to protect His **two witnesses**. Therefore, these **seven trumpets** last three and a half years during The Tribulation. You will see some of these **two witnesses** go into a **place of safety** while a remnant is martyred. Finally, after these **two witnesses** have prophesied for three and a half years (not in a physical place), they are martyred in Jerusalem and are dead in the streets while the world **"rejoices."** Why? Because of the catastrophes of **the seven trumps**. Then, after three days, they are **resurrected** and rise to the clouds. Why? This is **the seventh trump**, Christ **returns,** and they meet Him in the clouds. Now, John **shifts the story flow** to catch up with **the history** of God's Church.

REVELATION 12   Suddenly, just before Christ's **return** on Mt. Zion in Revelation 14 with The 144,000 Israelites, John relates the account of church history from **the birth of Christ** to the time Satan is pursuing the remnant of God's people who keep His **commandments**. This includes Israelites and The Church of God. Most of Christianity goes into safety and God seals them (Revelation 7:3 and Revelation 12:1-17).

The place of safety is **not a location** since **the entire** Church of God and Israel are in **the wilderness** (the world). Those sealed by God's Holy Spirit are protected by **the seven trumpets** with Christ as your **rock** of protection. Deuteronomy 32 reveals **the rock** protects The Church on The Wings of The Eagle (Jesus). Christ is **"the rock"** (I Corinthian 10:4). Jesus protects you even though chaos is all around you – **He is your refuge** (Psalms 91:1-9).

THE BEAST   Who does Satan, as the dragon, use to persecute the woman (church) in Revelation 12? This hideous beast arises out of the sea with seven heads and ten horns (Revelation 13:1). Who is this beast? This beast was like a **leopard**, a **bear** and a **lion** (Revelation 13:2). This is the same beast in Daniel 7:3-7. These three beasts were, also, like a leopard, bear and lion. In Daniel 8 and 9, three beasts fall leaving **the fourth beast**, which is Rome with **seven heads** and **ten horns**. These seven heads are seven Caesars in The Roman Empire with an eighth. Reread Chapter 4, 'Who is The Beast?'

Another **"beast with two horns"** who is Christian, speaking as a lamb, but is preaching everyone should worship the **image** of **the fourth beast** or The Roman **government** (Revelation 13:11-18).

The Roman **government** lasted only about six hundred years, but the image of **the fourth beast** has lasted until our **present day**. Chapter 5, '**The Mark of The Beast**' explains globalization with democracy but without **the true** God and His Son, Jesus. The whole world is in Babylon, with multitudinous religions centered in Jerusalem as their place of origin. That is why God tells all true Christians to come out of Babylon (Revelation 18:4). This Babylon is Jerusalem **in the end-time** (Revelation 11:8). This is where and when **the two witnesses** (144,000 and Church of God) are martyred.

The **two little horns** carry on the **two legs of Daniel 2**, which are The Western and Eastern part of The Roman **government**. Their **image** continues in The Catholic and Orthodox Churches, which are the **candlesticks** as Christ walks in their midst (Revelation 2:18-22). They go through **the great tribulation**.

All those worshiping this **image** of The Roman **government** have a "**mark**" and that "**mark**" is 666. The number "six" connotes being human and number three, making three sixes – 666 is **completion**. Therefore, 666 denotes the completion of human imagination or origin. These **churches** are ritualistic with human works. Their doctrines are of human origin and not from God or His Son. This religion is filled with "**many ways**" to worship God or Babylon. That is why there are so many Christian and Jewish denominations. You can pick "**the church**" of your choice. At this point in Revelation, all the inheritors and the enemies of God's "**kingdom**" are manifested. Now, to a critical time in world history. The **last days**, which are "**the days of the fourth beast**" in

Daniel 7, before Christ **returns** and smashes the **ten toes** (ten kings) of the great image in Daniel 2. Then Jesus **returns** and sets up The Kingdom of God upon Mt. Zion. This brings you to **the seventh trumpet** or **The Return of Christ**. This is the **beginning** of **the end-time** or **the end of time**. The time of the Gentile's rule is about to end and be **fulfilled**, and God's **"kingdom"** will take over.

THE WINEPRESS   After **the sixth angel**, **the seven trumpets** sound, an angel cries out and **one woe** is past with **two more woes** are to come. **The sixth angel** sounds, which is **the second woe** and The Euphrates River releases **four angels** to make way for the 200,000,000-man army to descend upon The Valley of Jehoshaphat or Armageddon. Notice, this **sixth angel**, comes from **the four horns** of The Altar, which is **the fourth beast** with ten toes of Daniel 2. "Horns" are "governments" and **"the altar"** signifies "sacrifice" or "shedding of blood" (Revelation 9:13-21). Even with the plagues of **the six trumpets** and The Battle of Armageddon, not one person who worships the beast's image **ever repents** (Revelation 13:21). Christ, The Lamb and 144,000 stand with Him on Mt. Zion (Revelation 14:1). This is **the seventh trump** – Christ **returns** (Revelation 14:14).

With Him in the clouds are **the angels**, along with **"the saints"** of The Barley Harvest, and they are **ready** to **rule** with **Christ**. They are Christ's Bride. These **saints** with the 144,000 are **the redeemed firstfruits** (Revelation 14:4). This is **the first resurrection** – **the barley harvest**. **Two more "woes"** to go. Revelation 14:14-20 states there are **two more harvests**. The angel thrusts in the sickle for **the wheat harvest** and the third, **a grape harvest** is **the winepress** of God's **wrath** (Revelation 14:19). **The seven last plagues** are about to be released as Christ with **the angels** and **saints** venting out God's **wrath** upon those with The Mark of The Beast. Reread Chapter 7, 'The Mystery Harvest' to better understand these events. This is the bitterness in John's stomach. This is the distasteful winepress before God's **"kingdom rules."**

The **first vial** is poured out and a grievous **sore** befalls those with the beast's **mark**. It is very similar to what occurred to Job. **The second angel** made the **sea blood; the third angel** made the **rivers** become **bitter**; then, **the fourth angel** caused the **sun** to **scorch humanity. The fifth angel** produced **total blackness**, which caused much pain. Instead of repenting, those with the **mark** of the beast will **not repent** (Revelation 16:11). Then **the sixth angel released those armies** from The East and Armageddon "commences" (Revelation 16:12). As these vials are unleashed in a very short period of time, the armies of Armageddon clash. This is in harmony with **the seventh trump**, and at the time of this last trump, **many voices** sounded (like Jericho), **"The kingdoms of this world are become the kingdoms of our Lord, and of His Christ and He shall reign forever and ever"** (Revelation 11:15).

"The seventh trump" and **"the seven last plagues"** occur almost simultaneously. The whole world, **all nations** from the ten world rulers descend (World War III) upon The King of The North (Arabs) and the **whore**, Babylon or end-time Jerusalem with its host of the world's religions (Revelation 16:14). Truly, a Babylon of confusion. Then a voice states, **"Behold I come as a thief. Blessed is he that watcheth,**

and keepeth his garments, lest he walk naked and they see his shame"
(Revelation 16:15). This is no secret. The world is fully warned! You
would have thought with **the seven trumpets,** which brings world
catastrophes along with the seven last plagues, should have caused a lot of
repenting. Instead, Satan, the beast and the false prophet have demons
coming out of them to cause the whole world **(ten kings)** to gather
together for the battle of that great day (Armageddon – Zechariah 14) of
God, Almighty (Revelation 16:13-14). Then, Jerusalem fell when a great
earthquake hit. The city (Jerusalem – Zechariah 14) is divided into three
parts as God pours out His **cup of wine** of His **wrath.** (Reread Chapter 6
'Babylon and The Two Grails'). Finally, **the seventh vial contains one
hundred pound hail balls** and still humanity **fails to repent** (Revelation
16:21).

Notice – it states **all nations,** not merely ten nations, as some erroneously
believe. This battle at **Armageddon** is **World War III** and includes **all
nations** of the **entire world** with their ten leaders (Zechariah 14:1-3). The
King of The North listed in Psalms 83 composed of The Arab Nations
coming against Jerusalem – **the end-time** Babylon. The terrorists finally
decide to attack Israel. These Arab countries take crafty counsel against
God's people, Israel (Psalms 83:3-4). They say, **"Come, and let us cut
them off from being a nation, that the name Israel may be no more in
remembrance"** (Verse 4). This is what The Jihadists have been saying all
along. Notice these nations listed in Psalms 83:5-18, are all Arab nations
mentioned as Assur (Verse 8). Assur is present day Iraq. Don't be
surprised if they change their name. When tidings come out of the north
(Daniel 11), the rest of the world, The Arabs prepare to battle in

Armageddon against Israel. **All the nations** (Zechariah 14) come against Jerusalem so The Arabs will not be able to take world control of their oil. World War III is about to occur as **the fifth angel** sounds and the army of locusts (military weapons) torments men for five months. These weapons do not kill but do paralyze the enemy causing excruciating pain (Revelation 9:1-13).

Then **the sixth angel** sounds to open up the armies from The North and East. This is the 200,000,000-man army coming for the final battle of World War III at **Armageddon**. Then **the seventh trumpet** sounds and **two woes** are past with the **third woe** is about to come, which is the beginning of God's **wrath, the grape harvest** or **God's winepress** (Revelation 14:15-16). Christ **returns** at **the seventh trump**. Revelation 10:7 states in the days of **the seventh angel, the mystery of God** is completed as He had declared to His servants, Israel and Christianity. The **witnesses** have finished their **witnessing.**

BABYLON, THE GREAT WHORE   Revelation 15:1-8 continues after **the seventh trump** and **The Return of Christ** with **the saints** and His **angels** to **unleash** "**the seven last plagues.**"   This is **God's** "**winepress.**"

As Christ meets His **saints** – The Bride of Christ, in the clouds, they release **the seven last plagues** (Revelation 16:1).   There cannot be a "secret" **Return of Jesus**. The **entire world will know** they were duped by Satan, the false religious prophet and the beast or **the fourth beast** in Daniel 7 and Revelation 13. Then **the seven angels** release **the seven plagues**. The **first plague** pours sores out upon those with The Mark of

The Beast or those who followed this worldly system of government and religion. All devised by humans who were deceived by Satan, The Dragon. **The second vial** made the sea turn to blood and killed those in the sea. **The third** contaminated the rivers with blood. **The fourth** made the sun "**scorch**" mankind. **The fifth** poured darkness upon Babylon or **end-time** Jerusalem and **the sixth** brought the northern armies. Satan, being demon-possessed, as is **the fourth beast** and **the false prophet**, deceiving all nations and bringing them together to Armageddon.

Then **the seventh angel** sounded and a great voice out of **the temple** said, "**It is done!**" A great earthquake strikes, which divides Jerusalem in half (Zechariah 14). This was the largest earthquake since humans had occupied the earth (Revelation 16:18). Then Great Babylon (Jerusalem), **the great city** breaks up into three parts. God is venting out His final wrath as a winepress squeezing its **grapes** – The Battle of Armageddon. A great hail came out of **heaven, each hail weighing a 100 pounds.**

Then Revelation 17 and 18 reveal The Fall of Babylon, **the great whore**. This is end-time Jerusalem who accepted **all the religions of the world**. A true Babylon or "**confusion**" just as in the time of The Tower of Babel. Everyone's choice of worship. This city was its very center or point of origin of all major religions in the world. "**Her plagues come in one day, death, and mourning, and famine, and she shall be utterly burned with fire,**" shall come upon her and the world will mourn (Revelation 18:8). All the world's **prosperity**, its **riches** and its **power** are coming to an end. Satan is finished. **The beast** (Daniel 7) and **the false prophet** are thrown into a Lake of Fire (Revelation 19:20). Satan is taken and bound in prison (hell–tartaroo) for **one thousand years** (Revelation 20:1-3).

THE BRIDE AND CHRIST   **"Salvation," "glory" and "honor" to God** (Revelation 19:1). The whore, Babylon (false human religions) has been avenged from all the blood of **The Prophets, "saints" and His "servants."** The final Battle of Armageddon will have so much blood spilled it will reach the bridles of horses (Revelation 14:20). Then all the rest of those with The Mark of The Beast in the battle will be slain by Christ and His armies (Revelation 14:21). A great number of fowl will devour the dead – so the fowl will have a great feast for themselves. The **Lamb's Bride** gathered from all of human history and **the two witnesses** – Israel and Christians are martyred and have witnessed Christ even at the expense of their own lives (Revelation 19:7). The Bride has truly made herself ready for the engagement period with her husband, Jesus, The Christ.

FATHER OF THE BRIDE   In most weddings, The Father of The Bride gives The Bride away. The Wedding Feast between Jesus because His Bride has no father in-law to give away The Bride. Why not?

RACHEL AND JACOB   The answer to this bewildering question, "Who is **the father** of The Bride at The Wedding Feast in God's **"kingdom"** is a startling one (Read all of Genesis 28 to 32). Jacob, who became Israel after his dream (Jacob's ladder), continued his journey to his father's kinsman's abode in Haran. When he arrives at a well near his relative's home, he meets Rachel. He tells her he is looking for his relatives. She tells him her father is Laban, Jacob's mother's brother. She takes Jacob or Israel to her home and Laban welcomes Jacob to the family.

After a period of time, he states Jacob shouldn't be working for nothing. Jacob tells Laban he loves Rachel and wants to marry her. So, Laban said, "Work seven years for her and she is yours." Jacob agrees. After seven years, he asks for Laban's daughter, Rachel in marriage. Laban agrees but fools Jacob and gives Leah, the elder sister instead. He said " it is not our custom to marry off the younger first." Laban then said, "Work another seven years and Rachel is yours." Jacob agrees. After one week, Jacob marries Rachel and then works seven years for her. Jacob **bought** or **redeemed** both Leah and Rachel as his wives. Remember, after Eve sinned in **the garden**, she became Satan's property. From then on, marriage meant the woman was to be a sex object for reproduction as any livestock. She was now the man's property after the god, Baal or Satan. That is why in The Law "**marriage**" allows divorce (Deuteronomy 24:1-3). The word for "marriage" in The Law is "**Baal**." Eve and all women are now daughters of Satan until Christ **redeems** them by giving His **life**. Laban and Jacob (Israel) are a good example.

When Israel, the nation, sinned under Moses, she had played the harlot and the engagement with God was broken. It was only after Christ gave His **life** and bought Israel and The Church of God back to be His Wife. These are **the two witnesses** or **two candlesticks**, The Church in The Wilderness and The Church of God.

THE JEWS Read all of John 8. When Jesus said to His Jewish followers or disciples: **"If ye continue in my word, then are ye my disciples indeed"** (John 8:31). The Disciples said they were **not** in bondage to anyone since they are the children of Abraham. Jesus said to them, if they were Abraham's children, they would do the works of Abraham. Then John 8:42-44 reveals the reason they don't hear Christ's **Word,** it is because they are the **children of their father, Satan** and not **God, The Father**. Why doesn't Christ's Bride have a father to give her away? Simply, Satan was her father (or Baal) and Christ **redeemed** her or bought her back just as Laban wouldn't give up his daughters to Jacob or Israel (Genesis 31).

In Genesis 31:29-42, Laban chased after Jacob when he was leaving with his wives Leah and Rachel. Satan does the same to his **two witnesses**. When Laban catches up with Jacob, he said, "You wanted to do me harm but God stopped you." Then Laban accused Jacob of stealing his "**gods**" or "**icons**." Rachel still believed in paganism and took Laban's images. Then Laban searched and couldn't find them because Rachel claimed to have had her **period** and couldn't rise. Laban left when he couldn't catch Jacob taking his "gods." Laban lost just as Satan, who was Israel's Father and The Church of God's "Father." Christ redeemed His Bride and bought her by giving His very **life** (Ephesians 5). Satan, at this point, is taken out of The Wedding Party and cast into prison for a thousand years (Revelation 20:1-3).

Why didn't The Father of The Bride, or Satan, give away his daughter, Israel and The Church of God? Because The 144,000 Israelites and The Church of God **came out of Babylon** (Revelation 18:4) and made herself ready (The Bride) for the marriage! (Revelation 19:7) Satan no longer was the father. Now, God, The Father, is The Bride's Father, as well. God will be at The Wedding Feast.

THE MILLENNIUM   Satan is bound for a thousand years and then God, The Father, is The Bride's Father as well as The Father of The Groom (Revelation 20).   Revelation 20:4-6 explains The Groom and The Bride's engagement period.   They reign together during the millennium or one thousand years as Kings and Priests (Revelation 5:10).

This is **the first resurrection** of **the barley harvest** and are God's **firstfruits**.   They have **eternal life** but also their **reward will be as Christ's Bride** at The Wedding Feast to come.   The second death, The Lake of Fire, has no power over them. During the one thousand years, Israel is **saved** (Romans 11:25-26).   Read all of Ezekiel 37-48.   In Ezekiel 37, **"the valley of dry bones"** prophesied a physical resurrection of all Israelites who had ever lived and they live for one hundred years both the young and the old (Isaiah 65).   They are all converted by keeping **The Letter of The Law with Christ's new temple on earth**.   Israel, as a nation, finally becomes God's witness to The Gentile Nations.   Gentiles begin to keep The Letter of The Law and The Holy Days of God.   Finally, millions are converted or **repent** and receive God's Holy Spirit and become His **sons** and **daughters**.

Those Gentile Nations farthest away from Jerusalem do not respond in keeping The Letter of The Law so they remain unrepentant. All they can see is the abundant riches and prosperity of Israel – especially Jerusalem. Satan, after the one thousand years, is released from his prison or place of restraint (hell) and sets about to deceive these very nations who have **not repented** (Revelation 20:7-9). Gog and Magog, those Gentiles of the most northern parts of the earth, form huge armies, and descend upon the very wealthy Jerusalem. God sends fire to the earth and consumes them.

The devil is cast into The Lake of Fire where **the beast** and **the false prophet** are. Now, everyone knows **the true** God, The Father and His Son, Jesus, The Christ, with His Bride (Revelation 20:7-10).

WHITE THRONE JUDGMENT The Great White Throne Judgment is the time of **the second resurrection** but includes **the two harvests** to come – **the wheat harvest** and **the grape harvest** (Revelation 14). Christ explains these **resurrections** in John 5:28. Jesus said **all** who are **in their graves** will be **resurrected**. Then, those who have done **good**, but are not in **the first resurrection**, receive **life.** Those who have done evil, receive **damnation**. The word "**damnation**," in The English language, is a gross mistranslation in the Greek language. The Greek for "damnation," is "krisis" or "**crises**." It does not mean to be "damned" but literally means "a point of crisis" or "judgment." Jesus defines some are **sheep** (repentant) and some are **goats** (unrepentant) (Matthew 25:31-41).

Some believe **The White Throne Judgment** has **two resurrections about one hundred years apart.** This is a big error as Jesus had stated, at the time of **this judgment, the division** is determined **all at the same time** (Matthew 25:32-33). Sheep and goats are all separated and rewarded or sentenced. **The sheep** enter God's "**kingdom**" as Guests while **the goats** are to be thrown into The Lake of Fire (Matthew 25:34,41). Prophecy shows you there were so many people at the time of this **judgment** that no place was found for them (Revelation 20:11-15).

God uses His <u>Book of Remembrance</u> (Malachi 3:16) to judge the people

(Revelation 20:12).   **Separation** between the **sheep** and **goats** is **determined** not by who **sinned the most**, but who **sought "the true" God and grew to "true repentance."**   It is very clear how God will judge! (Malachi 3:16)

Those not in The Book of Life or on an invitational list to **The Marriage Feast** are thrown into The Lake of Fire.   To understand the process of what happens to those in The Lake of Fire, read the book, God's Work. Remember, God makes no mistakes.   **God aborts no one** (Isaiah 66:8-9). But, only the **few are chosen** to be in or invited to The Wedding Feast (Matthew 22).   Most of humanity must go through The Lake of Fire to be "**saved**."   Also, Jesus said, "**Many are called to The Wedding Feast** [the church – the called-out ones] **but are deceived** [because they have not qualified]."   All Christians and Israel **must spiritually grow** or come out of Babylon (Revelation 18:4).

The **first** to be thrown into The Lake of Fire is "**death**" and "**hell**" or "**the grave**" (Revelation 20:14).   Before the **incorrigibly wicked** are thrown into the fire – death and the grave end.   Death no longer exists when the wicked are thrown into The Lake of Fire. Those not written into The Book of Life, to be in The Wedding Feast are thrown into The Lake of Fire, but they will not die (Revelation 20:15).   Read God's Work to learn how they repent and become "**babes in Christ**."

NEW HEAVEN AND NEW EARTH   God creates a **new heaven** and a **new earth** (Revelation 21:1-8).   This new paradise is so beautiful and wonderful no thought will remain of the former.   This **new earth** doesn't contain oceans – only lakes, rivers and creeks.   The earth will be vast.   It is so large – New Jerusalem is 1500 miles in each direction or four square just as **the temple** in **heaven** and **earth**. This is truly **paradise** with **no death**, no pain, sorrow or stress. Everyone will have complete liberty. Everyone can do whatever they choose or have total free will (Romans 8). Why?

As Christ said in Matthew 5 **"not one jot or tittle of The Law will pass until heaven and earth pass away."** You are now in God's **"kingdom."** There is no **temple** or **court** because God, The Father and His Son, Jesus, are **the temple**. Their **glory** is so brilliant, the very sun and moon are not necessary. Now, everyone who is invited to The Wedding, will be filled with God's **"glory"** or **"the shekinah."** No one sins because there is no longer any Letter of The Law to keep. Why? Because God is **writing His Law** in your hearts and minds. Your nature is God's Holy nature and God is **all and in all** (I Corinthians 15:28). This fulfills **God's real purpose** for you and everyone else. Everyone is at complete liberty or freedom to do whatever they wish because they are **now Holy as God** and will always do what is good to God and His Creation. Everyone will be creators, as **sons** and **daughters** of God – **eternally**. God will keep creating and growing only now through His Son, Jesus, you will be God's strength and continue to create, four, five, ten and even more dimensions than can ever be imagined. Since everyone is **saved**, what are the rewards.

THE WEDDING FEAST One of **the angels** who had **the seven vials** said, **"Look and see The Bride, The Lamb's Wife"** (Revelation 21:9). Then you read about New Jerusalem, The Lamb's Wife with all of mankind's **rewards** (Revelation 21). Everyone is **saved**, but there are different groups with varied rewards (Revelation 22). **All** but **one group** are invited to The Wedding. The left-out group is banned from entering The New Jerusalem and cannot have access to The Tree of Life.

The **One God, The Father,** only has **life** and is in the midst of New Jerusalem. God will make access to The Tree of Life exactly as it was in The Garden of Eden. God sits upon His **throne** and said He will make **all things new**. This **is a totally spiritual dimension**. Nothing is corruptible or can be destroyed (Revelation 21:5-7). Then, **the city** is described. God will make available to everyone **the fountain of the waters of life** freely, even those who were in The Lake of Fire (Revelation 21:6)0. This is **the true fountain of youth**. No one has to be called. It is freely accessible to everyone – even those who came out of The Lake of Fire (Revelation 22:17). Israel as The Twelve Tribes are **the gatekeepers** or **ushers** to The Wedding Feast (Revelation 21:12). The foundation of the city walls are The Twelve Apostles; and therefore, **the walls** are **the seven churches** who came out of Babylon and did not have The Mark of The Beast on them. They are The Bridesmaids. Forever a Bridesmaid, but never a Bride. The Guests are those who live outside The City of New Jerusalem, but will be The Guests at The Wedding and are in <u>The Book of Life</u> (Revelation 21:24). They continue to **spiritually grow** in God's "**kingdom**" because they must bring their growth to New Jerusalem to show God's "**glory**" from the light of The Lamb and The Father.

These will all have God's name, YHVH, in their foreheads or minds. They are The Sons of God and have the same name as The Father, YHVH (Revelation 22:4). The **Bride** are those who are **the righteous ones** or

saints who dwell with Christ, their husband in The Holy Place with "**The Menorah**" and the table with the shewbread. The Bride lived by every Word of God and was in **the barley harvest – the firstfruits**. The **witnesses** (Israel and Judah) and The Guests are **the wheat harvest – the sheep**. Who is left?

THE GRAPE HARVEST Then God's "**wrath**" – His "**winepress**" or "**grape harvest**" will be unleashed on those **not invited to The Wedding. This winepress ended in The Lake of Fire** (Revelation 14 and 15). These are the ones who will come out of The Lake of Fire as "**spirit beings**," but still only **babes** and are carnal (I Corinthian 3:1-2). They did **repent** and their bodies are completely gone – only ashes remain. Only "**the spirit in man**" is left, and now they receive a "**spiritual body**" – all are **saved** (I Corinthians 3).

Remember, only those who keep God's "**commandments**" in their "**hearts**" can enter The City of New Jerusalem (Revelation 22:14). Those who will be able to enter New Jerusalem will continue The Wedding Feast **eternally** by continually partaking of The Tree of Life. All those who went through The Lake of Fire cannot enter New Jerusalem until they eventually have God's Law in their hearts (Revelation 22:15). Until then, they will have **no access to The Tree of Life**. The "**abominable ones**" and "**the faithless**" must **spiritually mature** until they come to the stature of Christ! These are those who are **the least in "the kingdom"** (Matthew 5:19). How will they **grow spiritually**?

A great river will fill the earth with The Tree of Life on each side of this river. As **the leaves** from **the tree** fall off, these leaves along with the waters are for **the healing** or for continual **spiritual growth** of the nations who are **saved** and, also, those without the city (Matthew 22:1-2).

What is the **reward** of those who will then be **saved**, but still only **"babes in Christ?"** They will be crying in darkness and they are in grief over their stupidity for not coming to Christ (Matthew 22:13). They are the farthest from New Jerusalem and God's **"glory."** Without the sun and moon, they live so far away from God; they are in darkness. You could compare it to those at the two poles, getting six months of night with only some light during the day. They will have to continue living at this distance until they become **spiritually mature** and as they grow eventually they will be able to enter New Jerusalem with The Tree of Life and God's **"glory."** That is why Revelation concludes with only The Bride and The Holy Spirit inviting everyone to come and drink the **waters of life** freely! No Father or Christ calling, but The **Bride**, The Mother of **all** – New Jerusalem who will be nurturing everyone (Galatians 4).

CLOSING OF THE WILL This concludes the reading of Christ's **"will"** – The Book of Revelation! Notice the concluding warning; Anyone reading or hearing this **"will,"** better not tamper with it (Revelation 22:18-21). If you tamper with it, you will have your name taken **out** of The Book of Life and will have to go through **the seven last plagues**. Christ warns His **servants** – **"Israel"** and **"the seven churches"** (all Christianity) to come out of Babylon! (Revelation 18:4)

The Grace of Our Lord Jesus Christ be with you all! Amen!